MW00514230

Fund of Funds Investing

Founded in 1807, John Wiley & Sons is the oldest independent publishing company in the United States. With offices in North America, Europe, Australia, and Asia, Wiley is globally committed to developing and marketing print and electronic products and services for our customers' professional and personal knowledge and understanding.

The Wiley Finance series contains books written specifically for finance and investment professionals as well as sophisticated individual investors and their financial advisors. Book topics range from portfolio management to e-commerce, risk management, financial engineering, valuation, and financial instrument analysis, as well as much more.

For a list of available titles, please visit our Web site at www.WileyFinance.com.

Fund of Funds Investing

A Roadmap to Portfolio Diversification

DANIEL STRACHMAN
RICHARD BOOKBINDER

John Wiley & Sons, Inc.

Published by John Wiley & Sons, Inc., Hoboken, New Jersey.
Published simultaneously in Canada.

For general information on our other products and services or for technical support, please contact our Customer Care Department within the United States at (800) 762-2974, outside the United States at (317) 572-3993 or fax (317) 572-4002.

Wiley also publishes its books in a variety of electronic formats. Some content that appears in print may not be available in electronic formats. For more information about Wiley products, visit our Web site at www.wiley.com.

Library of Congress Cataloging-in-Publication Data:
Strachman, Daniel, 1971-
Fund of funds investing : a roadmap to portfolio diversification / Daniel.
Strachman and Richard Bookbinder.
p. cm.—(Wiley finance series)
Includes index.
ISBN 978-0-470-25876-7 (cloth)
1. Hedge funds. 2. Risk management. 3. Portfolio management. I. Bookbinder, Richard. II. Title.
HG4530.S8367 2010
332.63'27—dc22

2009023127

Printed in the United States of America

10 9 8 7 6 5 4 3 2 1

To my wife, Felice, my daughter, Leah, and my son Jonah
—Daniel Strachman

To my wife, Arlene, and my sons Jonathon and Douglas
—Richard Bookbinder

Contents

Acknowledgments ix

Introduction xi

CHAPTER 1
On the Road 1

CHAPTER 2
A Hedge Fund Is What? 16

CHAPTER 3
How Large Is the Market? 26

CHAPTER 4
Hedge Fund Investing 31

CHAPTER 5
Understanding Alternative Investing Is Both Math and Science 44

CHAPTER 6
Why Fund of Funds Work 57

CHAPTER 7
Understanding Risk and the Need for Due Diligence 73

CHAPTER 8
Redemption 95

CHAPTER 9
Fees 105

CHAPTER 10
Leverage Facilities and Risk Management 110

CHAPTER 11
Recent Lessons Learned and Current Trends 124

CHAPTER 12
New Products 134

CHAPTER 13
Multi-Strategy Funds versus Hedge Fund of Funds 144

CHAPTER 14
How Fund of Funds Source Managers 155

CHAPTER 15
Conclusion 159

Epilogue: Turning Points 167

Appendix 179

Glossary 193

Notes 203

Index 207

Acknowledgments

The idea for this book comes from a series of ice coffees and ice teas at numerous Dean and Deluca's near Rockefeller Center. Together we discussed how to create a book to fill a void in the marketplace. What you have in your hands is the result of many hours of work, many ice coffees and ice teas, and countless hours' research, writing, and interviewing.

This book would not have been possible without the fine efforts of our trusted colleagues Erik Buischi and Jacqueline Oring Rockman. We both are eternally grateful for their hard work and effort. We also thank the people at John Wiley & Sons including, but not limited to, Jennifer MacDonald and Pamela van Giessen.

With the understanding, insight, support, and love of our families this book became a reality. With their encouragement and motivation, this book was completed. With their inspiration, we just might try it again.

Daniel Strachman
Richard Bookbinder
New York, NY
June 2009

Introduction

The day is short, the task is great . . .

—*Ethics of the Fathers*, Chapter 2, Verse 20

In *Fund of Funds Investing: A Roadmap to Portfolio Diversification*, we take a brief look back at the history of the fund of funds industry, examine where the industry is today in the wake of the Madoff scandal, the credit crisis, and the failure of many hedge fund managers to perform over the past few years. Our goal is to provide both a roadmap for first-time investors looking for an entry point into the wacky, wild, weird, and exciting world of fund of funds investing and a resource guide for sophisticated investors who may not be certain what the optimum investment approach should be for allocating their assets.

According to our calculations, hedge fund industry assets exceeded $10 trillion (or was it really $2 trillion?) at year-end 2007 and dropped to $6 trillion by year-end 2008 (which we discuss in the book), and closely approached mutual funds in assets under management. This book will try to simplify things as much as possible and provide you with an even playing field for making decisions.

Asset growth in the hedge fund industry has been fueled by investors of all shapes and sizes, including pension plans, endowments, foundations, private banks, family offices, and high net worth individuals looking for returns that differ from those of traditional long-only investments. As institutional investors and their allocators look to find solutions to ongoing and future capital needs, many have turned to fund of funds to meet the needs of their constituent investors. Given the proliferation in the hedge fund industry, one of the drivers of the growth of assets has been the development of the fund of funds industry, along with the realization that assets do not always rise.

In the simplest of terms, fund of funds are investment partnerships that invest directly in a wide range of hedge funds. This allows investors to have a single entry point into a diversified hedge fund portfolio rather than creating their own portfolios that consist of a series of hedge fund investments.

Hedge funds and fund of funds managers have created large institutional complexes that directly compete with their traditional long-only asset management brethren. Due to the subpar results of many long-only strategies, "absolute return" has become the new investment paradigm in structuring investment approaches for portfolio management. At the same time, it requires an adjustment or refinement in the approach to investing.

As the capital markets have become more efficient, investors have experienced a moderation of returns, leaving them with questions about how to increase portfolio performance without increasing risk. *Fund of Funds Investing: A Roadmap to Portfolio Diversification* provides investors with a roadmap and a set of tools to understand and evaluate investments, and make thoughtful investment decisions.

Even though drivers have become accustomed to relying on navigation devices while traveling the roads of the world, nothing beats having a map and knowledge of the area and its terrain for getting from point "A" to point "B." The same is true for hedge fund investing. Making investment decisions is not as simple as inserting numbers into a spreadsheet to arrive at the desired results. Investing is not that simple and should not be taken lightly.

Fund of Funds Investing: A Roadmap to Portfolio Diversification provides a unique and insightful overview of this often misunderstood and opaque area of the investment community. Through a series of high-level interviews as well as direct industry insight, we have worked to give you access to this area of the investment marketplace that is often thought of as closed or secretive. Our goal is to provide you with what you need to make solid investment decisions.

In the following pages, we explain the how's and why's of fund of funds investing. Our intent is not to offer investment advice but rather to enable you to make good investment decisions—smarter investment decisions. We hope that you use this book as a guide to the fund of funds industry and alternative investment investing. Think of it as a resource that you can turn to repeatedly to become a better investor.

Daniel Strachman
Richard Bookbinder

CHAPTER 1

On the Road

When we (authors Daniel Strachman and Richard Bookbinder) started working on this book, all was right within the world of hedge funds, fund of funds, and alternative investing. Sure, there had been some hiccups—the credit crisis that started in the spring of 2007, the fire sale of Bear Stearns, the pending collapse of Lehman Brothers, to name a few—but nothing prepared us for the news of December 11, 2008.

While December 7, 1941, was a day that will live forever in infamy, many on Wall Street and beyond believe that December 11, 2008, was one of the worst days of all time. It was on this December 11, as the markets were closing on Thursday afternoon that the news broke that Bernard L. Madoff had been arrested for a massive Ponzi scheme. I (Daniel) remember exactly where I was sitting and what I was doing when Richard called me on my cell phone with the news of Madoff's arrest. Both of us were shocked, but as on December 8, 1941, when reports of the extent of the Japanese attack on Pearl Harbor began to come to light and F.D.R. made his famous speech, the news of the extent of the crimes Madoff had perpetrated on the thousands who had invested with his firm was simultaneously shocking, sad, and funny.

It was shocking because the initial reports named some of the most respected money managers and investors in the world. It was sad because the world learned that people had literally given Mr. Madoff all of their money and were now penniless. It was funny, maybe only to us, because some of the people who were listed as investors just a few months before—in one case, a few weeks before—had detailed the need for due diligence, research, and diversification. Yet, these same investors—fund of funds managers—had given the bulk of their funds' assets to a single manager who turned out to be a total fraud.

Of course, there is nothing truly funny about the Madoff situation, just as there is nothing funny about the events of December 7, 1941. Still, there is some irony in the events of December 11, 2008, that many people in the hedge fund and alternative investment community found somewhat amusing. The irony is that these people work hard to create products—funds—that deliver alpha (a term we'll define later), and yet they are not given the time of day by fund of funds managers or institutional investors because of a host of issues and items that cause the fund manager not to "fit the box" with the investor.

Given the Madoff news and the dismal returns within the stock market and the hedge funds for 2008, the prospects for the hedge fund industry in early 2009 did not seem all that good. However, we believe that as time goes on and the wounds inflicted by the losses from the Madoff fraud and the market heal, investors will continue to see the value in fund of funds investing. It is this premise that led us to continue our project of writing a book about this fascinating and often considered misunderstood and expensive segment of the investment community.

THE MODERN HEDGE FUND INDUSTRY

Since the late 1990s and the early years of the 21st century, hedge fund investing has been a topic discussed by investors around the globe. What were previously thought of as secretive investment partnerships among the wealthy are now front page news on a regular basis and are being sold by brokers, financial advisors, and others, often in as small as $10,000.00 increments.

Hardly a day goes by without mention that hedge funds are involved to some degree in moving markets, providing financing to troubled companies, capitalizing on downtrodden home owners, or making a hostile run at unsuspecting public companies. This, of course, does not include reportage of the spending habits of Wall Street's new elite, which is often found in the society pages and in the art sections of the media as these modern-day robber barons gobble up the finest and most tempting things money can buy. As the credit crisis spread and the economy weakened in 2008 and early 2009, hedge fund managers still were capturing the front pages with their largesse as well as their ability to capture profits and deal with losses no matter which way the markets moved.

Hedge funds, you see, have arrived. These unique investment vehicles are being poked, prodded, and probed by investors around the globe in order to create the most uncorrelated portfolios imaginable for institutions and individual investors.

The appeal of these investment strategies is simple: investors believe that hedge funds offer low or noncorrelated opportunities to traditional long-only investments. This theory, whether it is correct or not (we will deal with that later), has prompted investors of all sizes to look at, review, and analyze hedge fund managers to determine the alpha these investments can add to their portfolios and in turn fill their pockets.

Alpha is one of those great Wall Street terms that everybody talks about and many think is hard to understand; in reality, it is quite a simple concept that very few people are able to grasp. Our definition of alpha is "the difference between what a traditional investment earned compared with an alternative investment." For example, if an S&P 500 index fund earned 10 percent and a long/short equity manager earned 15 percent, the alpha is the additional five percent. Earning alpha is what every investor is looking for regardless of market conditions. It is the holy grail of investors and investment managers around the globe because alpha, you see, makes a difference. And the difference is rewarding not only to the investor, it is also rewarding to the manager. In later chapters we discuss fund structures, fees, and compensation, but for now remember this: hedge fund investing is one of the very few means whereby the interests of the client (the limited partner/investor) and the asset manager can be aligned. The client is the investor, and the service provider is the manager. If the manager makes money for the investor, both are rewarded; clients gain returns on their investments and managers gain fees earned on the returns on the investment. If managers fail to deliver for the client, they make nothing and the client pays nothing. It is quite simple. Suppose you go to the butcher to order a T-bone steak and tell him that you will pay a small fee today for the meat but only after you eat it and determine whether it delivered on the butcher's promise will you actually pay him for the meat. Think about how good the meat would be—no more fatty steaks for anyone!

Togetherness, if you will, is one of the key ingredients of hedge fund investing. It has been one of the main factors contributing to the growth of the hedge fund industry and is about the interests of the investors and the managers being completely aligned. Reread that last sentence, because that is what hedge fund investing is all about. It is what the powers that be at many of the large mutual fund companies in the United States don't get and it is why so many investors are looking to hedge funds for their portfolios regardless of what you read in the press or hear from the financial news channels.

WHERE HEDGE FUNDS CAME FROM

To understand how hedge funds have become so popular during the past few years, one needs to go back in time. The trip begins in 1949, when sociologist turned journalist Alfred Winslow Jones opened the first hedge fund—A.W. Jones & Co. in New York City. Jones launched his fund after realizing two things: (1) that he could not make enough money to live the life he wanted to and support his family as a journalist, and (2) that what the people on Wall Street were doing was not all that hard. The genesis for his fund came after he worked on an article titled "Fashion in Forecasting" for *Fortune*. His research for the article centered on how some stocks moved one way while others moved the opposite way, but regardless of which way the stocks moved, investors were making money. Jones took the data and hypothesized that if you created a pool of investments—some long positions and some short positions—you would be able to outperform the market regardless of which way the market moved.

In theory, when the market was up the longs would rise, and the increase on these investments would be greater than the losses associated with the short positions. The reverse, Jones believed, was true for the shorts when the market fell.

One shorts a stock when the investor makes the assumption that the stock is overpriced and will go down in value; this is the opposite of going long a stock, which is the move to make when you believe the price of stock will increase in value as the market puts a real worth on it. Investors buy stocks (or go long stocks) in expectation of a rise in the stock's price. On the flip side, if an investor believes that the stock price is high, the investor will simply sell the stock. But if the investor does not own the stock (or is not long the stock) the investor will short sell the stock with the expectation of covering the short (or buying the stock back) at a lower price sometime in the future when the price falls.

In order to go short a stock, you borrow the stock from your broker and sell it at the current market price. The proceeds from the sale are deposited into your brokerage account. At a point in the future when the stock has gone down in value, you go into the market and buy the same amount of shares you borrowed from the broker and replace the shares that were on loan and that you sold at the higher price. This, in turn, closes out the position. The difference between what you sold the stock for initially and what you bought it back for at a later date is the amount of money you make on the trade, less whatever commissions you are charged by your broker for executing the transaction and lending you the shares.

Shorting is often a difficult concept for many people to grasp. Most people do not understand how you can sell something you do not own and then buy it back later and have the potential for a nice profit. Shorting is something that is extremely common in hedge fund investing and is one of the characteristics that sets hedge funds apart from other traditional investment vehicles or mutual funds. Once you grasp the mechanics of the trade, you will find the concept easy to understand.

That, however, is not all there is to it. Shorting a stock or stocks successfully and consistently over a period of varied market cycles is extremely hard to do. Most people are not good at it because they don't understand what makes a good short as opposed to a bad short. When you are long a stock, the risk is that the stock can go to zero (if you buy a stock at $20 and it goes to zero, you lose $20). The loss is quantifiable. With a short, the stock can go through the roof, resulting in an unlimited loss (if you short a stock at $20 and cover the short at $100, $125, or $150, your loss is huge). Finding good shorts is extremely difficult, and most people get it wrong. Shorting is not for the faint of heart!

This book, however, is not about shorting. It is about hedge fund investing and, more importantly, investing in hedge funds through fund of funds, so we will not spend too much time on the subject of shorting. That being said, we are not done. We believe that it is our duty to make sure that you, the reader, understand the concept of shorting securities; therefore, we have spelled it all out for you in the following text. So bear with us; it is worth it, and frankly, you might learn something.

Shorting a stock is not simply deciding you like IBM and don't like Apple and therefore you are going long IBM shares and short Apple shares. Shorting a stock consists of looking at a company and deciding that the company is going to miss an earnings estimate, suffer from a poor Christmas or back-to-school season, or possibly even fail. Unfortunately, this makes shorting seem un-American or unpatriotic to some observers, because it is counterintuitive to everything we are taught about business, the markets, and the American way (betting and profiting on the failure of a company). This specific argument led the powers that be in Washington and other capitals around the world to ban short selling, in the summer of 2008 and into 2009, of some financial stocks and other companies as their respective share prices were hammered by the market; this was believed to be the work of short sellers. In essence, shorting equities is often based on the assumption that a company will fail and that its management is so bad that it will go out of business and the stock will go to zero. Alternatively it is based on betting that the stock will go down in price in the short term in response to a change in the near-term fundamentals of the company. If you really want to learn more about shorting, type the phrase "shorting a stock" into Wikipedia.org or e-mail us at dsrb@hedgeanswers.com.

A.W. Jones & Co. was all about capitalism and therefore believed not only in the concept of shorting but in the value of using shorts as a hedge to protect long positions during periods of down markets. "My father had this idea about how stocks moved and decided to put the theory into practice with his fund," said Tony Jones, Alfred's son. "The problem he learned early on was that he was not a trader or investor but rather a good marketer, so he ended up hiring the traders and focused on raising money for the partnership."

The Jones partnership was by many measures a successful venture for both the managers and the investors. Unlike most hedge funds today, Jones did not charge a management fee; he charged only an incentive fee. This, Tony said, is what he believed kept his interests clearly aligned with his investors. "The problem with [a] management fee is that you end up in the asset-gathering business rather than the asset-management business, my father believed," he added.

Today the Jones model—a portfolio that consists of both long and short positions—is the basic premise for all hedge funds and the most popular strategy in number and total assets. Unlike long-only investing of mutual funds or long-bond investments, which profit only if their respective markets rise, in theory, a hedge fund—because it goes both long and short—can make money regardless of which way the market moves. The concept is quite simple: create a vehicle that goes long and then short the market in an effort to make money, regardless of market conditions. The difference is that unlike Jones, who went long and short only with equities, today's managers invest in anything and everything: bonds, currencies, commodities, derivative products, and real estate loans. The concept is simple: deliver alpha and use whatever arrows are in your quiver to do so.

THREE WISE MEN

Although Jones is clearly the father of the industry, it is truly the success and investment prowess of three other managers that put hedge funds on the map. George Soros, Michael Steinhardt, and Julian Robertson are three individuals who, in our opinion, caused hedge funds to be so prevalent in the investment landscape today. No discussion of hedge funds is complete without focusing on their work in the markets around the globe as well as the following each has had for more than 30 years. Each of the three is unique in their own right except for one small thing—they call themselves hedge fund managers.

All of these "wise" men have had countless articles and words written about them in both the financial and the popular press. Some of the stories are right, some are wrong, and we will not go on any further about them except to describe them as the cement that glued Jones's foundation into place. It is reasonable to think that had Soros, Steinhardt, and Robertson not come along, hedge funds would not be where they are today. One hedge fund investor and industry observer said that he knew of no other individuals who touched so many different areas of the asset management business and who were responsible for the creation of so many funds. Each of their contributions is immeasurable.

And while these individuals put a positive spin on hedge funds, there clearly have been a lot of negative news items about the industry as well. The most prominent story—regardless of what happened in 2007, 2008, and 2009 in the wake of the credit crisis and the collapse of old-line investment banks Bear Stearns and Lehman Brothers along with Fannie Mae and Freddie Mac—is that of the threat of failure and subsequent Federal Reserve–orchestrated bailout of Long-Term Capital Management (LTCM, for those in the know). It is the handiwork of LTCM's founder and face, John Meriwether and his colleagues that has forever put the fear of global financial meltdown into every institutional investor and into every Tom, Dick, Harry, Selma, Louise, and Joan.

The unprecedented borrowing of the financial giant LTCM in 1998 was forgotten by all during the leverage buildup period of 2002–2007. Not only did Meriwether's LTCM shock the world with sophisticated models that did not work; the Wall Street community along with Fannie Mae and Freddie Mac repeated the excess less than 10 years later. The models of the geniuses of 1998 and 2007–2008 demonstrated that investors, regulators, managers, and the powers that be have short memories.

Again, this book is not about LTCM or its people. For that, we suggest reading Roger Lowenstein's *When Genius Failed: The Rise and Fall of Long-Term Capital Management* (Random House, 2001), which is a solid account of the before, during, and after of the LTCM crisis. There is really nothing we can add except to say once more, don't believe everything you read, and you should ask yourself, who can you trust?

So what can we add is what you are probably thinking: the answer is simple, we can add a lot about fund of funds investing. Not only are we capable, but we are willing. This, you see, is the fundamental subject of this book—fund of funds investing.

Our goal is to enable you to understand the pros and cons of investing in fund of funds by explaining how they work, how they can be used in a diversified portfolio, and where to find them. We are not going to give you investment advice, nor are we going to give you advice on specific funds. We will give you ideas and strategies on how to do due diligence on managers, but for that you need to read on. The idea is simple; this book will be a roadmap to learning about fund of funds and will serve as a reference tool to be used time and again as you look to these vehicles for your portfolio. It offers a toolbox of sorts that will provide you with the tools that you can use to decide who to trust your hard-earned money with in the wake of the recent mess in the investment world.

That being said, you are invited to read on to see how and why the hedge fund industry has evolved over the past decade or so.

SOPHISTICATED INVESTORS

We believe that the evolution of the modern hedge fund industry can be traced to the evolution of the sophisticated investor. The sophisticated investor is defined as an investor who believes two things: (1) that markets rise and fall, and (2) that they need professional money managers to deliver returns to their respected institutions or pools of capital.

The rise of the sophisticated investor can be traced back to the stock market crash of 1987. What happened in October 1987 can be connected with the economic slowdown that began one year earlier after the decline from record-high interest rates from 1981 to 1982. On that Monday, October 18, 1981, overvalued stocks got the ball rolling as investors sought to lock in profits, but the real culprits were program traders and sellers of portfolio insurance. Program trading was blamed for the wholesale selling that accelerated the pressure to get out at any price. Along with program traders, however, the recent introduction of portfolio insurance forced selling as the market moved lower and investors needed to make sure their losses were covered by the insurance.

Twenty years later, newly invented complex financial products created by Wall Street once again wrought havoc with investors, leading to the subprime and related credit crisis that began in 2007 and continues.

The collapse of 1987 is what caused investment professionals responsible for large pools of assets at endowments, foundations, private banks, and family offices to realize that to preserve capital during rocky markets they needed to invest in products or funds that could go both long and short the market. The belief was that to capture market inefficiencies as well as to be prepared on the down side should the markets fall, money needed to be invested in hedge funds. These investors believed that hedge funds could generate profits regardless of which way the market was moving and by putting capital with these managers they were protecting their assets. This belief on the part of the investment community, coupled with the realization by Wall Street that providing services to hedge funds could be an extremely profitable business, caused the market to flourish and blossom in the early 1990s and into the new millennium (see Figure 1.1).

In short, these two beliefs prepared the way for hedge funds to grow and become a massive force in the capital markets around the world. It was a glorious time to be offering services to hedge funds in the early part of the new millennium, and many Wall Street firms and service providers

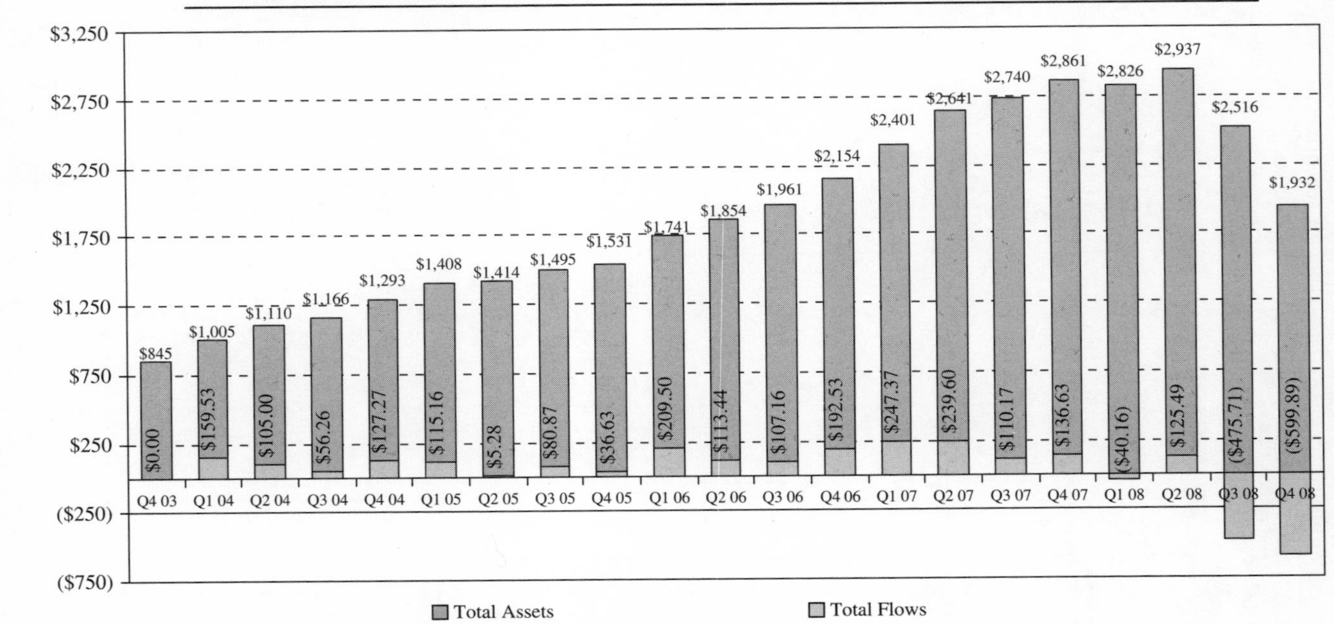

FIGURE 1.1 The Hedge Fund Industry's Growth 1990 to 2007
Source: Hedgefund.net.

(*continued*)

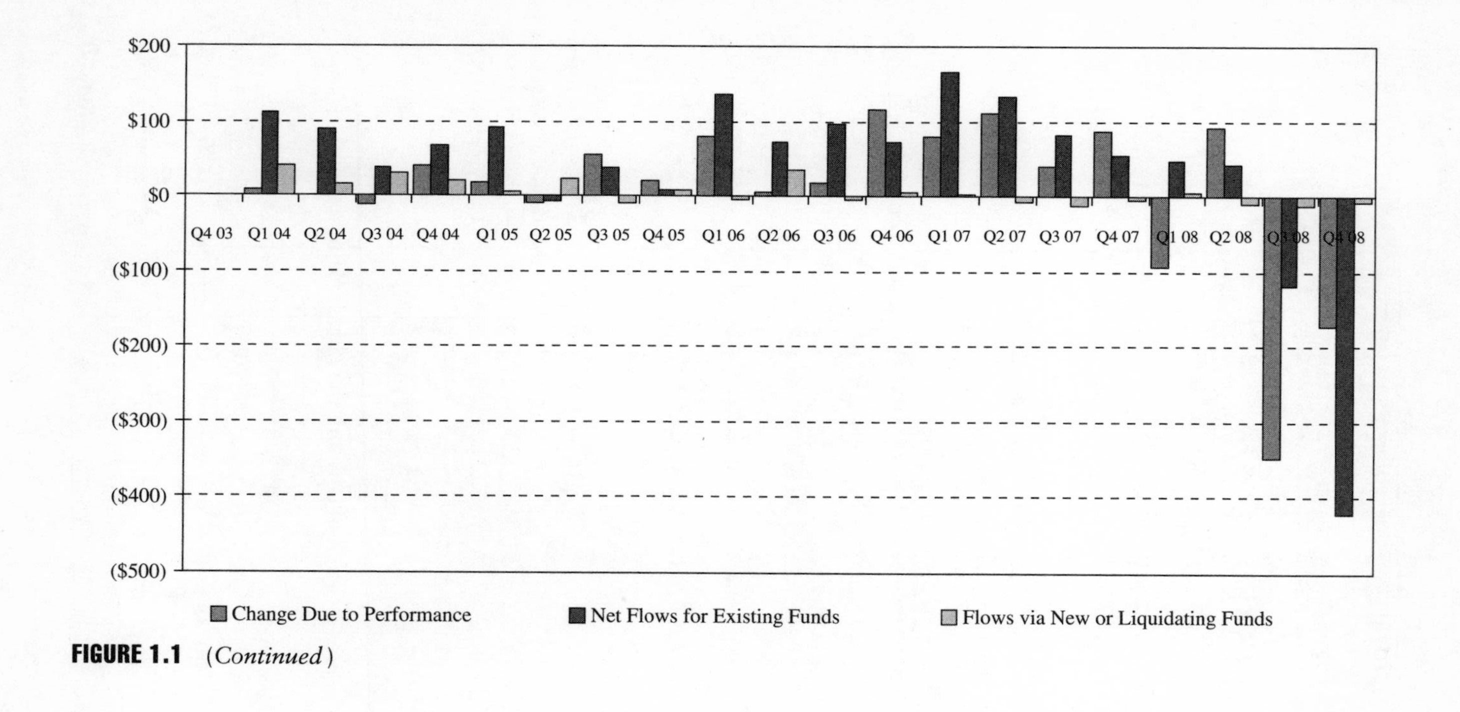

FIGURE 1.1 *(Continued)*

(companies that provide services to money managers but are not broker/dealers) were able to gain a toehold into a business that was about to explode and allow them to prosper.

HEDGE FUND BOOM TIME

"The 1980s was a wild time on the Street," said Peter Testaverde, a partner at Eisner LLP, a New York-based accounting firm, who specializes in working with hedge funds and broker/dealers. "However, it was nothing compared to what it was like in the mid-1990s when growth in the hedge fund industry was at its peak."

The hedge fund industry experienced the first of a series of turning points in the wake of the credit crisis or financial crisis known as the "Asian Flu" hit the economies of Southeast Asia in July of 1997: the Thai baht collapsed sending the country into economic tailspin as a result of the government's decision to no longer peg the currency to the U.S. dollar. Massive losses resulted in all areas of the markets; stocks, bonds, currencies and real estate got hit extremely hard in most of the countries in the region as prices fell and seemed to have no bottom. The losses in Asia traveled around the world hitting Europe and the United States forcing the markets down and causing many to think that a global recession would ensue. The falling markets continued around the globe in the spring and summer of 1998 and witnessed the bailout of LTCM. These events set the industry for massive growth.

Wall Streeters from all over the United States launched hedge funds in every conceivable strategy in hopes of taking advantage of investors' appetites for products that had low correlation with the public debt and equities markets. Investors were seeking ways to achieve positive returns regardless of the direction of the markets. To do this, they needed to augment the rest of their portfolios, which held stocks, bonds, and other investments that would profit only when markets rose.

The Birth of Alternative Investments

Around the dawn of the new millennium, the phrase "alternative investing" appeared not only in money management lexicon but in the popular press as part of the discussion of long/short equity managers and fixed-income arbitrage strategies. In the 10 years since the LTCM collapse, hedge funds have become the topic du jour for both sophisticated and not so sophisticated investors.

Hedge funds have always been Wall Street's forbidden fruit, and it seems that everyone on Main Street wants a bite of the apple. The ride has been tumultuous during the past 10 years, but for managers and investors alike it has been worth it. Fortunes have been made by managers and investors, and even in the wake of the losses resulting from the credit crisis, hedge funds have solidified their grip on the investment community. Hedge funds are here to stay; the ride is far from over. Long-only investors have learned that investing in products that go only one way is like riding a sled downhill with no brakes. Hedge funds, on the other hand, have tremendous braking ability. The reason for this is simple: Hedge funds are an engine that many investors—read institutional investors—need in order to meet the ongoing financial liabilities of their constituencies.

Since 2000, those who provide investment advice and guidance to the institutional investment community (i.e., pension funds, endowments, family offices, and insurance companies) have concluded that hedge funds are an asset class where these assets should be allocated. This realization has led to massive capital inflows by these investment behemoths. The genie is out of the bottle; hedge funds are here to stay. However, with these massive allocations (it was expected that these investors will have allocated approximately $1 trillion to hedge funds at the end of the first quarter in 2009 according to a report issued by The Bank of New York Mellon in April 2009), there are still many issues that investors need to have answered before their money is put to work.

In the early 1990s, sophisticated investors such as college and university endowments and foundations joined high net worth investors and family offices as early adopters of hedge funds, and large public retirement plans started to review this asset class. Despite the setback of the LTCM implosion, institutional investors started diving deeper into the so-called secretive world of hedge funds and looked for the best vehicle for an entry point. Seeking advice from investment consulting firms that previously knew the long-only world, early institutional investors into hedge funds started the migration to fund of funds in the period 2000–2002.

Although many concerns are constantly raised by investors and consultants alike about the validity of investing in products that invest in other investment funds, the list of reasons why it is an efficient and easy way to access the asset class is long. Some of the main points are

- It is a single point of entry into the hedge fund industry.
- Investors that lack extensive internal research efforts can use seasoned professionals at fund of funds to allocate assets among a series of hedge fund managers.
- Fund of funds investing provides diversification.
- Managers employ ongoing and constant risk management.
- Hedge fund investing through fund of funds delivers specific risk/return profiles unattainable through single-manager investing.

Investors use fund of funds investing to achieve the previously listed objectives. While the financial media often single out hedge funds as part of the "axis of evil," this is clearly not the case; it's a scare tactic used to sell newspapers and gain ratings points. The reality is that despite the setback of redemptions in 2008, hedge funds expect to experience massive inflows of capital from new and existing investors, both directly and through fund of funds, in the next several years.

WHY FUND OF FUNDS

In general, the first hedge fund investment option for many investors has been fund of funds. These investment vehicles provide a single point of entry into the hedge fund world, with instant access to a wide range of styles and strategies. Most fund of funds have research teams, portfolio management teams, and risk management teams that investors leverage by putting their capital into these products.

All evidence to the contrary in light of the Madoff situation, fund of funds also are thought to provide investors an opportunity to avoid the land mines of hedge fund meltdowns and frauds while also providing them with cover in the event of a blowup or fraud. Most investors at pension funds, endowments, and insurance companies, along with their boards of directors and their allocators, want to avoid "career risk" events. Fund of funds are thought to fill a large psychological and physical need for novice and experienced investors and to provide someone to blame if something doesn't work—either risk or reward.

However, over the past few years and specifically as of December 2008, fund of funds have been suffering from moderation of investment returns, and investment strategies have started to shift away from "mainstream" hedge fund strategies to activist investing, complex derivative strategies, and greater reliance on less liquid private equity strategies to deliver returns.

At the same time, many fund of funds investors have started to evaluate direct investment into hedge funds on their own rather than off-the-shelf fund of funds allocations. Even though fund of funds investments seem to have lived up to their description as "hedge fund investing with training wheels," more investors have started to branch directly into individual hedge fund strategies in hopes of limiting risk while increasing reward.

The first phase of fund of funds investors moving into single manager hedge funds occurred in the period 2005–2007 as hedge fund returns moderated and investors questioned the second level of fees that were being charged for portfolio management at the fund of funds. At the same time, fund of funds investors were clamoring for higher levels of transparency and thought that direct investing would provide this additional level of portfolio and position transparency. The result was that some institutional investors decided to go direct.

Poor returns by hedge funds and funds of funds in 2008 along with high-level blowups in fixed-income, arbitrage, and derivative strategies continued to push the more seasoned large institutional investors away from fund of funds and into hedge funds. Large investors believed that they were getting more customized portfolios that met their respective investment and asset/liability requirements, greater transparency by which to monitor the portfolio, and certainly a more favorable fee structure by going direct. Prior to the Madoff catastrophe, the well-publicized blowups of firms such as Amaranth, Zwirn, and Bear Stearns Asset Management forced many investment committees to think long and hard about whether to use fund of funds as a place to invest. Regardless of the determination of the investment committees and consultants, the research is clear that fund of funds (Madoff excluded) offer a level of diversification unattainable by direct investing. The ability to diversify through fund of funds investing limits the impact of a specific blowup or fraud on an investor's asset.

Diversification 101

Take, for example, the impact, described as follows, of investment by two pension plans of $100 million of their assets in a single manager and $100 million in a fund of funds. Investor one put all of its investment into Madoff—resulting in a total loss when the fraud was exposed. Investor two put all of its money into a fund of funds, which in turn allocated evenly among ten managers, resulting in a loss of $10 million. They both experienced a loss and were victims of fraud, but two clearly did better then one.

The lurking question, which we discuss in great detail later in the book, is whether the extra level of fees or costs associated with fund of funds investing is worth it. Our initial reaction, based on the preceding example, is yes—but read on to make sure you really see where we come out on the fee argument.

INSTITUTIONAL INVESTORS LOVE HEDGE FUNDS

As the thundering herd of institutional investors sweeps across the plains into fund of funds as their first foray into investing in hedge funds, many are no longer satisfied with the off-the-shelf products that these managers are offering to the masses. Many of these investors are demanding a separately managed account that is tailored to their specific investment needs or wants or expectations.

These investors also require a more sophisticated reporting process and risk measurement system to accurately assess risk and returns as well a way to determine the source of alpha—the one thing, regardless of the size of one's wallet, that all hedge fund investors want, need, and expect.

Alpha Is?

What is alpha? As described previously in this chapter, alpha is a performance measurement on a risk-adjusted basis that compares the risk-adjusted return according to an industry benchmark or index to that of the underlying investment.

Alpha is used as a measurement to determine the return of an investment versus an index. For instance, if the manager is up 15 percent in a calendar year, and the benchmark index S&P 500 is up 10 percent, the manager's alpha would be 5 percent. If both the index and the manager are up 15 percent, the manager's performance would be directly tied to the market, or in this case, directly tied to the index, with a resulting alpha of zero. In other words, the investor did not need to invest with the manager but could have invested directly in the index of an exchange-traded fund that mirrors the index.

Investors search for alpha, not to determine an investment's correlation to an index, but as the reason to invest in hedge funds as opposed to traditional long-only funds that have little or no chance of beating the index.

Going both long and short the market at the same time is the only way to truly insure success. However, having investment vehicles that go both long and short is something that, while confusing to some, represents a very important area of the capital markets that is here to stay. Over the past few years however, the hedge fund and fund of funds industry has evolved from a "trust me" attitude (thank you Mr. Madoff and others) when making investment decisions that could be sealed with a handshake, to one that now requires sophisticated due diligence, background checks, and peer group analysis before any investment is made, regardless of how much money is at stake. Therefore, to be most effective with your or others' assets, you need to think about due diligence, which is more than just making a decision to invest based on a relationship or marketing brochure. The next step for you and others is to turn the page and begin to understand the importance of hedge funds and manager due diligence.

CHAPTER 2

A Hedge Fund Is What?

Although this book is not intended to be a primer on hedge funds, one of the first tasks is for us to define the term *hedge fund*.

While there is no universally accepted definition, the term hedge fund generally refers to an investment vehicle that invests in a wide range of securities and other assets, and is not registered as an investment company under the Investment Act of 1940 (the 40 Act). As such, the hedge fund does not issue shares or units such as mutual funds to investors but instead offers limited partnership interests. Investments in hedge funds are not sold in a public offering like mutual funds, but through private placement offerings to investors that meet specific income and asset levels as defined by the 40 Act.

However, in light of the credit crisis of 2008 and the Madoff fraud, Congress is contemplating changing some of the requirements and guidelines mentioned previously and subsequently. At the time of publication, nothing had been made firm, and we don't know where things will end up. One thing is for sure: things will change sometime before the end of 2010. We don't know when it will come or what it will be, but we do know that things will change, maybe for the better, but quite possibly for the worse.

THE CREDIT CRISIS AND HEDGE FUNDS

It is important to understand the mechanics of hedge fund investing as they were in the early part of 2009.

Hedge funds are open to accredited investors and super-accredited investors that meet an income and asset test determined by the manager before he or she can accept the investor into its fund. As of this printing, the definition of accredited investors is individuals who have a net worth of $1,000,000 or more and an annual income greater than $200,000. Institutional investors must have a minimum of $5,000,000 in assets.

Hedge funds are prohibited from advertising under the Securities Act of 1933. Cold calling, advertising on TV, and using billboards or the Internet are prohibited.

Offerings can be made only by the private placement memorandum to accredited investors. In fact, all marketing material must include disclaimers and caveats regarding the risk associated with hedge fund and private placement investing such that any thinking persons who read the material completely would not be considered in their right mind if they invested in such a product. Think kitchen sink of risks and disclaimers and add about 10,000 words. If you would like to see examples of the disclaimer or have a question, send us an e-mail at dsrb@hedgeanswers.com.

While private placement memoranda vary from manager to manager because each is "individually" designed by the many different law firms around the globe that specialize in hedge funds, most private placement memoranda outline and state in broad terms the investment strategy practices of the manager, the pricing methods of securities in the portfolio, details of any conflicts between the investment manager and investors, and the risks and fees associated with the investment. The conflicts are usually few and far between and can include things like the manager places trades through an affiliated broker dealer instead of going to outside brokers. Other conflicts could be that he manages a number of funds that trade different strategies and one fund may take advantage of one thing that another cannot. Conflicts could also be employee related, and be a result of employees sitting on boards of directors or being involved in other businesses outside of the fund. The private placement memorandum also details whom the fund does business with and provides great detail on the manager and its organization. The section of the private placement memorandum that deals with fees is usually of great interest to investors. This section details how the managers make their money and how they are paid. As of this printing, the generally accepted fees for hedge funds consisted of a management fee of between 1 and 2 percent and an incentive fee of 20 percent. Fund of funds, for the most part, charge between a 1 and a 1.5 percent management fee with a 10 percent incentive fee.

HEDGE FUNDS ARE AN ASSET CLASS

Some critics of the hedge fund industry often state that hedge funds are not an asset class but merely a compensation scheme to reward managers. This is generally advanced by mutual fund managers who are deemed by most sophisticated investors as being not in the investment-management business but really in the asset-gathering business, given that they make fees only on assets under management and have little or no stake in the success of the fund's performance.

Hedge funds employ strategies to achieve an absolute rate of return by which the funds earn a positive return regardless of market environment. Hedge funds are not as concerned as traditional long investors in achieving a relative return through which the manager seeks to beat the benchmark index. A hedge fund manager is not content to state that "our fund outperformed the S&P 500 last year." Whereas a long-only manager would be content with results that are "only" down 5 percent while the index was down 10 percent, hedge funds seek to achieve positive results in all market environments. Remember alpha from Chapter 1?

Many hedge funds often use leverage to achieve higher returns while at the same time using sophisticated risk management tools to lower portfolio volatility. The most defining difference between hedge funds and long-only investing is the extensive use of shorting securities—stocks, bonds, commodities, and exchange-traded funds (ETFs)—to "hedge" long positions and to generate positive returns from the short positions. Shorting is accomplished by managers who sell securities short (stocks or bonds) that they don't actually own with an objective of buying them back at a lower price in the future with the stated intent of earning a positive return.

Many hedge funds use hedging as part of an arbitrage strategy, such as fixed-income and convertible arbitrage, to generate low-volatility returns that are consistent over a market cycle.

In addition to trading equities and bonds, hedge fund managers use strategies that utilize currencies, futures, ETFs, commodity contracts, derivatives, private placements, weather contracts, life insurance settlement contracts, asset-based lending, and trade claims. While the list could easily be expanded more comprehensively, the fundamental basis for hedge fund investing has been to exploit market inefficiencies and capitalize on gains that may be created in each respective market, all over the globe.

Unfortunately for hedge fund managers, globalization of the capital markets and the 24-hour trading day have improved the efficiency of the markets, forcing them to look under many more rocks than they needed to just a few short years ago in search of new and unique opportunities for undiscovered profit.

LIQUIDITY PRESENTS PROBLEMS

Certainly, the lower level of liquidity of hedge funds may present an additional obstacle for some investors. In a down market or period of market stress and dislocation, liquidity seizes up, the markets lock, and trade executions are stressed. Many hedge fund managers and investors experienced this in 2007, in 2008, and into 2009 as credit collapsed and everyone seemed to be hording cash, leading many to question what, if any, value hedge funds offer investors. On that issue the jury is still out; however, there are a number of issues that investors need to keep in mind above and beyond the recent events before an investment in a hedge fund is made:

- **Use of leverage.** As witnessed on several occasions during the past five years, hedge funds use leverage to "juice" returns in up markets, but that may cause the returns to be subject to downturns or large changes in standard deviation in the fixed-income and credit markets in a down market.
- **Underperformance.** While estimates of expected returns may not be achieved, some hedge funds may increase risk to increase return or recoup past losses.
- **Liquidity.** Investors must ask whether the liquidity terms and risk profile justify the investment.
- **Style drift.** Inflows of capital and generous compensation schedules for managers may not be enough to encourage managers to "stick to their knitting," or invest in strategies that compliment the managers' backgrounds. For example if they are long/short equity managers, they should not be trading fixed income securities.
- **Transparency.** It could result in economic damage to a manager if short positions were publicized or active buy programs were made public. Since all positions may not be known, investors with a lack of short positions must rely on incomplete portfolio modeling.

The strategies employed by hedge fund managers have considerable width and depth. Some of the most popular hedge fund strategies include:

Global macro

CTA/managed futures

Long/short equity

Sector-specific long/short equity

Risk arbitrage

Fixed-income arbitrage

Mortgage-backed arbitrage

Asset-backed arbitrage

Merger arbitrage

Statistical arbitrage
Convertible arbitrage
Regulation D exploitation
Credit arbitrage
Emerging markets
Multi-strategy
Event-driven
Distressed investing
Quantitative model
Asset-based lending
Short selling
Activist investing
Carbon emissions trading
Weather trading

Although most of these strategies have been around since the beginning of the hedge fund boom in the 1990s, spreads and returns have moderated as the capital markets have become more efficient, market participants have become much more sophisticated, and hedge managers continue to evolve and find ways to exploit market inefficiencies.

TECHNOLOGY HELPS THE INDUSTRY

One of the greatest contributors to leveling the playing field has been the growth, acceptance, and prevalence of the Bloomberg. This system has created a seemingly endless list of analytical tools for tracking and modeling most investment strategies and styles. As the Bloomberg moves from a box on a trader's desk to his home office, accessed through the Internet or BlackBerry, real-time around-the-clock, around-the-globe analytics became possible, thereby eliminating the edge that many money managers have used to extract profits from the markets.

Today, with a point and click of the mouse, you can literally get real-time prices and information about pretty much any security in the world. The proliferation of the Internet as a tool in the investment world has leveled the playing field between the haves and the have-nots in the money management world. Investors of all shapes and sizes believe that with the use of technology they can beat the markets. However, the data proves this to be untrue, and it has created an edge for managers or professionals to exploit.

As the markets continue to evolve, some conditions have caused various strategies to fall out of favor as opportunities wane and the ability to deliver returns vanishes. This has led Wall Street and others to develop and create new ways of skinning the proverbial cat.

Some Strategies Fail to Deliver

Take, for example, merger arbitrage, a stable and profitable strategy for much of the 1990s. However, as the deals dried up and merger and acquisition (M&A) activity during the technology bust of 2000–2003 all but disappeared, merger arbitrage returns declined and managers lost assets. Fewer deals meant narrower spreads and less profitability. Technology also played a part in the decline in merger arbitrage managers as modeling and new analytical tools and increased flow of information for announced merger deals came out in the open. Traders now can instantaneously price a new deal using Bloomberg, thereby reducing the advantage that old-school managers had with their ability to price deals before the evolution of the point-and-click trading turret.

The "new kids on the block" of hedge fund strategies in the post-technology blowup of the early part of the new millennium, along with those that have been successful despite the recent credit crisis, include credit arbitrage and activist investing. Investors seem to have moved away from the somewhat plain vanilla long/short equity and debt managers and good old-fashioned fundamental investing in favor of managers who use distressed and credit arbitrage strategies.

Investors believe that credit arbitrage managers take hedging to the next degree by buying or selling credit protection as a proxy for long or short positions in specific bond issues, or as a tool to increase leverage through the derivatives market. In the subprime meltdown, many victims—lenders, banks, and dozens of high-profile hedge funds—were wiped out, while numerous savvy managers who understood the subprime market, mortgage cash flows, and structure realized big rewards from big bets in short positions.

ACTIVISM IS A NEW BUZZ WORD

Activist investing has also become a more accepted strategy in the new millennium. Activist investing is fundamentally a long-only strategy that attempts to address the increasing institutional interest in corporate governance and to "enhance shareholder value" with substantial upside if the manager can be effective. Instead of just acquiring a large block of stock and trying to influence change within the company, many well-known managers/investors, including Nelson Peltz, William Ackman, Edward Lampert, Mario Gabelli, and Carl Icahn, have worked with management teams to "achieve shareholder value"; but they become more hostile if the perceived necessary steps are not taken and an increase in stock price is not achieved. These managers go for the jugular; they believe—rightly so, we add—that it is their company and that shareholder value needs to be maximized.

The U.S. Congress whipped the nation into a frenzy over the executive compensation practices of AIG and the banking industry, but activist investors have been on the forefront of leveling the playing field for many years. Activists may advocate asset or whole division sales, corporate divestitures, or increased dividends and share buybacks—anything and everything to increase the share price. However, with exceptionally large positions, liquidity is lessened and partnership returns may be subject to large monthly swings. In some cases, the egos of the money managers seem to get in the way of actually producing increased overall shareholder value, which can hurt both the company and the fund.

Other new strategies that are less trafficked but growing nonetheless include catastrophe bonds, carbon emissions trading, weather derivatives, insurance premium finance, life settlement contracts, and asset-based lending. As a result, hedge funds are playing a greater role in the growth of assets by becoming more like private equity funds in some cases. Hedge funds have started to get involved in funding transactions and running businesses in a host of industries and sectors. One of the most famous examples of this is in the automotive area with the purchase of Chrysler by the hedge fund Cerberus and its purchase of a 51 percent stake of GMAC and ultimate divestiture in 2009. Edward Lampert of ESL Investments fame got into the game of operating companies with his purchase of old-time retailers Sears and K-Mart. The Chrysler purchase came to a head when on May 1, 2009, President Barak Obama forced the company into bankruptcy in order to complete a deal with Fiat.

PRIVATE EQUITY AND HEDGE FUNDS

Similarly, in recent years several large private equity firms have set up shop in hedge fund land, blurring the lines between the two groups. In the past, private equity firms provided leverage for multibillion-dollar financings while the hedge fund brethren traded and financed billion-dollar recapitalizations and turnarounds.

In the spring of 2002, the SEC undertook a fact-finding mission to conduct a study of the hedge fund industry that included service providers and the related investors. The 2003 Staff Report to the U.S. SEC, "Implications of the Growth of Hedge Funds," dated September 2003 stated "Hedge funds often provide markets and investors with substantial benefits. For example, based on our observations, many hedge funds take speculative, value-driven trading positions based on extensive research about the value of a security. These positions can enhance liquidity and contribute to market efficiency. In addition, hedge funds offer investors an important risk management tool by providing valuable portfolio diversification because hedge fund returns in many cases are not correlated to the broader debt and equity markets."[1]

In short, the SEC seems to have come to the conclusion that the capital markets need hedge funds. The question is, how good can this study by the SEC be in light of the recent news of the regulators' failure on so many issues? Nevertheless we like it!

The intent of the SEC's report was to recommend that hedge funds, hedge fund advisors, and hedge fund of funds register with the Commission as Registered Investment Advisors. The report considers a number of issues surrounding the hedge fund industry, including

- Valuation, suitability, and fee disclosures
- Monitoring capital introduction services by broker-dealers
- Permitting general solicitation of offerings by hedge funds
- Embracing a "best practices" policy

The SEC is not the only group looking into how hedge funds operate; that is a topic being considered by regulators around the globe. The UK Financial Services Authority (FSA) and the International Organization of Securities Commissions (IOSCO) have both been advocating change to the industry. The IOSCO released a report in 2007 looking at valuations for hedge funds, and the FSA called for greater transparency regarding fees and redemption policies. There is no doubt change will come to this industry; the question is, will it solve any of the so-called problems or just create more billable hours for attorneys and an increased bureaucracy?

HEDGE FUNDS AROUND THE WORLD

Hedge fund acceptance globally is still in the early stages as more hedge fund outposts are established in Asia, Australia, the Middle East, and Latin America. The U.S. media and elected officials are not the only ones always quick to blame hedge funds for market volatility or price collusion; hedge funds have had a challenging time in Europe and Asia as well. In Germany, one public official called hedge funds "schabe" (translated into English, "cockroaches"). This comment illustrates the concern of the German government about hedge funds, causing regulators in that country and others in Europe to make it very challenging for hedge funds to raise assets and attract investors in this area of the free market.

In this case, Wall Street has done what it does best when faced with adverse working conditions; it comes up with a solution to get around the regulation or impediment. Accordingly, Wall Street created a series of structured products using bond-like investment characteristics, which in turn made it possible for many German and European institutional investors to gain access to hedge funds. Hedge fund wraps, including principal-protected notes and structures that resemble bonds, seemed to be acceptable as German investors look to capitalize on the returns of hedge funds and are not allowed to go direct by their government. This is just one example of Wall Street ingenuity finding ways to allow some institutional investors, including insurance companies and others who have restrictions on investments, to get around those restrictions and gain access to hedge funds.

ALTERNATIVE INVESTMENTS

Hedge funds are one type of investment vehicle included in what is now called the alternative investment universe. If we look at the maturity of the investment management industry and various investment buckets that assets are placed in along the investment curve, hedge funds should no longer be labeled "alternatives" in our opinion. Hedge funds had previously been called "other" by investment counselors and consultants; now, however, they are commonplace and not just accepted but expected as part of a diversified portfolio.

Alternative investments may be structured as limited partnerships, limited liability companies, trusts, or corporations. Included in alternatives in addition to hedge funds are private equity funds, real estate funds, leveraged buyout funds, venture capital funds, offshore fund vehicles, and of course fund of funds. Investors in these so-called alternatives include college and university endowments, foundations, pension plans, investment companies, family offices, high net worth investors, among others. The range of investment allocation to alternatives varies according to the risk profile of the underlying investor. Some investors may invest in a single hedge fund or a series of individual hedge funds, while many investors allocate to a specific range of hedge funds. The traditional fund of funds investor seeks portfolio diversification through the expertise of the fund of funds manager.

Many believe that hedge funds are still classed as alternatives, but probably they should not be. True alternatives are direct investments such as timberland, real estate, oil and gas, venture capital, and private equity. Investors seek hedge fund investments for absolute return with low correlation to the public markets or more traditional long-only investments.

Investors want and demand alpha! Unlike true alternatives, hedge funds can provide shorter liquidity, which generally ranges from monthly to annual, though in some cases, it may be as long as three to five years.

Even with skeptics characterizing hedge funds as lucrative compensation schemes for the manager to get rich (we believe the only people who complain about the fees are those who cannot charge them), the investor's mandate is to achieve a net of fee return and risk profile that meets the portfolio objective. Simply put, the manager and investor are in it to win it, together.

Hedge funds have been able to generate good returns for the investors and general partners with little direct regulatory oversight until recently. The subprime meltdown and the well-publicized extraordinary results of many hedge funds along with the sudden failure of the Bear Stearns external hedge fund in the spring of 2007 pushed hedge funds to front-page news. The collapse of Madoff's Ponzi scheme has kept them there. For the masses, the jury on the industry is clearly still out; however, managers continue to survive and thrive.

The use of structured products, illiquid private placements, and the ability of hedge funds to quickly react to borrowers' needs has led to new tools of financial innovation to provide higher levels of return for investors. Clearly, this is the new turf of market inefficiency, with only the most nimble being rewarded. From the perspective of a hedge fund or fund of funds investor, the higher noncorrelated returns and alpha produced are meeting investors' objectives, but a whole new set of due diligence and compliance requirements have arisen for all investors.

CHAPTER 3

How Large Is the Market?

It seems that everyone on Wall Street wants to work for or run a hedge fund. It seems that everyone on Main Street wants to invest in a hedge fund, and then there are some of us who just want to know how many hedge funds there are and how much money these capitalists are managing. While the two statements are true—it is impossible for us to get an answer to the last question.

HEDGE FUND DATA IS WEAK

Comprehensive hedge fund data is exceedingly deficient. Since there is no consolidated database and individual investment managers voluntarily report results to various databases, it is truly impossible to arrive at a true count of the industry. Unlike mutual funds, which are required by an act of Congress to report their returns and assets under management to FINRA (Financial Industry Regulatory Authority) on a daily basis, there is no such rule for hedge funds. This is a serious problem that Congress and the powers that be need to fix if they ever really want to get their hands around the hedge fund industry.

There are at least 10 recognized hedge fund databases that collect and report hedge fund data with some regularity. The most noteworthy include but are not limited to Credit Suisse/Tremont, Hedgefund.net, Morningstar, and Barclay Group. Many managers that are closed to new investment dollars or those that do not want to share performance results with the database simply don't list the existence of the fund and choose not to provide returns to the database companies. Because there is no reporting requirement and for the most part the databases operate on a catch-as-can basis, many firms with good performance histories report numbers and demand inclusion, whereas those with bad numbers simply don't. It is really ridiculous that the industry operates this way. It makes little or no sense, yet it is accepted.

Many service providers, including prime brokers and information sources such as Infovest21 and Lipper HedgeWorld, conduct surveys that allege to provide results that point to the size of the hedge fund industry, but the data is questionable. As recently as the summer of 2008 it was estimated that approximately $2 trillion dollars in assets was under management at hedge funds around the globe.[1]

Technology Is Helpful

One of the best indicators of the size of the hedge fund industry is an annual study done by PerTrac. Founded in 1996, PerTrac provides an analytical software solution for hedge fund investors to compile a range of statistical measures for portfolio construction and to generate reports to track performance for individual managers as well as universes of all hedge fund strategies. PerTrac aggregates 11 databases, including Barclay's, CogentHedge, CISDM, Eureka, Hedgefund.net, Hedge Fund Research, Lipper/Tass, Morningstar/Altvest, and MSCI Hedge Fund Indices, and has issued an annual study since 2003 that defines the size of the hedge fund industry. This study, which is generally issued in the first quarter of each year, has become a widely followed industry indicator. The results of the 2008 study are included in the Appendix.

In the report for the year ending 2007, PerTrac found that despite the overlap between the databases and the widespread growth among them, relatively few hedge funds report to more than two or three databases, and only one fund reports to all 11 databases. In fact, a significant number of hedge funds and fund of funds, about 12,000 in the 11-database sample, appeared only in a single database.

In 2007, the study found that new fund launches declined; although that information is interesting, it is unclear how many funds actually do not participate in the survey. Meredith Jones, a PerTrac employee, said that given the extraordinary growth rates of new fund launches in earlier years of the industry, the slowdown in launch rates was probably inevitable as the industry has matured.

"The decrease in new fund launches reflects the asset flow trends in the industry to well-known established large hedge funds and fund of funds," she said. "This acts as a deterrent for new entrants into the marketplace."

REPORTING IS WEAK

In addition to the reporting issues in the hedge fund industry, there is a second flaw to gauging the size of the marketplace, which is what the popular and trade press use when estimating the asset size of the industry. In short, leverage is not taken into account, and therefore the numbers could be off by a factor of ten.

The "total assets" number is, in reality, the total equity of the funds' equity, not total assets of the investments. Applying the actual total leverage used increases gross exposure of the manager and really represents total assets at risk. Hedge fund managers publish and notify investors of the "equity" in each respective fund.

Leverage

Long/short equity leverage generally employed by managers ranges from none to one-and-a-half times partner capital, resulting in .50 percent leverage. In other words, a manager with $1.00 of capital (or equity) invests $1.50 in assets, with many equity strategies employing higher levels of leverage, in some cases greater than 200–250 percent.

As an example, a long/short equity hedge fund that has $100 million in limited partner equity may be long $100 million in securities and short $80 million. Total gross exposure is $180 million, while net market exposure is low at only $20 million.

How does the total capital get counted and reported to investors and databases? The manager reports $100 million in partner capital, but available trading assets are really $180 million. Risk capital is actually $180 million. In reality, the manager actually has $180 million of market risk against which portfolio volatility must be evaluated, not the equity of $100 million. For every $1 price move, there will be a $1.80 move in portfolio price. In 2008 there were record levels of redemptions as investors witnessed the impact of leverage.

On the leverage scale of low to high, long/short equity managers' use of leverage is moderate. Fixed-income arbitrage and derivative strategies typically use higher levels of leverage, often exceeding 10 times the actual equity investments. Mortgage-backed securities managers often use higher levels of leverage, whereas many other arbitrage strategies, including convertible arbitrage and corporate bond arbitrage, use leverage ranging from two to four times. Leverage is used to enhance returns, period.

If we use the 2007 PerTrac results for the size of the hedge fund industry, equity capital is $2 trillion, and the total actual assets of the hedge fund industry are dramatically understated. When total assets invested are considered, the figure probably exceeds $10 trillion, closely approaching total mutual fund assets of $11.5 trillion[2] before the deleveraging of 2008 began.

Risk Management

Risk managers are concerned about systemic risk and volatility as well as leverage and always work to evaluate the portfolio exposure on both gross and net exposures of the assets. With $10 trillion in hedge fund assets and adding off–balance sheet items, including derivatives, swaps, special purpose entities, which in turn include collateralized debt obligations (CDOs) and collateralized loan obligations (CLOs), market exposure and volatility are certainly greater than the "accepted" industry asset estimates of $1.5 to $2 trillion.

In looking at the total size of the hedge fund industry, the correct benchmark must be to consider total market exposure, not total equity or total assets invested in funds. In other words, while the equity of the hedge fund industry may have been $2 trillion in 2007, the industry commanded control of assets in excess of $10 trillion at year end 2007. This represents the capital at risk for on–balance sheet positions, not including off–balance sheet derivatives or credit default swaps of other leverage vehicles. In short, hedge fund assets are becoming very cumbersome, and hedge funds no longer can be called a "cottage industry."

Based on the 2007 results of the report,

- 15,250 single-manager hedge funds were identified, along with 7,400 fund of funds in 2007, compared with 13,675 single managers and 6,100 fund of funds in 2006.
- 4,600 distinct general partners were identified, compared with 4,900 in 2006.
- 35 percent of the single-manager hedge funds were U.S.–based funds, with 66 percent offshore, essentially unchanged from 2006.
- 13 percent of the fund of funds were U.S. based, and 87 percent were offshore.

According to the data, fund of funds assets were about $980 billion, and one-third of the fund of funds manage less than $25 million.

Single-manager funds had $1.41 trillion in assets, with 250 having assets greater than $1 billion. One-third of single-manager funds manage less than $25 million.

INSTITUTIONALIZATION OF HEDGE FUNDS

As the industry has grown and the acceptance of hedge fund investing has spread, many have said the industry is becoming institutionalized. This has resulted in large hedge funds continuing to grow and expand, with more then 350 having assets of greater than $1 billion.

In reviewing the fund of funds industry, the story is a bit skewed. Assets in fund of funds have grown from $84 billion at year end 2000 to nearly $1 trillion in 2008. According to data provided by Freeman & Co LLC, a New York–based advisor to the financial services industry that provides M&A advisory services and strategic management consulting, the compounded annual growth rate of assets under management since 2000 has been 44.1 percent for fund of funds compared with 21.3 percent for hedge funds.

Freeman's data shows that 2,000 hedge fund and fund of funds assets were $491 billion in 2000 with 17 percent in fund of funds, and Q3 2007 results totaled $1.81 billion with fund of funds assets making up 55 percent of total hedge fund assets. Clearly, as investors gain access to hedge funds, fund of funds have gained the greatest share.[3]

One of the questions that is often raised about starting a hedge fund or fund of funds is: what is the barrier to entry? We have posed a different question that many investors have raised: what is the barrier to investing in fund of funds?

The existence of high fees or a second level of fees is the most often cited barrier to investing. This comment continues to be made quite vociferously in light of the Madoff mess. However, fraud aside, longer-term fund of funds investors generally seem to be more satisfied than new investors. We believe that criticism of the extra layer of fees, while based on reality, is unfounded given that seasoned, committed fund of funds organizations play a vital role in portfolio management for a diversified pool of hedge fund strategies. Of course the Madoff situation has caused many to question whether and how managers allocate assets. While fees are always a sticky subject, we say once again that the only people complaining about fees are those who cannot charge them. In short, you get what you pay for; therefore, make sure you pay for what you are buying and vice versa.

Even if the fee issue is not enough to deal with, the other major concern is transparency. There are too many views on this subject to comment completely about it in this chapter. We will deal with transparency later on; however, it must be said that transparency is important and cannot be overlooked. Therefore, you should ask questions, get answers, and make sure you understand what is being said. If not, you could end up in a Madoff situation, a Tremont situation, or a Fairfield Greenwich situation. And while the jury is still out on the last, everyone knows, unfortunately, what happened with the first.

CHAPTER 4

Hedge Fund Investing

The crossover or convergence of hedge funds and private equity has provided new opportunities for investors and managers to work together and extract profits from the markets. However, as the convergence has occurred, investors have raised many questions and concerns about how their money is being managed. All marketing material for hedge funds, as well as for other investments, states "past performance is not indicative of future results." In the changing environment, investors are betting on better future results.

PRICING PROBLEMS

One of the challenges of hedge fund investing is subjective and periodic pricing of the portfolio. Pricing of the individual positions in portfolio or "marking to market" can be a complex issue for illiquid or less frequently traded securities (i.e., private equity holdings). Managers will generally use pricing obtained from publicly available sources as well as from proprietary sources from the prime brokers or administrators. The Wall Street dealer community also provides pricing data to the manager. In less liquid or illiquid positions, the challenge is different.

To standardize the pricing and reduce the need to manage pricing and monthly performance results, the Financial Accounting Standards Board (FASB) introduced FASB 157 for Fair Value Measurements to define fair value within the annual auditing process. The purpose is to reduce the risk of mark to market bias by managers by addressing three issues: definition of fair value, methods used to establish fair value, and providing additional disclosure and its results.

Accounting Rules

To define fair value, the FASB established a three-level system of classification for the portfolio and set a requirement for each level. Level one inputs are quoted prices or "observable prices" in active markets. This is easy for companies that are quoted on a stock exchange. Level two inputs are "observable for the asset or liability, either directly or indirectly." Level two prices may not have an observable price, but the prices are based on input for financial instruments such as interest rate swaps. Level three includes "unobservable prices," such as private equities, real estate loans, or complex derivatives. Level three may require using a model to price the position and to consider when selling the position. This would include taking the current market pricing and liquidity into account for the pricing, even though the position may have no market and no resulting liquidity. Most hedge fund managers would argue that the value is unchanged, given that there is no known market and the value has held up, because no deterioration of the credit has occurred despite the change in market liquidity.

Illiquid Securities

The greatest challenge for hedge fund investors traditionally had been the pricing of illiquid securities, but the introduction of FASB 157 in 2007 presented a new wave of issues for hedge fund managers and the U.S. commercial banking industry. While the auditors and bank examiners forced depository institutions to "mark down" the prices of hard-to-value securities and to take a hit to equity capital, the issue was not as clear for the hedge fund industry. Now being holders of private equity comparable to longer locked positions, investors who seek liquidity have found pricing to be a major issue. This was never more evident then in the waning days of 2008 and the early part of 2009, when investors who experienced massive losses from pretty much all investment strategies demanded redemptions for their underlying hedge funds and fund of funds. Many large hedge funds chose to limit or suspend redemptions, stating that the prices in the marketplace were simply not correct or that fund managers could not execute sales at prices that were acceptable or at reasonable price levels. Many fund managers put in place a little-known item in their private placement memorandum called a *gate*.

The gate provision allows a manager to limit or shut off redemptions for any investor, based on the idea that to allow one investor out, he or she could be wreaking havoc on the portfolio and causing other investors to suffer. The suspension of redemptions and the use of gates caused quite a stir in the popular press and, more significantly in the hedge fund investor community during the second half of 2008 and the beginning of 2009. Apparently, many investors believed that managers were not necessarily acting in the best interest of investors when they used their ability to gate the fund and suspend redemptions and were really only acting on behalf of themselves. It remains to be seen how investors will react to fund mangers who used gates or suspended redemptions. The reality is that some managers will suffer for their decisions and others will thrive. It comes down to their ability to communicate why it was necessary to take the action in the first place.

HEDGE FUNDS AND THE PRESS

Whenever hedge funds make front page news, finger-pointing is renewed about the ability of "secretive" hedge funds to move markets and alter the course of both financial and political history. Hedge funds have always been described as "secretive," but a quick search using Google shows results of over 11.3 million pages with the term hedge fund in it.[1] (By the way, Google found these 11.3 million pages in less then 0.21 seconds!) With the press continuing its vicious attack on hedge funds by publishing successive negative reports on these investment vehicles and the wizards who run them, many hedge fund investors seeking refuge from the onslaught from their own peers have started to separate the myth from the reality of hedge fund investing. Unfortunately, we have found that no discussion of these sought-after investment vehicles is complete without listing a few of the most important, influential, and interesting myths that prevail in the marketplace.

The Failure of Large Hedge Funds Will Have a Major Impact on the Markets

As we witnessed with the 2006 implosion of Amaranth, the impact was restricted to the direct investors in the strategy. While $6 billion of investor assets evaporated overnight and direct Amaranth hedge fund investors were impacted severely, one-month returns for fund of funds were only slightly impacted as a result of the overall portfolio diversification. With most fund of funds averaging more than 20 different manager positions, a wide range of exposure to different strategies, sectors, and managers provides a risk-reducing tool for fund of funds investors. When Amaranth imploded, the rest of the capital markets barely yawned because of the wide diversification of exposure. During the final three months of 2008, hedge funds globally were selling massive amounts of securities across all asset classes to meet year-end redemptions, but traditional long-only investors were dumping as well as investors who sought the safety of cash.

While hedge funds were one component of the sell-off, the cause was not the failure of a large fund but a crosscurrent resulting from the combined selling by all investors. The reality is that because each and every market is so intertwined, there is probably no single fund or group of funds that could cause the financial markets to collapse. In the aftermath of the announcement of the $60 billion Madoff fraud, the markets did not flinch. Even though the Madoff affair provoked considerable discussion and debate among investment professionals, the staggering losses it caused did not move the markets. However, it is fair to say that as the markets become more and more intertwined, large fund complexes can move markets—and that they do. Total and utter destruction is not something that is likely to be created by a fund manager; most managers simply have decided to leave that up to their respective governments.

Hedge Funds Are Dangerous Because They Use Derivatives

Because the use of derivatives is highly complex and depends on the underlying development, creation, and analysis of quantitative models, the use of derivatives is limited to sophisticated investors, including hedge funds that have specialized staff to analyze these positions. When used as hedging vehicles, derivatives generally lower portfolio volatility and also offer a cost-effective methodology to reduce risk. If used to make big bets, derivatives may raise portfolio volatility to higher levels. Simply put, nobody really knows how to define the impact of derivatives on a portfolio, because to do so one needs to know the extent to which these contracts are being used. In some instances, with levels of leverage, derivatives can cause massive problems for the fund and its investors. In other situations, the use of derivatives can add significant alpha. The reality is that not all uses of derivatives are bad; when used appropriately, derivatives are an important part of the capital markets.

The Use of Leverage Is Bad

Most hedge funds use no level or limited levels of leverage to extract opportunities from the marketplace. In the case of traditional Jones-style long/short equity, all managers are able to use the same leverage amounts as defined by Regulation T.[2] Reg T as it is known in the industry, is the Federal Reserve Board's regulation that governs how much credit or margin a brokerage firm can give to a customer to buy additional securities. Most individual investors regardless of size can borrow up to 50 percent of their holdings. This includes the amounts that individual investors can use in their brokerage accounts as well. While some funds such as traditional fixed-income or mortgage-backed securities arbitrage funds use higher levels of leverage, the use of leverage peaked in 2007 when managers were able to borrow as much as 12 to 15 times the value of their underlying securities. Now, in light of the current credit crisis and decrease in leverage mandated by banking examiners, the numbers have been dialed down considerably; in 2009, most fixed-income managers are able to get 3 to 10 times in leverage. Two things seem funny to us when the discussion turns to excessive leverage. First, leverage is nothing more then borrowing; most Americans use leverage every day when they buy a home or a car or use the plastic card in their wallets. Furthermore, it was the excessive use of leverage by the traditional banks and the investment banks—often more then 25 to 30 times their balance sheets—that many believe is to blame in part for the credit crisis and the economic havoc that taxpayers around the world were being forced to deal with in early 2009.

Hedge Fund Strategies Are Niche or Quirky

Hedge funds are often viewed as being the extension of the highly guarded proprietary trading desks of Wall Street firms of yesteryear. After all, some of the best hedge funds were born at Wall Street's biggest trading desks. That is where creative minds were able to exploit market inefficiencies and capitalize on the large capital base and distribution capability of the investment banks to earn massive profits for their shareholders. As hedge fund entrepreneurs develop their business models, the key is to be able to replicate the style and strategy of their former shops and then grow the new hedge fund business franchise. Hedge funds of today have replaced many of the proprietary trading desks of yesterday, because hedge funds answer only to their investors and the regulators. Today, most investment banks have either merged into traditional banks or are themselves in the process of becoming traditional banks. As such, each is no longer able to put capital at risk, and the risk takers have been replaced. Hedge funds now fill this crucial area of the capital markets. They pick up where Wall Street left off.

Hedge Funds Are All-Day Traders Using Nonpublic Information

As the hedge fund industry has become more globalized and trade less liquid positions in many strategies, the holding periods for securities have grown longer and longer. Financial information is available to all who ask for public information, and Regulation FD[3] (or Fair Disclosure) has leveled the playing field. As investment returns have moderated, hedge funds are looking for less-trafficked ideas, many of which are longer term. Because of the growth in the number of hedge funds since 2000, market liquidity has increased. New financial products such as weather derivatives or investments in private equity and real estate have provided financing for many projects that have unique funding requirements, with financing coming from hedge funds. Many of these trades are not covered by traditional rules regarding disclosure.

However, most funds discuss transactions as they relate to the overall performance of their fund. Furthermore, in light of some of the insider trading cases that have been prosecuted in New York and other jurisdictions over the past few years, it is clear in the minds of many that there is a clear distinction between what is and what is not public information, including the ramifications for disclosing nonpublic information to those who can profit from it. The Securities and Exchange Commission, regardless of the lapses manifested in the Madoff situation, takes quite an aggressive stance against trafficking in nonpublic information.

Hedge Fund Fees Are Too High

While hedge fund fees have moved up, returns have met investors' objectives, as demonstrated by the growth of industry assets to nearly $2 trillion by the end of 2007.[4] The hedge fund industry contracted during 2008 and the early part of 2009 as a result of significant levels of redemptions due specifically to poor performance, and fees are once again on the minds of many investors. Let us just say this: it seems that, for the most part, the only people really complaining about the fees are those who cannot charge them. When investors demand a decrease in fees, the fees will decrease. 2009 will probably usher in a new era of lower fees.

Hedge Funds Don't Tell Us What They Invest In

With the institutionalization of the hedge fund industry, this is no longer true; hedge funds managers understand the need for investors to be able to perform specific levels of due diligence and use risk models to analyze their portfolios. As such, hedge fund managers are providing a greater flow of information surrounding their investment strategies, with most providing position-level transparency. If a manager is not receptive to providing an acceptable level of transparency, investors should simply take a pass.

Fund of Funds Charge a Second Level of Fees, Which Reduces Returns

This statement is correct. However, the argument for the additional fees is that fund of funds managers provide a level of service and expertise that some investors cannot accomplish on their own. Direct investing through single-strategy managers requires a significant internal expertise and substantial investment in infrastructure. The fund of funds fee should more than offset the resources that the fund of funds provides, including research, due diligence, ongoing monitoring, appropriate portfolio diversification, and risk reduction for the investor. The problem is that some fund of funds don't do what they say they are going to do and provide little if any value for their services. Choosing a fund of funds is right for some and wrong for others. The key is making sure you are getting what you pay for.

Hedge Funds Dislike Fund of Funds

While hedge funds are receptive to receiving new assets and want to grow, if you ask most hedge fund managers what they think about fund of funds' assets, their answer is not always positive. Most hedge funds will respond that fund of funds are "information hogs," "always looking for fee concessions," or "constantly rebalancing managers" (or is that a case of heading for the exit after a few poor months?). This is problematic, because managers don't like investors that take up a lot of their time, demand lower fees, and move in and out of the fund based solely on performance. In reality, fund of funds spend considerable resources and time and are reluctant to make changes to their allocations unless the strategy currently being pursued is no longer viable or changes have taken place within the organization that merit redemption. Hedge funds prefer "sticky" assets, such as foundations, endowments, or pensions, which are interested in longer-term investing over a cycle rather than quarter to quarter. However, many fund of funds that have deliberate, comprehensive due diligence processes that are developed over a long period of time to identify strategies are welcomed by many hedge fund managers as sticky investors. Many investors, including a small number of fund of funds, are constantly searching to find the next hot strategy and will jump from manager to manager in search of perceived or untapped alpha. Frankly, these managers just don't succeed and usually burn out. Hedge funds want stable assets! Many hedge funds compare these sticky assets to core deposits in the banking industry, where depositors are looking for a full-service relationship rather than a rate and term for the cash.

THE FUND OF FUNDS VALUE PROPOSITION

Fund of funds managers provide a basic service that most investors are unable to provide: the ability to construct a portfolio of diversified hedge funds that offer attractive returns and liquidity terms in a cost-effective investment vehicle. Many investors will state that it is easy to start a fund of funds because the start up costs that constitute the main barrier to entry are relatively low. The reality is that to be successful, the fund manager needs significant assets to manage to make the business viable.

There are significant economies of scale that can be realized by the manager once assets cross the $500 million mark. However, before those levels have been reached, some fund of funds have difficulty competing in the marketplace. Size does matter. The manager must be able to fund the infrastructure and staff in order to source, review, allocate, and monitor the portfolio of hedge fund managers, not to mention handling the day-to-day tasks of running the business.

Fund of Funds Investors

In light of the poor hedge fund performance in 2007 and 2008, capped by the Madoff scandal, many investors have soured on fund of funds. That fund of funds managers were in the marketplace offering "diversified portfolios," when in reality all or most of the assets were with a single fund or strategy is, in our opinion, criminal. This has been an unfortunate wake-up call to remind many of us that we're just getting over the blowups at Amaranth and D.B. Zwirn, along with the fraud of Bayou. There is no level of due diligence or regulation that will totally wipe out fraud or blowups. These are natural occurrences. However, managers who cut corners by not completing background checks or operational evaluations make the situation even worse. The reason fund of funds make sense, are important, and are worth the fees is that investors are buying services that are too hard, too costly, and too time consuming to perform on their own.

FEES

As of year end 2008, by our unscientific albeit straight-to-the-point exercise, fund of funds averaged a 1 percent management fee and a 10 percent incentive fee. Fund of funds are often criticized for this so-called additional layer of fees, but unless the investor is prepared to build out an investment, due diligence, research, legal, accounting, and reporting team, the fees are actually low. Fund of funds managers provide a unique and specialized service as portfolio managers. Our research shows that most fund of funds managers' operating expenses exceed .50 percent, which means that the fund of funds business is a low-margin proposition. However, because the business is scalable, the business proposition continues to improve as assets under management continue to increase. As long as fund of funds are able to achieve higher than average returns with lower volatility, there is, in our opinion, sufficient justification for the level of fees that are charged by the manager.

Many fund of funds managers offer various arguments to justify their fees—arguments that we do not subscribe to. If you are provided with such arguments, in our opinion you should ask, "How?" Ask this question if the managers claim to be able to

- Access closed managers.
- Access managers generally below the radar screen.
- Achieve above-average performance results.
- Discover new and emerging managers as well as up and coming strategies.

The fund of funds manager is supposed to access closed managers, access undiscovered managers, and uncover new strategies. Nothing stated here would make a fund unique. But these statements must be met with skepticism.

ALLOCATION STRATEGIES

One of the ongoing challenges of individual hedge fund selection and allocation is the size of the underlying managers. Many investors like to claim that they have been the first to discover and allocate to the newest, greatest manager that no one else knows about. Still, the question is really one of capacity. The new, emerging manager may have a great pedigree, but no track record. He or she may have capacity constraints and may not be able to run a business. Fund of funds managers and other large institutional investors constantly ask, "How much capacity will you reserve for my fund?" This is usually one of the final questions of the due diligence process. Since fund of funds are quick to point out the ability to source new up-and-coming managers, size may be the biggest challenge to performance. Most strategies such as small-cap or sector-specific strategies may have size constraints; most large fund of funds have size constraints before allocating initial capital, or requirements placing a maximum amount of capital that may be committed to one manager.

The challenge of the fund of funds manager is the ability to commit capital to managers that will not restrict asset terms while at the same time not diluting returns. If this is an issue, fund of funds managers will look at larger managers that can accept unlimited amounts of capital. Unfortunately, in this scenario many fund of funds will start to look like other large fund of funds as they continue to invest in all of the same "household names." The redundancy of the same positions in the large fund of funds portfolios may cause a problem in markets that do not function as modeled or when a blowup occurs. In the wake of the Amaranth blowup, many fund of funds investors quickly discovered that while they had invested with different fund of funds managers to achieve portfolio diversification, many of the fund of funds actually owned the same Amaranth position in each of their portfolios. Amaranth was a widely respected hedge fund with great pedigree, and it would have been smart to include it in a diversified strategy. Redundancy of positions by several fund of funds for large institutional allocators can actually prove to be counterproductive

One investment trend today is for allocators and their consultants to invest in "bulge bracket," or multibillion-dollar fund of funds only. As a result, investors may not place a premium on the research ability of the fund of funds manager to find new undiscovered managers because the manager has a capacity issue and can allocate only to larger hedge funds that have the ability to accept larger inflows of capital. As an example, small-cap equity managers that are always looking for new companies with a unique edge in the market by researching companies that are not widely covered or followed are hedge funds that large fund of funds may not be able to utilize. The question then becomes, "What is the value added to an equity manager who invests in large-cap companies such as Microsoft or IBM where most of the relevant research data is in the public domain?" The answer is "little or none." Therefore, we believe it's best to shy away from large fund of funds that cannot distinguish their strategies because their size limits their ability to perform.

Fund of funds managers that research and access small-cap managers or other specialized strategies are able to charge higher fees than the larger funds, given that the cost of discovering and allocating to new, emerging managers is more challenging. At the same time, many of the large multi-strategy managers are starting to look like fund of funds, further clouding the waters.

When looking for hedge fund managers, fund of funds are looking for managers with a competitive advantage. According to Robert Schulman, former president of Tremont Advisors, a large fund of funds that got caught in the Madoff scandal, "You are looking for managers to reach a decision and gather knowledge that nobody else is finding. That is not done with published material or shared by others." Schulman believes that most fund of funds should be paid to discover the next generation of hedge funds or strategies by knowing their industry.

BOUTIQUE INVESTING

As the institutionalization of the hedge fund industry continues, this former cottage community of small, secretive boutiques is now morphing into large asset management firms that perform investment banking transactions, engage in commercial lending, and finance real estate, all the while managing large portfolios of global securities. As a result, these large hedge funds are becoming some of the largest investment banking clients of Wall Street. These once small companies of a few have adopted many of the same attributes as the large, well-respected Wall Street investment banks, including

- Risk management systems to monitor and stress test portfolios
- Technology to support the firm's investment process and internal investment system
- Transparency to access a client base of highly regarded investors
- Enhanced distribution from strategic partnerships with well-respected financial institutions
- Shared ownership by a range of employee ownership to demonstrate an alliance of interests
- Forward-looking vision for the company

At the close of 2007, there were nearly 7,200 fund of funds in the marketplace, according to the most recent PerTrac Study.[5] The recipe for success for a fund of funds is different from that of a hedge fund, with distribution being a major ingredient.

Institutional Names

According to Eric Weber, chief operating officer and managing director of Freeman & Co., brand name is key. He notes that no independent fund of funds is among the top nine ranked by assets under management and only one in the top 16 is an independent firm. Each of the largest is a part of a large money management complex. The independents are not able to grow because the market doesn't want the perceived risk associated with a small firm. Remember, nobody ever got fired for buying IBM computers. The same can be said for fund of funds. Nobody ever got fired for investing in Goldman Sachs, Bank of New York, or JP Morgan Chase fund of funds.

Finding distribution channels is a significant challenge for smaller fund of funds.

Weber said that many large asset managers and private banks in the United States and outside the United States offer distribution relationships, and it's hard for smaller participants to compete. Consultants also provide a key role in the education of clients and consequently provide a different level of distribution of fund of funds for their clients.

As the hedge fund industry grows and well-publicized frauds and blowups escalate, the need for greater transparency increases. Larger, better-capitalized fund of funds are able to develop state-of-the-art risk management systems and greater in-depth research staffs to analyze and conduct due diligence for newly created strategies. These efforts require a higher level of financial, legal, and regulatory oversight and come at a cost. At the same time, many midsized fund of funds, firms with assets of less then $1 billion under management, are picking up assets because of their ability to achieve better results than some of their larger peers. While hedge fund and fund of funds investors are always looking for market correlations or low correlation to major strategies and indices, one fact is clear: There is a positive correlation between a fund of funds' size and growth rate. Critical mass is the major ingredient for growing assets, and many fund of funds are primarily concerned with growing with the masses.

With $750 billion in assets under management as of 2008, according to PerTrac, the fund of funds industry is really a story of the haves versus the have-nots.[6] Eric Weber believes, "many small funds are stuck at sub-scalable asset levels."

Weber's firm has been working hard in the mergers and acquisition marketplace to conduct transactions with fund of funds for quite some time. Weber and his colleagues have helped buyers enter markets, helped entrepreneurs sell their businesses, and helped parent companies divest their fund of funds holdings.

IVY AND BoNY

A catalyst for the industry was The Bank of New York's purchase of Ivy Asset Management in 2000. With $2.7 billion, the Ivy/The Bank of New York consolidation has demonstrated the benefit of having a strong distribution partner that is also a strong strategic partner with global recognition that has enabled assets to grow to over $15 billion by year end 2007.[7] However, recent developments, including poor performance and other issues, have caused the fund complexes' assets to drop significantly since 2007; at the time of this writing, many in the industry had put the firm's assets at less than $5 billion.

According to Freeman, there have been over 35 fund of funds transactions with funds over $1 billion in assets through 2007. The motivation for sellers has been the need for liquidity or succession planning; pressure from a parent company or outside shareholder; or, as is usually the case, the need for greater distribution, greater size, or increased branding. On the other hand, buyers of fund of funds have been motivated by a need to enter the marketplace quickly, rather than trying to build out an organization, track record, and brand. Buyers also want to gain product expertise and immediate presence in the industry. Most buyers want to capitalize on the brand and distribution capabilities of the acquirer as opposed to building it themselves from the ground up.

In The Financial Services' *Executive Forum First Quarter 2008* survey (released by the American Banker in connection with Greenwich Associates LLC), of 315 banking and financial services executives conducted in February 2008, the conclusion was that banks have an advantage over other financial institutions when it comes to trust and confidence.[8] The trust level shown here is slightly higher than that shown in a similar survey performed in the third quarter of 2004. With banks gaining an advantage over other financial services firms, it adds firepower for banking institutions to continue along the growth path of acquiring or building out alternative investment platforms.

Madoff

Some of the questions that arose in the wake of the Madoff scheme were: What happened to the fund of funds? How did the due diligence fail or become so fooled? Why did the fund of funds fail to uncover the fraud?

The answer to all of these questions is simple. According to data from the Madoff Receivers' office, less than 100 fund of funds actually invested with Madoff. In an industry that has a global head count of more than 7,000 fund of funds at year end 2008,[9] this means that slightly more than 1 percent of all fund of funds allocated to Madoff. It seems to us that the fees that Madoff paid to his investors were the major issue that caused allocators to avoid the strategy. The final reckoning on the Madoff situation is still to come, but one thing is for sure: there is clearly more to it then we all know at the time of this writing.

In the end, the question that investors must ask is whether the cost of returns is justified by the large fund operators, or can smaller, niche fund of funds provide greater alpha by not increasing risk to an uncomfortable level and offering different levels of portfolio diversification. It really comes down to what one believes and where one thinks benefits will come from with the allocation of assets.

CHAPTER 5

Understanding Alternative Investing Is Both Math and Science

To evaluate the performance results of individual hedge fund managers and the consequent aggregation of results of a portfolio of hedge funds, it is necessary to look at and understand the major influences on or drivers of hedge fund returns. Investors learned in the wake of the technology bubble's burst during 2000–2001 that the returns of many hedge fund managers, whose performance results in previous years had been skewed by participation in the high volume of initial public offerings, were mediocre at best. These investors believed prior to the market collapse that they had invested in a new breed of outstanding money managers.

Unfortunately, as technology stock prices fell, so did the value of many of their investments. As Warren Buffet once said, "you only find out who is swimming naked when the tides goes out." Investors learned who did and did not have the right stuff. The reason investors use or invest with a fund of funds is because they believe that the manager knows how to evaluate and decide who is and who is not swimming naked.

HEDGE FUND RETURNS

Hedge fund returns are driven by many factors, including

- Performance of the stock market
- Shape of the yield curve
- Credit spreads
- Direction of interest rates
- Volatility

Stock Prices

Global stock prices clearly drive performance. As many say, "A rising tide lifts all boats." In a bull market, all managers look brilliant. But what happens when the market heads south? Which manager really has the skill set to profit from short positions? Or which manager has the exceptional talents and the conviction to identify trends, such as subprime, before the herd comes thundering through and early on establishes short positions in anticipation of a meltdown while the conventional wisdom is to be long?

Yield Curve

Hedge fund returns are also driven by the shape of the yield curve. An upward sloping curve is good for the economy and stock prices, but it is especially advantageous for arbitrage strategies including convertible arbitrage, fixed-income arbitrage, and capital-structure arbitrage. There are many ways to attack these markets when things are on the rise. A flat or inverted yield curve creates a nightmare for arbitrage investors; it creates few opportunities for investors, because the markets are not moving or are moving in the wrong direction. While declining interest rates benefit corporate balance sheets and earnings, rising interest rate environments present a challenge. A flat-rate environment with an upward sloping curve is beneficial to many types of fixed-income arbitrage.

Credit Spreads

Credit spreads also play an important role in hedge fund returns. As credit spreads widen, bond prices come under pressure, as we witnessed in the corporate scandals of 2002 and with the subprime meltdown of 2007–2008. While managers can profit from being on the "right" side of the trade, which can take many different forms, they may also benefit from spread tightening. No directionality in credit spreads is a challenge for returns; when markets don't move, it is harder to make money.

Interest Rates

With the globalization of the capital markets, most markets are linked, and as we learned in 2007–2008, most markets are positively correlated. Simply put, a problem in the United States is a problem in Europe, and so on and so on. It is has been an unwritten rule of Wall Street and the world that when the United States sniffles, the rest of the world catches the flu. As we write this book, the world markets seem to be using a lot of Vicks NyQuil.

During the 1950s and the 1960s investor sentiment said, "What's good for GM is good for the country." Unfortunately, we learned a mere forty-odd years later that this is no longer true.

Volatility

Market volatility is another factor that comes into play with hedge fund returns. The most popular measure of volatility is the Chicago Board Options Exchange Volatility Index, often referred to as the VIX or the Fear Index.

This index reflects an estimate of future market volatility. In a market environment of low volatility, conventional wisdom would suggest that profit opportunities are strong. However, a spike in the VIX can lead to wide swings in return. Hedge fund results have been best in years when the equity markets were calm (see Figures 5.1 and 5.2).

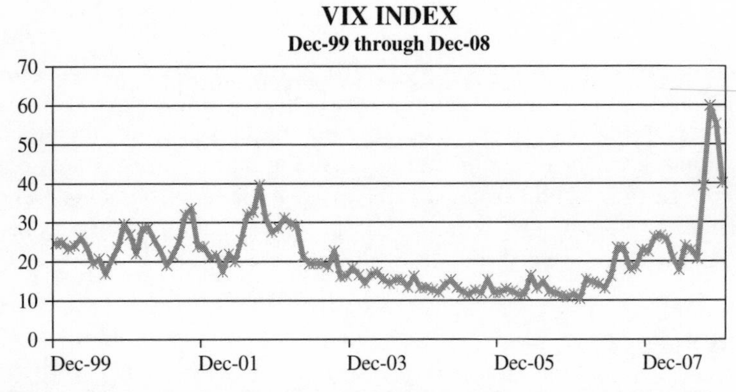

FIGURE 5.1 Annual Equity Market Volatility as Tracked by the VIX Index

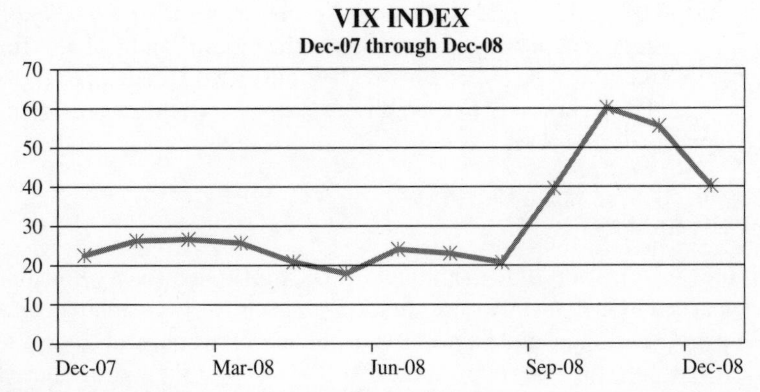

FIGURE 5.2 One-Year Measure of the VIX Index Movement from December 2007 to December 2008

The best performing managers in volatile markets are dedicated short sellers and managed futures. The short sellers are making investments that profit from the market moving downward. Managed futures managers profit from the spike in commodities prices that occurs when equity markets go down and investors look to gold, silver, oil, and other commodities as a source of returns. Unfortunately, our data concludes that these two strategies represent just 5 percent of all assets invested in hedge funds at the close of 2008.

DELIVERING ALPHA

While each of these factors contributes to returns and delivers alpha to investors, a change in one factor alone does not ensure overall profitable results of a portfolio or an investment. As an example, a price increase of 2 percent on a 5 times levered portfolio results in 10 percent gain on that portfolio. However, on the flip side, a 3 percent price decline on a 5 times levered portfolio results in a loss of 15 percent and possibly more if the manager is forced to sell positions to meet a margin call from the prime broker or Wall Street investment bank. However, a combination of capitalizing in the change in several of these factors along with the acumen of the manager should result in profit for the investor.

The bottom line is due diligence. When performing due diligence, investors must weigh the results of the manager in light of the factors previously listed. Asking a credit manager how he made money while credit spreads tightened is a good idea. Or how did the fixed-income manager make money while the curve was inverted or flat? Or with a flat and declining VIX, how did a convertible arbitrage manager have extraordinary results? Were there factors to drive the returns other than those listed in the marketing material or offering documents? One lesson that everyone has learned in light of the events of 2008 is that if something is too good to be true, it probably is; therefore, investors must ask questions and demand answers. If the answers don't add up, don't invest. Period. End of story!

A Short but Sweet Case Study

During a recent due diligence exercise, we met a convertible arbitrage manager with high teens performance results in a year when the convertible arbitrage index was slightly positive. After extensive questioning, he revealed that he had several positions in PIPEs (private investments in public equities). Generally, these are illiquid private placements, difficult to price, and initially priced at a substantial discount to the public market. Upon continuing our discussion, it became apparent that in reality, this manager was not really a convertible arbitrage manager, but a PIPE fund who still advertised as a convertible arbitrage manager. We took a pass.

To reiterate, look at the results of each manager and compare the results to what has happened in the real world to gain a greater understanding of the source and repeatability of returns. There is no excuse for not doing the work—after all, it is your money.

INVESTING IN A FUND OF FUNDS

In our experience, fund of funds are marketed using several main channels of distribution. For the record, marketing and distribution are synonymous with raising money. However, because many in the investment industry look down on the phrase "raising money," it has negative implications for some people; the industry has adapted the alternative terms *distribution* or *marketing*.

In the beginning, most investment managers, fund of funds, or single strategy managers, go after the "low-hanging fruit." This money is from friends or family or former colleagues; there is some direct personal connection, and the money manager, regardless of track record, style, strategy, or infrastructure, believes that he or she will be able to get assets into the fund. The reason it is called low-hanging fruit is because this sort of fruit is the most ripe. It is ready to fall to the ground. The manager's first pitch for assets is to those who are the most ripe.

Once this list has been gone through, the manager will market the fund to a wide range of high net worth investors and institutional investors who the manager knows has some interest in what he or she is doing. Most managers try to build relationship upon relationship on relationship to reach out to and access as many potential investors as possible. Distribution, or one's ability to raise assets, is the one and only means to growth and success of the business. Unless the fund of funds manager has a large marketing staff with strong global relations—or a niche fund with a specialized strategy such as emerging markets, emerging managers, or sector-specific strategy—raising capital is usually done internally and is often the biggest challenge to success.

Asset Gathering

Many managers rely on the "if you build it, they will come" theory of raising assets. They sit around and tell themselves and their colleagues that as long as performance is good and risk is kept in check, investors will seek them out. They believe that word of mouth from other friends and colleagues or other investors in the fund will magically cause investors to line up at their doorstep. It is, without a doubt, the most ineffective way to raise assets—one that reaches the smallest audience of potential investors.

Included in the methodology is the belief that data mining by prospective investors, those who hunt through databases looking for fund of funds that meet a specific investment criterion, will find a fund and invest. However, our experience is that data mining usually is helpful only to those with long track records and significant assets, say in excess of $1 billion under management.

THIRD-PARTY MARKETERS

Fund of funds managers may utilize the services of a third-party marketing firm to present the strategies to investors. Third-party marketers are companies or individuals who act as hired guns to raise money for a fund or fund complex. For the most part, their success is very limited given that many of these "marketing professionals" are usually not fully versed in the inner workings of the fund's investment strategy, have limited knowledge of the details of the strategy, and are unable to communicate the benefit of investing.

Besides not being well-versed in strategy details, many third-party marketers do not like the lower fees associated with working with fund of funds. They find the compensation schedule unacceptable and therefore put little effort into a capital-raising assignment. Fund of funds fees are typically a 1 percent management fee and a 10 percent incentive fee based on a hurdle rate. This fee structure is much lower than those employed by single-manager funds, and it reduces the amount of money a third-party marketer can earn working with a fund of funds.

It is our experience that the fees, along with the fact that one needs to know the direct investor (e.g., pensions, foundations, endowments, or consultants), cause many third-party marketing firms to shy away from trying to establish a marketing relationship with a fund of funds. Remember that third-party marketers are only as good as their relationships or ability to create relationships. If they are marketing a single-manager fund, they can target individuals, institutions, and fund of funds. However, if they are marketing a fund of funds, they lose one-third of their potential investors.

WHERE THE MONEY COMES FROM

Hedge funds, fund of funds, and alternative investments are the new capital-raising, income-generating model. It's the most recent trend for Wall Street, and it's here to stay.

Looking at the contraction of municipal bond dealers, which has shrunk from over 35 major firms when the space was profitable in the 1980s to a handful of investment banks today with narrow underwriting spreads, trade recaps of bond pricing made the market more efficient. The list of primary dealers reporting to the Federal Reserve has shrunk from 46 in the 1990s to 19 today.[1]

From the 1970s to the 1990s, most investment banks and commercial banks wanted to have large municipal bond departments or large government bond departments. What does that do to the outlook for hedge funds when Wall Street senior management teams decide that hedge funds present too much risk or too little profit? Has Wall Street learned from past mistakes? In 2009, the landscape is changing.

The success of each of the Street firms when raising capital for hedge funds shows how valuable the strategic partnership with hedge funds and fund of funds can be. The math of the joint venture makes sense for both parties, but is it in the best interest of the investors? Sharing (or recapturing) 2 and 20 percent from a hedge fund is a lot better than the 50 or 75 basis points these firms earn managing long-only money.

Given the proliferation of new investors looking for new ideas and trying to identify outstanding managers, investors must rely on intermediaries to identify investments and to perform sophisticated analysis and due diligence. At the same time, global financial institutions and private banks are getting increasingly more involved because they, too, see the writing on the wall, regardless of recent meltdowns. Investors understand the need for investments that can go both long and short the market and allow their portfolios to grow regardless of which way the market is moving.

Raising Capital

Since raising capital is the key to success for both manager and banks, the questions are, how far does the "Street" firm go to market the product? Is there a higher payout for the internal product? Or is it better to go to the "open architecture platform" that is more independent? These questions are ones that baffle many who work on the Street as well as those who are constantly trying to raise money. The second question asks whether the solicitor is a sales agent, an advisor, or just a marketing person tasked with raising money.

While many changes have been made in the post-Madoff period, sales conflicts are still prevalent in the current Wall Street model. The model is currently still somewhat broken. It is clear that sales agents and their client's interest are not always aligned. Our concern is that investors believe that because a product is being marketed or sold by individuals employed by some of the most powerful and respected investment firms in the world, they have a false sense of security. We hope that if Madoff taught us anything, it is to question everything. We believe that firms need to be more up front and transparent about their financial arrangements with the funds that they market. Investors need to ask the questions and get the answers.

In the wake of the market meltdown of 2008, we believe that investors need to have a greater level of transparency regarding their holdings. The problem, however, is not getting the information or data, but knowing what to do with it. It is all fine and good that Congress believes that the Hedge Fund Transparency Act will bring a new level of transparency to the industry. But what are investors supposed to do with this data, how are they to use it, and what is the value of having it? Many people believe that hedge funds will not provide transparency and are afraid of giving out data. To that, we say hogwash. The managers will provide the information; the question is, what does the investor gain by having it? Also, in light of Madoff, we now have to question the accuracy of the information. However, this last point will be covered later in the book. For now, assume the data is accurate and that one knows what to do with it.

These are tough questions to get answers to, and many have a hard time asking the questions and demanding the answers before they invest. This is the reason people invest in fund of funds. Fund of funds on the outside are supposed to do all this when they invest investors' money. Their job is to do the due diligence, pick the managers, and deliver returns. It is what you pay for, and it is their job.

And while that is all well and good, another interesting trend that has developed in the last few years in the funds of funds industry on the part of institutional investors is the use of fund of funds as a tool to find new, exciting, and emerging managers.

THE NEW NEW MANAGERS

There are a number of fund of funds that invest in "undiscovered names." When discovered, the fund of funds redeems and moves onto to new undiscovered names. The investment premium of the fund of funds is lessened as the investor starts to allocate away from the fund of funds. While immediate access to a fund of funds may be a marketing strength to some, to many others the idea of finding a manager when that manager is small, undiscovered, and not on everybody's radar screen is the edge that that manager offers to investors.

Selecting a fund of funds that is right for your assets is a process that takes place over a period of months—and in many cases, years. It begins with a series of phone calls, continues to a series of on-site meetings at the manager's office and meeting all of the senior people along with the support staff and research analysts. It includes checking references; checking service providers; and hiring independent firms to perform background checks on the people who run the company, pick managers, and handle the money. It is not easy, it is not fun; it is work, and it is worth it because it is your money!

Due Diligence?

Many believed prior to the Madoff revelation that institutional investors and their consultants applied a more rigid process of scrutiny and due diligence to asset allocation because of the nature of the source of funds. However, in light of the losses that pension plans, endowments, family offices, insurance companies, and their advisors experienced with their allocation to Madoff, it appears that due diligence has been lackadaisical and a smoke screen of sorts to a small percentage of hedge fund investors. This cannot, should not, and hopefully will not continue.

Managers, both single-strategy and fund of funds, must understand the decision-making process and the need for independent evaluation of the firm during the marketing process. While most fund of funds and hedge funds meet the expectations, many investors report negative experiences in dealing with the marketing individuals and teams at the firms. Attitudes, arrogance, and annoyance are often quite prevalent. Don't put up with it—it is your money. If they don't want to answer, are annoyed, are arrogant, or have an attitude, don't hire them; then e-mail us at dsrb@hedgeanswers.com.

Marketing is nothing more or less than a sales job. Some people get it, others don't. It is not a good or bad thing, it is just a thing. There is little, if any, glory in sales, and many fund companies seem to have a revolving door when it comes to their marketing staffs. There is clearly a shortage of experienced institutional marketing professionals relative to the size of the market. Don't be surprised if one day you talk to one person only to find out a few days later you are dealing with someone else.

The marketing phase takes place over a long period of time, and personnel changes are common at both the investor and the consultant level. Therefore, fund of funds marketing professionals must be able to provide an intense level of detail regarding the fund's strategy and organizational structure. Equally important is the fact that investment strategy education is critical, because many investors may be first-time investors, and constituents of the investment process may be time constrained.

Asking Questions

As basic as it may sound, the most effective marketing question that should be asked by a fund of funds professional to potential investors is: What are their investment needs and their expectations of the investment? On the flip side, an investor should ask what the stimulus for firing or redeeming a manager is and when was it last triggered.

Meeting with key investment and risk managers of the fund of funds organization should provide a high level of comfort in the decision-making process regarding the portfolio. However, you need to go deeper than a couple of meetings. Interaction between the fund of funds and its investor provides many with a high level of satisfaction, but satisfaction is not enough. You need to get documents, meet the accountants, and perform background checks. There are many people who say that Madoff would never have passed their investment test; however, there are even more who are considered serious hedge fund and fund of funds people who got caught in the fraud. Although the jury on the level of their involvement is still out, maybe they knew, maybe they didn't. One thing is for sure: had they looked into the accounting firm that allegedly performed the audit and net asset value calculations, some alarm bells should have gone off signaling that something was not quite right.

Getting Answers

Fund of funds must be able to plainly explain the difference between their strategy and that of other firms and to demonstrate where they can and do add value. It is more than a matter of a few basis points here or there. Many fund of funds are accustomed to bringing armies of analysts to hedge funds during the due diligence process. This can be a smoke screen. It is nothing more than an appearance that work is going to be done. We believe that the manager should bring only senior representatives, including a decision maker, to the meetings—that is, the people who have a role in the funds management process and understand the investment process. Too many cooks spoil the soup.

In keeping with Wall Street customs, most investment managers think that he who has the biggest "pitch book" has the best fund. While size may be contested, it's really all about content and the synthesis of the information. Since the decision makers' time is limited and the manager may get only 30 minutes of the busy schedule of the investor, the fund of funds should simplify the presentation, review several of the pages—certainly not the whole book—and encourage an open dialogue of questions and answers.

Investors want to know about risk management, the research process, the background of the investment team and senior professionals, access to managers, and how the funds of fund will fit within the overall portfolio. Investors also want to understand the current investment climate and how the fund of funds is positioned; they want to receive a bird's-eye view of the economy and to be told how the fund of funds plans to adapt to changes in the economy and markets that may lie ahead.

After screening various databases for fund of funds according to predetermined quantitative requirements, the investor or consultant will follow up with on-site due diligence to meet prospective managers. In addition to meeting key investment personnel, operational staff, and legal and compliance personnel, the prospective investor should feel comfortable that the investment philosophy and strategy had been well articulated by all the people involved. When reviewing the investment portfolio of hedge fund managers and strategies, the investor should understand the flow of information and how the best ideas make their way into the fund of funds portfolio. Ask about postinvestment monitoring by the fund of funds manager; this is important to ensure that the "advertised" risk management system is real and that they are paying attention.

The Due Diligence Process

One of the most effective tools used (as well as abused) as part of the research and due diligence process in identifying managers is the Request for Proposal—RFP in the vernacular. In the world of asset management, the RFP was originally intended to be an invitation for an asset manager to submit a proposal to a prospective investor who was conducting a search for a specific investment mandate. Investors, through their investment consultants, would advertise that a search was being conducted for managers that met the specific criteria and would invite managers to complete an RFP and possibly make a formal proposal stating why each firm's strategy was better than that of its peers. They would then patiently await a favorable response from the prospective investor.

Many financial publications such as *Pensions and Investments* advertise classified notices of current investment requests for proposals. Each RFP has a unique set of questions in which the manager lists performance history, the background and experience of the firm and its principals, legal structure, fee structures, investment process, and risk management systems. RFP questionnaires can range from 15 or 20 pages to 50 to 60 pages.

Many of the large hedge funds and fund of funds have staffs charged with the sole purpose of completing RFPs. As the hedge fund industry has matured, the RFP has taken on a life of its own. It is now used as a primary marketing tool by hedge fund managers. It is a textual presentation of the "pitch book," the PowerPoint version of the marketing book. In short, it consists of words instead of pictures.

While managers are proud of the hours spent by a staff of designers and analysts who insert the graphs, performance charts with peer group comparative results (always showing the manager in the top deciles or quartile), org charts, and all biographies, the RFP is nothing more than a long-winded document that looks about as interesting as any printed page.

The consulting industry, along with other direct investors, now ask or request an RFP to obtain all of the information relating to the manager and strategy as the first step in the due diligence process. It provides concise data in a format that will provide investors with the opportunity to fill in the blanks with a standardized format. Whether the information is actually directly used to evaluate managers as part of the due diligence process for the current RFP or is used simply to aggregate data that can be used for creating internal databases, in many cases consultants and fund of funds will boast that they have "x" thousands of managers in their database, but only allocate to a smaller percentage of "y" dozen managers. Size, it seems, matters here as well.

One of the issues that concerns managers is that the RFP is considered to be a marketing piece and must be reviewed and approved by legal counsel prior to dissemination to potential or existing investors. Since hedge funds are prohibited from advertising, each manager and the legal staff must be prudent about the content of these documents and safeguard the information being provided to both qualified and unqualified investors. The lawyers are really sticky about this point. Some managers require the completion of a nondisclosure agreement (NDA) to prevent distribution of the information to those outside of the direct investment process at a potential investor's firm or organization.

Ongoing Monitoring

Once the decision to invest has been made, it is important to follow up. Ongoing monitoring should include spending time with the key investment professionals and being provided with interim reports that describe the prior reporting period. Updated RFPs should be received and reviewed to determine what changes have been made since the last written report. The information should also detail any changes that occurred to the portfolio during the prior period as well information on expected changes to the portfolio. In addition, the fund of funds manager should notify investors of any personnel changes, including key hires or departures and commentary on performance results.

Remember the following three rules and you are assured to be safe:

1. If it appears too good to be true, it probably is.
2. Anyone who does not use well-known, well-respected, and industry-experienced service providers is someone you don't want to invest your money with.
3. If you ask for information and don't get it in a timely manner, don't invest.

These rules apply not only to investing in hedge funds, fund of funds, or private equity funds but to all investments. It is your money, you worked hard for it, and you deserve to have it managed properly, ethically, and as described. Ask questions and demand answers; if you do not like what you hear or receive, go someplace else. There are plenty of smart, sophisticated people who will do the right thing; you must do your work and find them.

CHAPTER 6

Why Fund of Funds Work

The primary investors in fund of funds are high net worth investors, family offices, foundations and endowments, and institutional investors. This is essentially the same investor base as hedge funds have, with the newest large entrants being public and corporate retirement pension funds globally. Hedge fund investors are typically looking for an investment vehicle that meets one of the following requirements:

- No or low correlation to the public debt and equity markets
- Outperformance (i.e., no losses) in down markets, while capturing a significant portion of upside returns when the market rallies
- Investment in sectors that are not user friendly to investors that lack specialized skill sets (fixed income or credit) or may not have a team of investment professionals analyzing individual hedge fund strategies
- Intention to invest in hedge funds to lower overall portfolio volatility and market exposure

THE EARLY ADOPTERS

Early institutional adopters of hedge funds in the 1990s were foundations and endowments. Historically, this group has been more visible in hedge fund investing than most other institutional investors, given that there is a requirement to make distributions of a fixed percentage of assets annually—and higher—consistent returns were required to meet this stated mandate.

Family offices with substantial assets were also early to invest in hedge funds and fund of funds. While the global macrostrategy employed by famed hedge fund managers George Soros, Julian Robertson, and Michael Steinhardt was the dominant strategy pursued during the 1990s, many family offices recognized the need to diversify into other asset classes and less frequently adopted investment strategies. As a result, this group of investors needed help in identifying hedge fund managers. Our research tells us that all but a few family offices had the capability of identifying new and established managers in the fragmented and unfamiliar hedge fund universe. Most of this was done through word of mouth or through connections through the country club and other social settings. (Sound familiar?)

During the early 1990s, several fund of funds were being launched and were struggling to raise capital and to form infrastructures for the early phase of building out their businesses. This resulted in an unlikely partnership between fund of funds building new firms and looking for capital and family offices with capital to invest, and searching for hedge fund managers. It was the beginning of the relationship for several different family offices that have since dominated the fund of funds of industry and have consequently built very strong investment companies that invest in hedge funds. This enterprise of cooperation was a good fit, because the larger family offices resembled larger institutional investors in the early developmental stage. This was probably the beginning of the convergence of private wealth management with institutional assets; everybody everywhere, regardless of asset size, was looking to hedge funds for alpha.

Manager Selection

The coupling of family offices and fund of funds managers was the result of investors' wanting to learn the art of manager selection and due diligence. These investors were happy to invest with a fund of funds to learn the skills and to determine who the new managers were and what they were doing to extract profits from the market. A second benefit that this partnership offered was the ability of the investors to acquire the tools necessary to find new managers and gain access to a community they otherwise did not know. Since many family offices were started by successful entrepreneurs, these investors were and still are willing to invest with new managers that lack a long and seasoned track record if the family could thereby gain an additional advantage in the marketplace.

One of the first family offices to use this approach was Trip Samson of Landmark Management, Inc., a multifamily office located in New York.

Trip's firm manages the assets of several family offices and has allocated to hedge funds since the mid-1990s. The investment objective for his portfolios was to diversify away from the risk of the public markets and several large concentrated equity positions that were held by several members of his families. As Trip started to look at hedge funds, he met two financial services veterans who were both starting their own new fund of funds. Both needed capital, and both also wanted to expand the relationships that they had. Trip had capital, and he wanted to get his feet wet in hedge funds and thought that this relationship would be beneficial to both parties. The results turned out to be worth it. At the time, fund of funds returns, like those of hedge funds, were quite strong during the early years of his organization. The gamble paid off.

Capitalizing on the benefit of the relationship with the start-up managers, Trip has since expanded into direct hedge fund investing. The results have achieved the investment objective of each client, and they also preserved wealth during the technology meltdown of 2000–2002. He found that the fund of funds became overdiversified during this same period, and he now does all hedge fund investing direct with managers. In short, his enterprise has become a specialized fund of funds.

As a result of interaction with many family offices, fund of funds have come to the forefront with many first-time investors like Trip Samson or those looking to gain a toehold in hedge funds without hiring a team of seasoned professionals. Since family offices are often very knowledgeable and not hesitant about paying for outstanding investment talent, many have also moved into direct investing while still maintaining relationships with fund of funds as an extended research resource. In general, family offices are concerned more with customization of the portfolio rather than the low volatility that other, more traditional institutional investors seek through hedge fund investments. Many families like "high-octane" returns and seek to capitalize on this aspect of hedge fund investing. They also like the greater tax efficiency of long-term holdings that may be realized through the customized portfolio rather than the greater diversification of an investment into a fund of funds directly. When investing in fund of funds, many family offices prefer niche strategies such as emerging markets, distressed investing, or specialized areas (e.g., financial services or technology).

WHO INVESTS

While each family office has different—some might even say unique—investment criteria, one fact is clear: High net worth and family office assets are growing globally; regardless of market turmoil and fraud, assets from this group of investors will continue to flow into hedge funds and fund of funds (see Figures 6.1A and 6.1B).

One of the unique aspects of family office investment mandates is that they are not as institutionalized as other institutional investors; they usually report directly to the senior family members, who are quicker to complete the due diligence process and make investment decisions. This is good for both the investors and the investment managers who receive the allocation. Many other institutional investor groups move at a slower, more

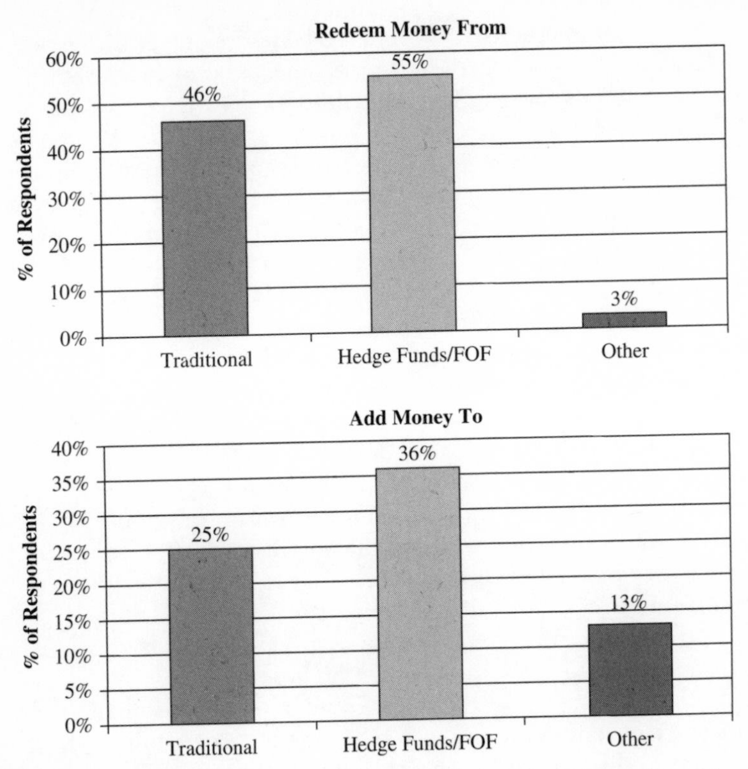

FIGURE 6.1A Percentage of Investors Who Expect to Redeem Assets from Managers
Source: IPI Family Performance Tracking® Survey 2008.

methodical pace and work within guidelines set by boards of directors that know as much about investment strategy and portfolio management as most of us do about brain surgery and changing a carburetor. That being said, one group of investors that has been pushing industry growth forward in the past few years has been large-state pension plans.

Large-state pension plans are massive pools of capital; clearly the biggest boys on the street. They know it, they use their size, and people respect them. Several of the names include Alaska Permanent Fund, Massachusetts Pensions Reserves Investment, and Pennsylvania State Employees Retirements System—all large-state employee pension funds.

Hedge funds are similar to private equity funds in that both are considered lightly regulated as compared with mutual funds and have limited periods of liquidity; most importantly, both structures permit investors to invest alongside of those who are actually managing the money. In the hedge fund

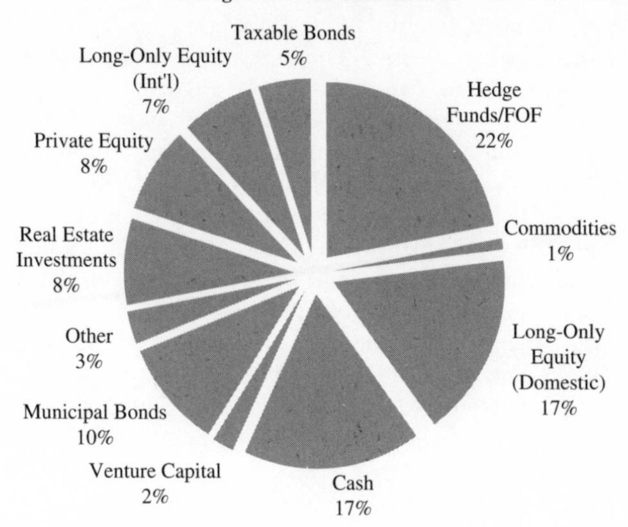

FIGURE 6.1B Percentage of Investors Who Expect to Add Assets to Managers
Source: IPI Family Performance Tracking® Survey 2008.

industry, as in other areas of the investment universe, this concept is known as "eating one's own cooking." As prospective fund of funds investors or their advisors review strategies and meet with the managers, question number one for the hedge fund should be, how much do you have invested? Similarly, investors should ask this question of the fund of funds managers if they are looking to allocate to their fund.

As hedge funds and particularly fund of funds have grown, many of the largest funds are now starting to resemble mutual fund organizations, and the question arises, is this just a marketing organization, or is it an investment management organization? Most mutual fund managers are in the asset-gathering business, not the asset management business. They get paid for assets under management, not performance. Therefore, it is to their advantage to manage to the mean or the index that they benchmark their fund against. They are not rewarded for outperforming. Their survival, since many are public companies with shareholders, depends on their ability to gather money, not on what they do with it.

GROWING ASSETS

For an investor, the objective is *returns*, not distribution of assets or the ability of the firm to grow its assets. A well-defined organizational infrastructure is required to protect partner assets while meeting the portfolio investment objective. Investors must be aware of exceeding large capital inflows and of any organizational changes that will impact the strategy to determine whether investors' interests are still aligned.

Foundations and endowments have also been early adopters of hedge funds and fund of funds. Two major direct investors in hedge funds are Harvard and Yale, who have been investing directly in hedge funds for many years. However, most smaller foundations and endowments have not made the financial commitment to build out investment organizations that can tackle hedge fund allocation and therefore use fund of funds to gain access to these managers (see Figure 6.2).

In reviewing the results of the study, it is interesting to note the higher percentage of alternatives with larger institutions, but the shift has been for smaller participants to increase allocations over the past several years as they cite the need for portfolio diversification, downside risk protection, and improved portfolio returns.

How Hedge Funds Work

"Fund of funds investing has been the first step to understand how hedge funds really work," states Bob Boldt of Perella Weinberg Partners LP, a New York–based financial services firm. Most investors, including foundations, endowments, and pension funds, are looking to achieve alpha in more innovative ways. The role of the fund of funds manager is to separate alpha from beta—to buy beta cheaply, and to achieve alpha using different strategies. While the large-state pension plans are looking to stick their toes in the water with allocations of 3 to 5 percent of plan assets, foundations and endowments are more aggressive in seeking higher returns. Fund of funds represent a good first step, but as the alternative industry matures, these groups will migrate to directly investing into hedge funds.

The big behemoth waiting in the wings and moving ever so slowly is the combined assets of the individual state retirement plans. As baby boomers get ready to enjoy their golden years, these investors are looking to protect assets through investments that go long and short the market. However, it might be a little too late now for some plans.

As of January 2009, the top 1,000 plans saw their assets under management drop by nearly $1 trillion as a result of the volatility in the equity markets. The top 200 defined-benefit plans lost nearly 16.5 percent of their assets, while the top 200 defined-contribution plans lost nearly 13.7 percent,. It was the worst decline in 30 years, according to *Pensions and Investments* magazine, which tracks the industry.[1]

2008 NACUBO Endowment Study © 2008 National Association of College and University Business Officers

Investment Pool Assets	Average Asset Class Allocation of Total Assets*								
	Equity %	Fixed Income %	Real Estate %	Cash %	Hedge Funds %	Private Equity %	Venture Capital %	Natural Resources %	Other %
Greater Than $1 Billion	39.4	10.8	6.4	1.4	22.6	10.0	3.6	5.3	0.5
>$500 Million to ≤ $1 Billion	42.5	14.6	6.1	1.9	19.2	7.7	2.8	3.5	1.7
>$100 Million to ≤ $500 Million	50.4	16.5	4.1	2.5	16.4	4.3	1.2	3.0	1.7
>$50 Million to ≤ $100 Million	54.1	20.3	4.2	4.4	11.5	1.8	0.5	1.9	1.4
>$25 Million to ≤ $50 Million	57.6	20.8	4.1	3.4	10.4	1.0	0.3	1.2	1.1
Less Than or Equal to $25 Million	55.9	27.1	2.2	8.1	3.3	0.6	0.3	0.4	2.1
Public	51.7	21.4	3.5	4.8	11.0	2.9	0.8	2.4	1.6
Independent	52.0	18.1	4.4	3.4	13.8	3.5	1.2	2.2	1.5
Equal-Weighted Average	51.9	19.2	4.1	3.9	12.9	3.3	1.0	2.2	1.5
Dollar-Weighted Average	40.0	13.1	6.5	0.5	21.0	8.4	3.2	6.5	0.9

*774 institutions provided investment pool asset class data.

FIGURE 6.2 Average Asset Class Allocation of Total Assets

(*continued*)

2003 NACUBO Endowment Study © 2005 National Association of College and University Business Officers

Average Asset Class Allocation of Total Assets*									
Investment Pool Assets	Equity %	Fixed Income %	Real Estate %	Cash %	Hedge Funds %	Private Equity %	Venture Capital %	Natural Resources %	Other %
Greater Than $1 Billion	44.8	18.6	4.2	1.8	19.9	5.2	3.0	1.9	0.7
>$500 Million to ≤ $1 Billion	54.4	18.2	4.2	1.4	13.4	4.2	2.7	1.1	0.4
>$100 Million to ≤ $500 Million	56.5	23.5	2.9	2.7	8.3	2.2	1.3	0.8	1.8
>$50 Million to ≤ $100 Million	58.7	27.2	2.8	4.9	4.3	0.6	0.3	0.1	1.1
>$25 Million to ≤ $50 Million	60.2	27.7	2.6	3.5	4.2	0.2	0.2	0.1	1.4
Less Than or Equal to $25 Million	57.0	29.8	2.2	6.6	1.6	0.2	0.1	0.0	2.5
Public	58.1	27.9	2.1	4.0	4.3	0.9	0.5	0.4	1.6
Independent	56.7	24.9	3.1	4.0	6.9	1.5	0.9	0.4	1.6
Equal-Weighted Average	57.1	25.9	2.8	4.0	6.1	1.3	0.8	0.4	1.6
Dollar-Weighted Average	49.4	21.4	4.5	1.5	13.5	3.8	2.7	2.4	0.8

*705 institutions provided investment pool asset class data.

Source: 2008 NACUBO Endowment Study; 2008 National Association of College and University Business Officers.

FIGURE 6.2 *(Continued)*

In short, their investments did not work. A change is needed, and it is believed that many will continue to look to alternative investments to right a sinking ship and get the plans to the promised land—a place where the return can achieve the returns of the actuarial tables.

Pension Plans and Hedge Funds

Hedge fund assets of the top defined-benefit plans increased 51 percent to $76.3 billion, including direct hedge fund investments of $38.6 billion and fund of funds investments of $37.7 billion, as compared with $3.2 billion as of September 2001. This indicates that large plans favor fund of funds but are starting to diversify into single-strategy funds as well to seek more customized solutions to achieve their investment mandate.

Bob Boldt said, "Pension allocations should be larger than 3 to 5 percent, but many don't clearly understand the role of hedge funds and will remain highly dependent upon their consultants. The challenge is for the consultants to provide a high level of education to their clients."

Boldt's comments are even more important in light of the Madoff scandal. Investors need to be educated and need to understand what is happening to their assets. Unfortunately, many do not have the time or specialized background to do the work. As a result, these plans in particular seem to rely heavily on consultants and others to make decisions and put money to work.

Internal Concerns

For those pension plans that have made the infrastructure investment with staff, direct investing is the logical next step. Boldt believes that foundations and endowments have made the investment in staff, and their increased allocations to hedge funds demonstrates the need for higher returns for foundations and endowments. Foundations and endowments need to earn a higher return and are willing to assume a different risk profile than other investors who use fund of funds to meet their hedge fund allocation needs. Boldt is aware of some institutions that hold hedge funds in their traditional allocation buckets as an alternative to long-only managers.

Each investor views hedge funds differently. While most investors view hedge funds as an asset class, some view hedge funds as a structure. This approach is a way of gaining exposure to a range of asset classes, and it provides the flexibility to shift market exposures to "where the action is." Hedge fund managers have broad mandates and the flexibility to seek new opportunities. Of course, this is not without risk.

There is no single model that distinguishes the risk level for a hedge fund investment program; this will be determined by the investor's risk profile and asset/liability requirements. However, investors should try to get up to speed in order to understand this asset class in greater detail along with the concomitant benefit and risk.

Foundations and endowments have spent the last decade educating their investment committees (or being educated by the investment professionals of the colleges and universities) and are in a position to assume a different risk profile than some more traditional hedge fund investors. Pension funds seek the security blanket of a consultant to blame if something goes awry such as a blowup or a fraud. While the likelihood of that is small, the plan administrator can always tell the trustees that the overall allocation to fund of funds was small and the consultant is responsible.

"Consultants fit the psychological need for having someone to blame," said Leslie Rahl, president and founder of New York–based Capital Market Risk Advisors. "With direct investing, the stakes may be higher, but the investors are able to customize the portfolio, make independent decisions, and understand why they have created the portfolio, and what the cost is."

EVERYONE IS INVESTED IN THE SAME THING

Why do consultants consistently recommend the same large fund of funds in most searches? While a few consulting firms have built dedicated hedge fund and alternative practices, most have not. Putting resources into building the infrastructure with senior investment professionals who have hands-on hedge fund experience has not been the objective of most of the gatekeepers. Many simply don't have the expertise and consequently rely on the herd concept. If the fund of funds or hedge fund is big, has a long track record, and is used by many other respected investors, it must be good! However, a new generation of consultants has grown up in the alternative arena who have the skill set required to delve deeper into hedge funds, transitioning from fund of funds into direct hedge fund allocation. That being said, in light of the losses of 2008, it is safe to assume that investors will increase due diligence and will no longer take consultant reports or information for granted. This means the industry will be viewed under a microscope for some time.

Hedge funds and fund of funds are still classified as alternative, because they go both long and short the market as compared with traditional investments that take only long positions. This belief has led many first-time institutional investors to be unhappy with the results of their allocation to fund of funds. Given that many of the institutional allocations have been made at the suggestion of a consultant, the first weakness may be due to the lack of complete understanding of the hedge fund industry or to incomplete education on the part of the consultant. The skill set to review, monitor, and select hedge fund investments differs from that required for traditional long-only investing, and both the consultant and investor may not have been up to speed as needed to understand the strategy of timeliness of reporting. A second weakness may also be attributable to the fund of funds manager, who may not have been fully aware of the unique reporting requirements for the new class of institutional investors and the need to explain the strategy, liquidity, investment process, and reporting expectations in greater detail.

Managers and investors alike who understand each other's approach are usually more satisfied with results, reporting, and fee arrangements.

Consultant Issues

Consultants must meet three challenges, right now and for the near and distant future. The first is to demystify the risks of hedge fund investing. At the same time, consultants must educate clients about the risks and benefits of hedge fund investing. The second is to acquire the talent needed to provide high-level research and dig into the opaque strategies that hedge funds employ. As a result, fund of funds remains the path for many consultants as they search out large managers with large research staffs that they think they can rely on.

Bruce Graham of Clearbook Investment Consulting, who works with pension plans, endowments and foundations, said that client education is what allows new investors to embrace the use of hedge funds. "Getting up to speed for foundations and endowments is quicker, usually a one-year process, but can be two to three years for large pension plans," he said. "However, both need the education before they can do anything, and that is our job."

Unfortunately, Graham's experience with many institutional investors may be limited to a series of phone calls and a three-hour semiannual meeting that covers a wide range of subjects; often, the discussion of hedge fund investing is reduced to a short time slot. Despite the time challenges, lack of experience, need for education and risks, Graham is often an advocate for clients adding hedge funds and fund of funds as alpha generators for their overall portfolio.

The third challenge that all investors face is the ongoing monitoring of both the funds selected and the prospective funds for future inclusion in the portfolio. Part of the postinvestment monitoring is to continue to update the client on changes with the manager, periodic performance reporting, and attribution of returns. Why was a fund up (or down) when the rest of the market did so well (or poorly) is a frequent question asked by investors.

Investors must speak with their hedge fund and fund of funds managers on a regular basis to ensure that managers deliver as promised. Put differently, if a manager will not talk to you, will not provide you with information, or is unwilling to respond to requests for a meeting, then redeem immediately. Managers who say that they cannot discuss their strategy with you because doing so is a risk to the portfolio are not managers to invest your money with. The follow-up risk management and monitoring is as important as the selection process. Read that again; it is important and we don't want you to miss it.

Consultants must be proactive; they must anticipate the questions that you pose and make sure that they are properly equipped to answer them, More importantly, they must be prepared, and required, to act should the information you receive not meet with your expectations. Simply put, it is your money.

EDUCATION

Clearly, the education process is critical. Many different moving parts are included in today's diversified portfolio investment products. These include derivatives, credit default swaps, and maybe some Term Asset-Backed Securities Loan Facility (TALF) money, rather than traditional stocks and bonds. You need to know what is going on with your money, and there is a lot to learn. The markets are global. We all live in a 24-hour investment cycle with nonstop media coverage, and you need to be prepared when the wheels come off the cart. One lesson we can say we learned in 2007 and 2008 is that the unthinkable is possible and we need to pay attention at all times. Consultants who got their clients up to speed with the ongoing developments of the past 24 months and continued to provide assistance as market gyrations occurred certainly earned their keep. As for the others—oh well, time to find a new consultant.

During the past year, institutional interest has pushed investment management consulting firms to increase their capabilities in hedge funds. Although many consultants have provided investment recommendations in real estate and private equity through the years, the increasing demand for education and follow-up exploration in hedge funds has been a drain on consultant talent during the past 24 months. The need for understanding hedge funds has pushed consultants to reassign staff from traditional long-only investing or to hire new staff to fill this gap.

Increasing institutional acceptance of these products, along with creation of new products, has also contributed to the evolution of hedge funds from alternatives to mainstream investing. Because of the unique nature of hedge fund strategies and the lack of standardized reporting requirements, the research has become more challenging than that required for traditional long-only investing.

One of the major components in recommending and evaluating hedge funds and fund of funds investing is investor education. Included in this is the demystification of what a hedge fund is in today's marketplace. This is very difficult, and something that many people struggle with on a daily basis. It does not help that the there have been blowups and that the press, for the most part, blames all that ails the financial world on hedge funds.

Many pension trustees are reluctant to make the leap into hedge funds and do so with some trepidation because of headline risk. Few are willing to make the time commitment required to understand the strategies, structures, and managers involved and believe that the headline risk is not worth the potential returns. It also does not help that the consultants, for the most part, drop the ball when it comes to investor education vis-à-vis hedge funds. In many cases, the consultant's representative is a young, ambitious, and up-and-coming analyst or marketing person looking to move up the ladder to the next job rung. This is a nightmare for both the investors and the managers. Trustees cannot put any faith in these people and often do not. Consistency in marketing and education may be challenged, and it serves to lengthen the education cycle of the prospective investment board.

"Investing directly in hedge funds requires knowledge, timing, and rolling up your sleeves to understand how the money is being managed," said Leslie Rahl. "If the investor is not willing to do the work, they better stick to fund of funds."

Education in hedge funds is much like understanding bond math. For many, understanding the relationship between interest rates, yield, and prices is as challenging as learning to speak Chinese. Do you ever wonder why most financial publications always include a sentence that says something like "when the price goes up, the yield goes down" in every bond story they publish. If the investor has trouble with that concept, the path to strong trustee stewardship will be a challenge when it comes to hedge fund investing. This role in theory should be filled by the consultant and others from the consultant's firm. It is their job to educate, explain, and make sure people understand what is happening with their assets.

Since the technology blowup of 2000 and the destruction that occurred in 2008, trustees and consultants alike have become aware of the benefit of hedge funds as an investment management tool to manage risk. Hedge funds that actually hedge provide a better tool to manage volatility and to produce alpha than traditional investment products. At the same time, the accounting industry has finally convinced trustees that the pension plan is a liability and is becoming more so. While hedge funds and fund of funds provide tools to lessen volatility, the plan sponsor should be willing to pay for hedge fund vehicles that dampen volatility as well.

Many of the early hedge fund adopters who were exposed to these strategies through fund of funds are now moving to the next generation of hedge fund investing. This is by way of direct investing with the managers through coinvesting in as many of the past successful arbitrage hedge fund strategies that have themselves become "arbed" away. While some institutional investors may choose to invest on their own, several are working with fund of funds on customized mandates in illiquid funds or strategies to coinvest with the manager in areas in which the investor will rely on the expertise or background of the fund of funds managers to vet the strategies. In addition, a few specialized fund of funds managers are creating managed accounts as investment vehicles with hedge fund managers to provide greater oversight, transparency, and ownership of the securities.

A Pension Investor

Specialized mandates are increasing as investors seek to capitalize on non-mainstream global investment opportunities and to take advantage of niche strategies in far-off lands.

One of the largest investors in hedge funds is ABP, the fund for 2.7 million Dutch retirees with assets over €208.9 billion or $277 billion in 2007. APB was an early adopter of hedge fund investing. Its management team has been actively investing in alternative strategies for the past seven years. It has an impressive track record for pension assets and currently allocates over 20 percent of assets to hedge funds.[2]

According to a PricewaterhouseCoopers report issued in March of 2008, ABP expects to raise its alternative exposure to 26 percent by 2009. This would put its allocation to these strategies at nearly the same level as the endowments of Harvard and Yale. It is unclear as of this writing whether the management of ABP was still planning to increase its exposure to alternatives in the wake of the turmoil in 2008.[3]

University Endowments

Kathryn Crecelius came to Johns Hopkins University in the newly created position as chief investment officer for the university's endowment in October of 2005. She had previously built the alternatives portfolio at MIT. At Johns Hopkins, she "untethered the university's assets from fund of funds and reallocated to single-strategy managers." Her team works hard to monitor, source, and allocate assets to alternatives.

Crecelius does not see the value in fund of funds. Her belief is that the reason she was hired by the university and in turn built an internal investment team was to manage money. "It comes down to who is running the foundation or endowment," she said. "If the team is in place and can do the job, then they should do the job."

Johns Hopkins has created a staff to manage its assets internally, but many other institutions continue to do it by committee, and that is a nightmare. Many colleges, universities, and secondary schools have investment committees, endowment business staff, and external advisors including trustees who are active in the financial services industry. Of course, in almost all cases, the foundation or endowment relies on consultants to provide unbiased information and investment advice as well as someone to blame should things go awry.

Drivers of Growth

Eric Weber, who is not in asset allocation and is not a consultant but a mergers and acquisitions professional, believes that hedge fund asset growth is demand driven.

"New allocations into hedge funds and fund of funds are coming from investors who want out of bonds or traditional investments," he said. "The consultants tell them that hedge fund allocations should be increased and the allocations are increased."

In our experience, the learning curve for hedge fund investing for pension funds appears to be five years. As soon as the pension fund staff can absorb the knowledge imparted by the fund of funds, the training wheels start to come off and they start to make selective, independent, direct investments into managers.

Leslie Rahl says that prior to making direct investments, the consultants' role fits the psychological needs of the trustees or powers that be at a specific organization. As well, it provides a person or entity to blame when performance falls short. "After all, the new hedge fund investor may not have the skills or knowledge to do the work to allocate directly," she said. "At some point, they wake up and say that they are ready, and sure enough they go direct."

GOING DIRECT

As investors move away from fund of funds and into direct investing, institutional investors want to invest only with firms that have good reputations and that are large enough in size to accommodate large flows of capital.

While most investors gravitate toward the large firms, there are thousands of good, smaller firms that fly below the radar screen.

Unfortunately, many investors miss these opportunities, and investments continue to flow to the biggest funds. The bigger will continue to get bigger, and brand names will gain greater acceptance. Since hedge funds are not permitted to advertise, finding managers is a word-of-mouth business, and in this industry branding is important.

To be "accepted" and to appear on an unofficial "approved" list, branding comes from investors telling other investors that the manager is "good." The problem is that market perception or brand acceptance is usually not worth all that much in the end. Nothing can replace good solid ongoing due diligence. Brand or no brand, due diligence is what matters most.

CHAPTER 7

Understanding Risk and the Need for Due Diligence

The term *systemic risk* is generally used to describe a series of interactions between financial institutions and the capital markets, and the risk of the failure of one market participant among other financial institutions. The demise of Long-Term Capital Management (LTCM) in 1998 in the aftermath of the Russian default of debt has come to be recognized as the first large-scale event that created major market dislocations as a direct result of systemic risks.

LTCM ISSUES

While many books have been written about "genius" failing, LTCM, started in 1994 and led by Salomon Brothers alumni, achieved unprecedented 40 percent plus returns for investors after fees. LTCM's managers simply thought they could master the investment universe. With a team of academics, traders, and former Federal Reserve officials, John Meriwether and his team used leverage to increase LTCM's asset base from $1.25 billion under management to more than $100 billion of investments in the markets. After thousands of arbitrage trades across the global markets and among various investment classes were made, the bottom fell out for the firm in the summer of 1998. The investment managers had significant exposure to many different markets. They were investing in developed markets and emerging markets, along with fixed-income and equity markets, and they used many varied and complex investment models. Coupled with the leverage, this was a recipe for disaster. When the Russian government defaulted on its debt and the Asian flu spread like wildfire, the fund's positions fell in price, margin was due, and wholesale selling of the portfolio began. The margin calls could not be met, and ultimately the fund was bailed out by a Federal Reserve–brokered deal. The genius, in short, failed.

At the end of September 1998, the Federal Reserve Bank of New York, having no choice, summoned the executives of the Wall Street investment banks and commercial banks to its headquarters to come up with a solution to the LTCM mess. LTCM was deemed too big to fail by the powers that be; as a result, a solution had to be put in place to ensure that the firm did not default on its loans. The Federal Reserve "encouraged" 14 banks to provide a $3.6 billion lifeline to the firm that would enable LTCM to unwind positions and provide an orderly liquidation of fund assets. The belief was that this lifeline would reduce both the shock to the financial system and the risk of a chain reaction of a failure of the banking system.

It was believed by LTCM's management that their financial models would be able to generate noncorrelated returns and that the leveraged portfolio would enhance returns. In the aftermath of the Russian default and the subsequent flight to quality, liquidity and credit became the top concerns to investors. Suddenly, all of LTCM's trades and positions were correlated; selling pressure exacerbated the situation, and the fund could not weather the storm. The systemic risk was the failure of LTCM along with the subsequent downward price spiral of global capital markets, which put pressure on financial institutions globally. Had the 14 banks not stepped in, the decline might have been much more dramatic and might have had a far greater impact globally, causing significant stress on the markets worldwide.

The bailout of LTCM was followed by the corporate governance issues of WorldCom, Adelphia, Enron, and Global Crossing in 2001–2002, once again putting stress on the financial system's circuit breakers.

LTCM's downfall was the first to highlight the link between the capital markets, the banking industry, and the financial services industry. Many banks and investment banks actually operated as hedge funds with their proprietary trading desks.

As we witnessed once again in 2007 with the beginning of the subprime meltdown and moving into 2008, we were reminded of the linkage between hedge funds, the banking industry, the capital markets, investment banks, and the man in the street. In a period of less than six months, Bear Stearns, Lehman Brothers, and AIG ceased to exist as independent entities and were joined by the "conservatorships" of Fannie Mae and Freddie Mac.

WHAT HAPPENED?

Lessons learned in 1998 and again in 2002 were once again thrust into the marketplace by the villain of subprime debt in 2007. Subprime debt is a term made popular by Wall Street during a period of providing mortgages to borrowers who could not afford the debt. Lenders, including commercial banks, savings banks, and Wall Street investment banks, with the encouragement of elected officials, have traditionally provided mortgage financing to borrowers in search of the American dream—home ownership. However, in the period immediately following the tech bubble, investors realized that the only place that they could make money was in real estate, because "it always goes up," or was "the safest place to put money since real estate never goes down." Seizing the opportunity, and with the creativity and distribution of Wall Street, lenders determined that they could provide the dream to current and prospective borrowers, many of whom could ill afford the debt of home ownership. Many firms created products to make housing more affordable, many of them appropriately called "teasers."

What Really Is Systemic Risk?

Fannie Mae and Freddie Mac had strict underwriting standards for residential mortgages for many years, and this included a loan-to-value requirement of a maximum loan amount of 80 percent. In other words, a borrower was required to place a 20 percent down payment for a home and would be required to complete a rigorous underwriting and financial review process administered by the lender. However, subprime borrowing changed the face of residential lending; loans were offered that included 100 percent loan-to-value underwriting, and incomplete (or no documents, or limited documents) underwriting. In addition, loans were offered at a below-market introductory rate (teaser loans) that reset to higher rates on future adjustment dates, making it more difficult for borrowers to meet future debt service requirements.

Even though lenders were being called predatory for inducing borrowers with inadequate information, loan origination moved to record levels. With nothing down (or little, in many cases), borrowers went on a spending spree, and residential builders complied with projects all over the country. Banks were happy to make loans to developers, Congress was happy because of the growth in their home districts, and borrowers were happy with cheap and readily available credit terms. Fannie and Freddie were happy because of the new loan volume for conforming loans (meeting their strict guidelines), but they also wanted to get into the new subprime game of originating loans that were easier to underwrite. In an effort to improve margins and earnings, Fannie and Freddie readily bought these loans into their portfolios as well.

Who were the happiest among the participants? You guessed it—Wall Street and the hedge fund community. First, Wall Street loved subprime loans because they would be able to use the specialized skills of the "financial engineers" that they had hired from the top universities in the world to create mathematical assumptions to reengineer cash flows and payoffs and expected default models to determine a value for the loans. The ability to assemble and aggregate pools of mortgage loans into different tranches of securities, with cash flows coming from various geographic areas of the country that would create different investment requirements of different classes of investors, became an exciting model for profit.

What could be better? Wide margins for the lender, wide margins for the structuring investment bank, and big commissions for the underwriter and distributor—a true match made in heaven. The major ratings services, Moody's and Standard & Poor's, loved it as well. The increase in product meant an increase in volume of debt that would be financed, and each deal needed an assigned rating before it could be sold to investors. The financial engineers ran models that made a series of assumptions and sold deals based on the assumptions.

In the far outposts of the hedge fund community, many hedge fund managers had their financial engineers as well and knew that the Wall Street assumptions were wrong. The lenders' underwriting was worse than it was thought to be. Borrowers would suffer extreme pain as the teaser loans or "liar loans" with incomplete documentation came home to roost and reset to higher interest rates, while the Street was starting to suffer from indigestion and was having difficulties selling some of this paper. The paper, which has since become known as "toxic waste," seems to be living up to its name.

The SIV

Much of this paper made it into structure investment vehicles (SIVs), a term not known to many until the summer of 2007. SIVs were offshore funds created by banks to sell short-term debt and were used to buy various mortgage products. The product was designed for yield enhancement for short-term investors. The SIV sold short-term debt, usually through the commercial paper market, and bought longer-term debt, providing higher yields to short-term investors. Most SIV investors probably did not know how the product was financed or why the yield was higher than traditional money market rates, but who really cared? Citibank and a host of other well-known banks were marketing the products that were rated AAA—therefore, it must be okay. Okay, that is, until investors stopped buying SIV commercial paper.

The event that triggered the SIV crisis was the debacle several months earlier at a Bear Stearns mortgage hedge fund. The fund invested in a wide range of mortgage products and collateralized debt obligations (CDOs). As mortgage delinquencies started to creep up in early 2007, cash flows of the underlying securities became even more unpredictable. Since the Bear Stearns fund used leverage to enhance returns, the fund's performance returns came under pressure. Suddenly, investors became uncomfortable and wanted to redeem. Unfortunately, the manager faced two of the biggest problems that a hedge fund fears—pricing and liquidity. Given that Bear Stearns, the investment bank, was a major factor in the mortgage market, the fact that it could not price and then sell these assets created a problem.

Wall Street prime brokerage firms that had lent money to the hedge fund decided that they too were concerned and needed protection for their assets; consequently, they seized some of the collateral that they had lent to the fund. Other banks decided to pull credit lines that previously had been used for financing facilities when all the while the fund was desperately seeking liquidity for positions. The fund suddenly faced a massive liquidity crisis because of systematic risk from many segments of the financial market.

Thus, the first two chapters of understanding systemic risk have been written. While LTCM seems like a generation ago, we will try to shed light on what happened in 2007 and 2008 and project what to look for in the future, even as history is being written.

LEVERAGE AND LIQUIDITY

The major themes that emerge from these well-known events are the relationship of leverage and liquidity and the correlation of all of the instruments that are supposed to be uncorrelated. As we are reminded by the wise old fixed-income bond geek who said in the wake of the most recent 2007 liquidity blowup, "Using leverage is like never having to say you're sorry." Systemic risk shows the inner relationship of hedge fund strategies and underlying risk exposure.

Many hedge fund strategies rely on leverage to produce higher levels of return. In addition to Wall Street proprietary trading desks, Fannie Mae and Freddie Mac used high levels of leverage to generate returns. Surprisingly, hedge fund leverage of 5 to 10 times of assets under management at many fixed-income firms was less than that used by Wall Street firms and government-backed entities such as Fannie and Freddie.

The hedge fund positions are generally larger than the amount of collateral that is posted to support the underlying positions. Therefore, leverage turns small profits into larger profits, or small losses into larger losses. When credit spreads widen, defaults increase, or rates rises the market value of the collateral is reduced, and margin calls for additional collateral are required.

In many cases, credit requirements are raised by the lender, and forced liquidation may occur over a short period of time thereafter. For portfolios that contain less liquid positions or positions that the lending counterparty—a bank, a Wall Street firm, or a prime broker—reprices, and selling pressure to meet margin calls increases. Suddenly, the non-correlated assets are correlated—hence, systemic risk.

The Credit Crisis

The spring and summer of 2007, leading into 2008, was a case of déjà vu all over again in the capital markets, reminiscent of the summer of 1998. The unwinding of hedge fund leverage to meet margin calls with ABS and MBS collateral that could not be priced, led providers of credit—prime brokers and banks—to reprice collateral lower. Unfortunately, market professionals suddenly did not know what the value of the positions was. In a span of a few weeks, bond prices plummeted from par to 70, 60, and 50 or less. As a result of this selling pressure, investors began selling plain vanilla securities that were readily priceable and marketable to raise capital to meet margin calls of the less liquid positions. At the same time, credit spreads of corporate bonds widened, and additional selling pressure kicked in. Many funds faced the inevitable death spiral. The rest is history; the major issue is that the more illiquid the investment position, the larger the price impact will be of forced liquidations or sales. And leverage just adds another kicker.

As market participants unknowingly learned very quickly, pockets of subprime paper that had been distributed globally for many years were marked down dramatically, and the U.S. financial contagion swiftly spread around the globe. As we discovered quickly, it was not restricted to the fixed-income markets. And so, as we review the list of well-publicized casualties, their downfall began with the thirst for the yield of subprime securities that included over 100 global mortgage companies and well-respected financial firms. Among them were

- New Century
- Bear Stearns
- Northern Rock
- Lehman Brothers
- Countrywide
- Merrill Lynch
- Fannie Mae
- Freddie Mac
- AIG

- Wachovia
- Washington Mutual
- Bradford & Bingley
- Indie Mac
- Hypo Real Estate
- Fortis

As we have witnessed, systemic risk can be defined as the domino effect of the failure or near failure of the financial system because of the confusion, the lack of liquidity, and the selling of assets by institutions that hold similar securities. It is then exacerbated by the selling pressure of nonrelated assets as other investors seek liquidity in their portfolios. Academics and economists will debate the subprime contagion for years, but it was lack of liquidity for securities that were highly leveraged and impossible to price that led to the downfall. As the risk moved from Wall Street to the banking community to Main Street, the credit markets approached a state of near freezing in 2008.

UNDERSTANDING DUE DILIGENCE

Understanding systemic risk is a very important piece of the puzzle; second is understanding due diligence. It is critical to establish due diligence controls that are in place before a specific manager is chosen and investments are made. Both investment and operational procedures of top-down and bottom-up analysis must be integrated into the evaluation to determine whether a potential submanager meets the portfolio's risk/reward profile.

Due diligence involves a two-part process of quantitative and qualitative analysis of the fund and the investment style of the investment manager. For the investor, it includes an evaluation of the investment process of the fund. Both reviews are accomplished by multiple on-site visits to manager's front and back offices as well as reviews of the key tax, regulatory, and legal issues.

One of the most often used and misused terms in hedge fund land is *due diligence*. Among the white shoe, investment banking brethren, due diligence describes the process of investigating a potential investment or merger of companies in which the bankers review all aspects of a company's business, including operations, management, and financial information. In hedge funds, it has taken on a broader meaning, one that includes identifying managers, meeting with the management team, and completing a laundry list of questions, all of which leads to the ultimate decision whether to buy, hold, sell, or avoid a hedge fund manager or fund of funds manager. In short, due diligence can best be described as everything involved in the search for stellar managers.

Due Diligence Around Risk

Here are some guidelines to follow:

- Successful investors seek opportunities across multiple strategies and asset classes but should recognize that since it is often better to avoid a strategy rather than invest, some opportunities should be avoided.
- It is essential to understand and review the character and background of a manager.
- Investors should avoid strategies that they do not understand.

All investors use a variety of approaches and procedures before making the investment decision. Many investors have established policies and procedures that are continually evolving over a period of years to select managers and alternative investment managers. Generally, the process for hedge fund selection is different from traditional long-only investing with much more deep diving. Most sophisticated investors have developed robust proprietary quantitative and qualitative analysis that includes due diligence questionnaires and a strict approval process by the fund of funds manager and institutional investor.

Why Fund of Funds

The process of selecting, monitoring, and then valuing and reporting the returns of a portfolio of hedge funds requires extensive knowledge and experience. Fund of funds are paid to be in this business and to continually upgrade the quality of the research and follow-up monitoring. The firm should maintain a group of professionals in all aspects of the fund's management business who possess the knowledge and background commensurate with the complexity of the strategy.

Portfolio construction should focus on researching various investment ideas and ultimately the selection of superior investment managers. Each underlying hedge fund manager and strategy should be evaluated in the context of the overall portfolio well before final portfolio selection. Each manager should be evaluated against peer benchmark indexes as well as in the context of the broader portfolio objective to minimize downside risks with low correlation to other managers and the peer industry benchmarks.

Some investors, including foundations, endowments, and family offices often rely on outside third-party firms and consultants to perform or to validate due diligence, but even so, they should have similar procedures in place. On the other hand, fund of funds have built extensive research staffs with many analysts who specialize in specific parts of the due diligence cycle. In many of the larger fund of funds firms, analysts specialize in fixed-income, derivatives, and long/short equity. While investors may be willing to accept market risk with regard to position risk, they should have little tolerance for operational risk.

In either approach, the investor is required to perform sufficient due diligence to make an informed investment decision that has been effectively documented and approved by a stringent review process of related investment decision makers. Many investors use customized questionnaires to gather preliminary data about a potential investment. (Readers are invited to review the sample form in the Appendix.)

Getting Dirty

Who is doing the research at a firm is a question that needs to be asked and answered constantly. Unfortunately, the story for many investors seems to be that young, well-educated professionals are meeting hedge fund managers, but they don't really understand the assets in this asset class from a hands-on perspective. Most have no experience in managing money, nor do they have experience in actually investing in hedge funds, much less equities or bonds. Still, they are making buy and sell recommendations for the constituent investor groups. We often hear from investors that the old people should go out and do all of the leg work, including the first meeting, and let the young people work in the office, transcribe notes from meetings, and answer the phone. Unfortunately, some investors often believe that more is better, and experience is overlooked.

In some industries, that is not the case. In the fund of funds industry, investors should favor organizations with older, more seasoned investment professionals. Gray hair is a plus. The better performing organizations, in fact, have fewer research and due diligence people but more seasoned veterans who understand how money is made. The prospective fund of funds investor should ask whether an organization with 60 young analysts is preferred to a more concentrated staff of 12 seasoned professionals

In the volatile period of hedge fund returns of 2007–2008 in which we witnessed many hedge fund closures and countless more with unexpected extreme return fluctuations, there were a number of fund of funds managers who were able to limit risk simply by sticking to strategies that they understood.

Subprime-related strategies were marketed to a wide range of sophisticated foundations and endowments as well as fund of funds; in the end, either the strategy was not fully understood or the assumptions were not correct. Losses were heavy and continued to mount. Similarly with Madoff, nobody seemed to really understand a split strike conversion strategy, but they believed that it worked, regardless of market swings. Still, thousands gave him money. In the end, everyone knows what happened.

UNDERSTANDING HOW MONEY IS MADE

When it comes to trying to understand obscure strategies, avoidance may be the best approach. Many strategies such as distressed investing and small-cap equities are idiosyncratic in nature; a review of the returns should demonstrate the correlation to the broad market indexes. While most strategies adopted in the period 2007–2008 exhibited correlation to the markets and correlation to other supposed "noncorrelated" strategies, on-site due diligence and a random review of files with individual positions might have revealed what the manager was actually doing, rather than what he said he was doing. It is a good idea to gain a complete understanding of the manager's analytical process.

Hedge fund returns should capitalize on market inefficiencies, and an analysis of position holdings and holdings of other hedge funds may show crowding in both longs and shorts on the part of equity managers. Stress testing by the manager should also show that he or she has evaluated the potential for loss in volatile markets.

The second phase of the due diligence process continues long after the initial investment has been made, with follow-up analysis and review. While several hundred man-hours may be involved in the initial research process, due diligence, and investment, it is routine to spend 75 man-hours in continuing review. Ongoing analysis of the investment returns and risk/return objective that continues long after the initial investment goes hand in hand with monitoring the manager and the changes that take place within the organizational structure. Peer group comparisons should be done to evaluate the invested manager against the performance of other managers in the same sector.

Ongoing due diligence should also address growth in the hedge fund organization as asset size increases to ensure that the manager continues to make a strong financial commitment to build out the firm. Monthly or periodic investment letters and marketing material must be reviewed to determine whether changes have taken place in the organization since the initial investment. In addition, annual financial statements and K-1s should be reviewed to see whether auditors were changed (and why), review changes in valuation policies, and determine whether there are a large number of illiquid investments or side-pocket investments. Also key is to review general partner flow and transfer of capital to ensure that "LP's interests are aligned with the GP."

In other words, if the General Partner withdrew significant amounts of money from the partnership, it would be appropriate to ask why he withdrew funds from the strategy. Was it to pay for his children's college tuition, to buy a new G-4, or to pay bonuses to his staff? It's always good to determine how dedicated the manager is to the continuation of the growth of the firm.

Transparency Issues

Hedge fund investors always seek a high level of transparency despite the fact that managers want to provide as little information regarding the portfolio as possible. Hedge funds may not be subject to the Freedom of Information Act, but investors must feel comfortable with the level of data being provided concerning strategy and position-level transparency that is necessary to make an informed investment decision.

There are several factors that contribute to shoddy due diligence during the overall research process. In most cases, seasoned professionals were born into the investment industry before most of these gadgets were used and understand the value of time spent with the manager. Fund of funds should be encouraged to make a few due diligence calls with the fund in order to gain greater insight into the manager's *actual* process, not just the manager's *reported* process.

Clocks When meeting a manager, forget about the time for the next meeting. If the investor or research guru is looking at the clock to make the next meeting, then delay or cancel it. Hedge fund managers are much like athletes, and when the manager gets into a groove and starts to talk in greater detail, revealing facts and details that were not discussed earlier in the meeting, don't leave. Just listen. The next meeting can always be rescheduled. An initial meeting should take about one hour. The purpose of the first meeting is to gather as much information as required and determine whether a second meeting is needed. In the initial contact with the manager, the fund of funds team should have determined that a follow-up on-site visit is required. Don't ask who the portfolio manager is or who the CFO is. That should have been stated in the marketing material that should have been reviewed before the meeting. Ask how the CFO interacts with the staff, request some of the risk reports, or ask the PM why he uses ETFs to hedge and does not short stocks.

BlackBerrys Put your BlackBerry in your pocket and turn it off. Even though this may be the era of multitasking, due diligence and research involves listening and writing above all. Unless the home office is e-mailing questions to the research team, there is no need for the BlackBerry to be on. If the manager uses a BlackBerry during a meeting, that's another issue. Ask why. Is he in the middle of a big trade, or just bored meeting with investors? If the manager does not provide 100 percent to prospective investors, how accessible do you think the manager will be once he or she has your money?

Turn Off the Internet It may sound irreverent or sacrilegious, but too much time is wasted on the Internet and looking at skateboarders' or politicians' missteps on YouTube. Productivity declines. Back in the office, look at databases, do peer group comps, or find out why investing in emerging markets is growing or could be career threatening. Turn off the iPods. Turn off ESPN. There are enough distractions today, so try to reduce them during interviews or during the work day. On the other hand, a tour of the hedge fund manager's trading floor or a visit to research analysts reveals a lot. If the Internet is on the screen, what is the person viewing? Edgar, Bloomberg, or a company position is great, and asking a few questions about the page viewed can provide additional insight.

The Key Components

There are many questions that must always be asked relating to the overall due diligence of the fund of funds manager. Many are similar to information obtained by the fund of funds in researching the underlying fund managers. Relevant topics include

- Organizational structure and recent changes
- Quality of research and due diligence personnel
- Quality of financial and operational personnel
- Complexity of structure
- Fund of funds key terms
- Investment decision process
- Liquidity analysis, including redemption periods, gates, and side pockets of underlying funds
- Use of leverage
- Quality of risk management
- Investor base
- Nature and complexity of each strategy
- Review of recent financial statements

- Review of professional integrity of the fund of funds management team
- Internal controls, policies, and procedures
- Risk management
- Off-site disaster recovery
- NAV reporting and timeliness
- Transparency
- Management's objective

Most of the listed points are obvious, but we shall discuss the final two in greater detail.

Transparency Transparency is the term in hedge fund land that always strikes a nerve with hedge funds and investors. Many hedge funds have been reluctant to provide a high level of position transparency, with some actually requiring the signing of a nondisclosure document. Transparency may be defined as the secret sauce that managers use to make astute investment decisions. Although the concern of some investors may be to take this position information and act on it, the prime issue for investors is to request and obtain some degree of position transparency to ensure that the manager is actually investing in the types of securities that he has specified within the investment strategy. It may also be a warning sign if a manager states that he has a diversified portfolio, but in reality has four positions that each represent 15 percent holdings.

For fund of funds investors, position transparency is much the same. Fund of funds managers are reluctant to divulge the names of the managers that they allocate to for fear that investors may now have suddenly identified either hedge funds that are well known or other funds that have been subjected to the fund of funds manager's painstaking due diligence and vetting. Just as an equity hedge fund manager may not want to inform prospective investors of new, large positions, many fund of funds also restrict information about large positions of undiscovered managers. However, an investment decision by a prospective investor should be thwarted by the lack of candor on the part of a fund of funds manager who is unwilling to provide this level of position due diligence.

Financial Objective of the Manager The next issue is to determine the financial objective of the manager. Is the fund of funds manager in the business of managing a portfolio or in the business of managing a business? The answer is critical. While the economics of managing a hedge fund with a 2 & 20 fee structure are rewarding to those who achieve consistent, above-market returns, the reward can be great as long as the manager remains active in the money management process.

For a fund of funds, the economics are different; they call for using a smaller asset-based management fee that may also be underpricing pressure from larger pools of assets of the large, institutional investors. As a result and with consolidation within the fund of funds industry by larger, traditional asset management firms looking for an entry point into hedge funds, some managers are more concerned with distribution than with portfolio management. While this may be more difficult to detect in the due diligence process, firms that are expensing more on marketing than research may have fallen into the distribution trap. With fund expenses that may approach 50 basis points to manage and operate a business enterprise, the level of critical mass of the fund of funds manager grows as the infrastructure grows.

MANAGED ACCOUNTS

The events of 2008, including but not limited to the Lehman bankruptcy, the precipitous equity and credit market decline, the Madoff Fraud, the imposition of gates and outright suspensions of redemptions at a number of well known hedge funds called into question the typical hedge fund structure. Many investors believe that it was time to rewrite the rules of hedge fund investing. (In other words, how do I enhance the protection of my hedge fund investments through an alternative structure because there is too much risk to simply invest in a fund. One alternative comes in the form of a managed account. The term "managed account" is often misused with the term "separate account," which refers to a portfolio of hedge funds created for a single investor. Separate accounts are typically for a large investor who is seeking a customized mandate or the perceived safety of having their own fund without the risk of being lumped in with other investors. While the managed account structure has been around for quite some time, dating back to the 1980s, the rise in interest in this structure picked up considerably following the events of the second half of 2008.

Typically, most hedge fund investors, including fund of funds, have invested through the traditional structure, known as a commingled fund, where all investors own shares or limited partnership interests in a particular fund. These investors receive the same investment terms, including fees, liquidity, and lockups and will have limited levels of position transparency, if at all—basically they are beholden to what the managers tell them. In this structure, the hedge fund manager manages the investment portfolio and the operational side of the business while selecting counterparties for specific transactions, and the hedge fund owns each of the underlying portfolio positions. Managed accounts are very different.

Managed accounts address several shortcomings of the traditional hedge fund structure. One key difference is the degree of transparency that each structure provides the end investor (whether it is a fund of funds or institutional investor). Unlike a traditional hedge fund investment, the managed account investor has full position level data, which provides better information for risk management and portfolio monitoring purposes. For example, the investor can examine the actual position overlap among several long/short equity managers when deciding to add or remove an investment. The high level of transparency also provides the investor with the tools to detect style drift. If a long/short equity manager says they are a financial stock focused, the managed account investor can see if they are buying stocks like Wal-Mart Stores Inc., which is not part of their mandate. In the traditional structure, the investor would only know about the investment in Wal-Mart Stores Inc. if the manager inadvertently told them.

Beyond the transparency benefits, there is complete asset protection and control whereby the investor, not the fund, owns the underlying assets in the managed account thus being able to reduce the risk of fraud. While market risk losses certainly remain, operational risks can be reduced dramatically. For example, the investor, not the hedge fund manager, selects service providers such as administrator and auditor. In examining recent hedge fund frauds over the past decade, one or both service providers played some role in the fraud on several occasions. Furthermore, the managed account assets are segregated from those of the hedge fund manager, which are held in their commingled fund. While the investor exercises control over the assets, they still allow the hedge fund manager to focus on managing the individual portfolio positions. This is made possible by a legal contract that allows the investor to revoke the hedge fund managers' trading authority and also provided customized guidelines under which the manager is required to operate. Unlike a hedge fund offering memorandum that is very broad, the contract between the investor and the hedge fund manager in a managed account structure is much more specific.

Gating and suspensions was also a hot topic at the end of 2008 and into early 2009—with a managed account, these tools do not exist. The investor can have the positions sold at any time, and if the manager does not want to do so, they can be removed from the account; the investor can appoint a new manager and do as they wish with the positions in the account. In light of the losses of 2008, investor calls for greater transparency and the need to reduce the uncertainty of liquidity, managed accounts have gained traction with certain hedge fund investors.

Another benefit is that an investor can allocate to a manager without dealing with their business-related risk. Frank Napolitani of Concept Capital, a division of SMH Capital, Inc., a mini-prime broker, said that managed accounts provide investors with more comfort in allocating to early stage managers or smaller managers by reducing the operational and administrative risks. "After all, anything that can allow investors to sleep well at night is a positive," he said.

In fact, managed accounts are the preferred method to invest with new and emerging managers or seasoned hedge funds with smaller asset bases so that the investor does not need to be exposed to operational risks associated with smaller businesses. While investors may be reluctant to invest with a small hedge fund in a traditional fund structure with managed accounts, they do not have to.

Lighthouse Partners is a well-respected global fund of hedge funds in operation since 1996. Lighthouse has made use of the managed account structure since 1999 and has made the growth of this structure a key strategic initiative for the past five years. With over $5 billion in assets under management, the firm has developed a comprehensive infrastructure to manage many of their hedge fund investments through a proprietary managed account they built. According to Kelly Perkins, co-Chief Investment Officer of Lighthouse Partners, "Each managed account is a separate and distinct entity owned and controlled by Lighthouse. The assets are not comingled with the assets of other investors of funds, and therefore not subject to the behavior or turnover of other investors. In addition, administration, valuation, NAV calculation, and audit services are provided to the managed account by independent service providers selected by Lighthouse. This structure allows each underlying manager to focus exclusively on their portfolio management expertise."

The Lighthouse managed account structure creates several advantages that do not exist in the typical comingled fun investment, including: daily position transparency available for investment analysts to oversee, unencumbered impediments such as gates, suspensions, delays or side pockets, stronger investor protection against fraud via better asset control and ownership, and the authority to terminate a manager "at will" if necessary. With an experienced investment and operations team capable of handling a higher level of oversight, Lighthouse has positioned the firm to provide investors fund of hedge fund products that they view as a superior way to invest in hedge funds.

Managed accounts, however, are not for everyone. When an investor considers transitioning traditional hedge fund assets to this structure, there are three challenges they must overcome. First, it is imperative that the investor have the experience and infrastructure to establish, monitor, and execute the managed account structure. As is the case with Lighthouse, their process has been built over several years; they did not just decide to start offering this structure in the wake of the 2008 financial crisis. Those who consider such a structure now must take this into account—do I have the right people and infrastructure to operate this structure?

The second challenge is economic. What is the minimum size account that a hedge fund manager will accept? Generally, larger hedge fund managers dictate minimum asset sizes of $25 million to $50 million or more for managed accounts, reducing the number of allocators that may actually qualify.

The third challenge is that not all managers are receptive to the managed account. Strategies that use illiquid securities with complex pricing issues and hedge fund managers that are large and can raise adequate money through their commingled funds may not be interested. In the end, as hedge fund allocators look to align the interests of investors with their hedge fund managers, the managed account model represents a newer and better approach to hedge fund investing.

Managed accounts do not replace the need for ongoing due diligence. Rob Swan, Lighthouse's Chief Operating Officer gives a resounding "no." "Both investment and operational due diligence remain the fundamental backbone of our process. The managed account structure enhances this process by providing full position-level transparency and asset ownership, but ultimately these tools are dependent on the ability of our people to conduct the work and make better decisions."

With hedge fund performance rebounding in 2009, there are now fewer calls from investors for managed accounts than there were earlier in the year. While some may call the structure a "fad" or a gut reaction to the financial crisis and related aftermath, for those able to offer the structure in a scalable and efficient manner, it can offer a superior way to invest in hedge funds for those investors.

WHAT TO LOOK FOR FIRST

One of the first common sense determinants of hedge fund (or fund of funds) credibility is the auditor. While it is always comforting to see one of the large global accounting firms perform the annual audit, there are many other nationally recognized accounting firms with dedicated hedge fund practices that perform this function as well. The first rule is to invest only with an investment manager who uses an accounting firm with a nationally recognized accounting practice; no deviations are permitted! In nearly every hedge fraud that occurred during the past 10 years, the auditor (and we use the term loosely) did not have a dedicated practice and was, in fact, a small or even a two-person firm. In fact, there was not a dedicated accounting practice as well.

The second common sense determinant is the background check. How can investors allocate capital before completing a check of the individual manager of firm? As recent history has shown, there are many shady characters that misrepresent their backgrounds, hide past legal infractions, and may even lie about the college or university that they attended. They may even state that they are CFAs when, in fact, they never even took the first part of the exam.

Randy Shain of First Advantage Investigative Services performs background checks for investors completing the final (or first) stages of the due diligence. As Randy said, "Background due diligence, a critical component of a broad due diligence program, is often performed so poorly it is amazing that the institutional investment community has any idea what they need when seeking effective background reports. As I explained in great detail in my book, *Hedge Fund Due Diligence: Professional Tools to Investigate Hedge Fund Managers*, on investigative hedge fund due diligence, knowing what to ask of your due diligence providers affords you great power. No longer must you feel vaguely or even totally dissatisfied with the results of background searches, without any means of addressing this feeling."

With a new fraud seemingly being exposed more frequently, now more than ever it is imperative for any institution investing in hedge funds—or advising others to do so—to understand the risks involved. Proper background due diligence, in conjunction with proper operational due diligence, is all about cutting risks. Cheap, data-dump, commodity-type background reports, however, are more about cutting corners than cutting risk. Smart institutions have long recognized that the question is not whether they can afford comprehensive due diligence, but whether they can afford not to do it.

It is interesting to note how many investors do not use this service before investing. But, then again, who would think that a prospective investor would not contact the prospective fund's auditor to get an overview as well. We recently spoke anonymously with an auditor for a new hedge fund to get some background on the prospective manager. While there were no surprises, a surprise did come when we asked how many other prospective investors call him concerning all of the other hedge fund clients that he serves. The answer was shocking: 15 percent.

FEE CHANGES

For a fund of funds in the post-2008 era, the economics have changed with the introduction of a smaller asset-based management fee that may also be underpricing pressure from larger pools of assets of the large, institutional investors, putting pressure on margins. As a result and with consolidation within the fund industry by larger, traditional asset management firms looking for an entry point into hedge funds, some fund managers are more concerned with distribution than with portfolio management. Although this may be more difficult to detect in the due diligence process, firms that are expensing more on marketing than on research may have fallen into the distribution trap. With fund expenses that may approach 50 basis points to manage and operate a business enterprise, the level of critical mass of the fund of funds manager grows as the infrastructure grows.

Many investors take different approaches to fund of funds investing. Gregoire Capital LLC is a New Jersey–based investment manager that has been investing in fund of funds for institutional clients for more than 10 years. Gregoire typically allocates to 8 to 10 individual fund of funds and has created a fund termed F3—fund of funds of funds. Although the extra layer of fees may appear to be counterintuitive, Scott Wolfel, co-manager of the F3 portfolio, states that the overall fee is less than that charged by the majority of other fund of funds. By receiving a fee discount from the underlying fund of funds in which they invest, Wolfel says that the F3 fee of 0.25 percent brings total fees to approximately 1.21 percent. Many large institutional investors are able to capitalize on large flows to fund of funds and receive terms that are different from the posted terms in the legal documents of the fund.

Gregoire scrutinizes the diversification process and believes that the F3 provides additional diversification. More importantly, through their due diligence process, they are able to evaluate and reduce redundancy in holdings among the different fund of funds, something that most investors and consultants are unable to accomplish. Wolfel said, "avoiding an undesirable level of overlap is important to us. We don't want too much concentration in sectors. We track exposures to make sure that the exposure level is not too great."

Tactical Asset Allocation

Hedge fund managers may produce positive results—even outstanding results—due to two factors: luck or tactical allocation. Within a narrow context of understanding the level of risk for underlying funds, Gregoire screens over 3,000 fund of funds to identify managers that meet the investment parameters for their clients.

Jim Gregoire, founder, says that "quality is not proportionate to size of assets." While size is important, Gregoire looks for fund of funds managers that have an edge or a niche product.

Access to specialized or different strategies is key to delivering positive alpha. While some investors will say that "getting the right call" from Wall

Street is the key to success, strategy allocation is critical. At the same time, active management of strategies is helpful. For example, one of the best (or worst) strategies is investing in emerging markets. During the past 10 years, investing in emerging market strategies has consistently been either the best or the worst performing strategy. Depending on the growth of world economies, emerging markets have performed in direct correlation with global growth. There are times to invest in emerging markets strategies, and times to avoid them. For the fund of funds manager who actively manages his fund, turnover will be high in this strategy as the manager seeks to add performance and reduce risk in periods of economic slowdown.

In evaluating fund of funds managers, the process is similar to that involved in the analysis of hedge fund managers. The following questions should be asked:

- Who are the people, and do they know what they are doing? This was the principal factor several years ago before the growth spurt in hedge funds, and it is still relevant for smaller, less institutional shops today.
- Is there a systematic process? Does the investment team have the tools to identify and evaluate talented managers and understand the investment thesis and approach? Or is it just a matter of checking the box and completing due diligence questionnaires?
- Does the manager have a strong and developed infrastructure with good systems to monitor and control risk?
- Does the manager have a thorough understanding of the portfolio and the risk and liquidity imbedded in the portfolio?

One of the issues of due diligence is reporting. Fund of funds managers and investors alike both have similar needs—timely and accurate reporting of fund information, portfolio performance, and position analytics. In the early years of hedge fund growth, both hedge fund managers and fund of funds managers alike provided portfolio analytics, monthly performance results, net asset value calculations, and investor communication. However, much of that responsibility is now provided by an external administrator. While much of the data is derived from the prime brokers, the industry has been moving more to the outsourced and independent administrator model. While some funds still use an in-house platform, the technology and cost advantage available to large global administrators has caused managers to rethink the most effective means of communication.

Performance results are still sent electronically as flash numbers from the manager, but investors demand greater and more accurate service. Investors should ask when preliminary monthly performance results are sent;

followed up with final monthly or quarterly NAVs. The shortest period for dissemination of information is critical to meet investors' needs. Monthly flash results should arrive a few days after month end, with final NAVs arriving around midmonth, along with relevant portfolio analytics. Investors should also ask what the past history has been for completion and mailing of K-1s and annual statements to see whether this is satisfactory for the underlying investors in the funds.

If K-1s are historically mailed in midsummer, that may be unacceptable for investors and may preclude investing in that fund. On the other hand, if K-1s, or at least drafts, are completed before April 15 and annual statements are sent shortly thereafter, the decision to invest may come more easily.

It may be straightforward to define the profile of the perfect hedge fund or fund of funds, but the investor (e.g., institutional, high net worth, or family office) bases, the investor perspective, and the outcome will vary. While track record, volatility, and terms may vary from manager to manager, the buy or sell decision will vary according to investor type. Depending on investor type, there are trade-offs in the due diligence process. Institutional investors have more rigid investment requirements, and the due diligence period is much longer. As a result, investors will ask what the trade-offs or sacrifices will be in order to issue an investment commitment based on the following terms:

- Length of track record
- Liquidity and fees
- Risk/return profile
- Internal management team
- Level of transparency
- Internal pricing policies
- Manager history
- Headline risk
- Total assets under management

Institutional investors require a longer track record, lower fees, and a high level of transparency; they desperately want to avoid headline risk. Although high net worth and family office investors also seek the same terms, many will forego rigid standards at the expense of higher returns for a shorter time horizon. While portfolio transparency may be lessened, process transparency should not be. Investors must evaluate an intelligent evaluation process by the fund of funds and have a healthy understanding of the process and the portfolio.

Where Are All the Managers?

One frequent characterization of the weak spot of the fund of funds community is a shortage of qualified experienced analysts. As a result, it is important for investors to seek fund of funds organizations that have knowledgeable analysts and firms that are continually building out the firm infrastructure. As any college student asks about the student/faculty ratio, investors should also ask about the number of analysts as opposed to the number of managers and should compare the turnover ratio of managers in different fund of funds. Furthermore, let's not forget to compare the results of funds with different levels of manager turnover.

In the end, you get what you pay for. The fund of funds manager provides a valuable service, and to keep investors satisfied, strong performance results with defined risk parameters are required. The fund of funds must have a strong client service/investor relations department that is a unique added value of the strategy; however, some managers are willing to shortcut the process.

As a well-known institutional allocator anonymously stated, "Make sure that you meet the genius who hired Amaranth. And the Bear Stearns mortgage fund. And Sowood! These yahoo MBAs are not quite ready to hire hedge fund managers." That is for the professionals.

CHAPTER 8

Redemption

Having an understanding of what drives the hedge fund manager is critical for investors and their assets. Managers must want that understanding; they need to be able to articulate what it is that causes them to buy or sell a security. It is the drive, ambition, and ability to maintain their edge that separates good managers from mediocre managers. While the main challenge of hedge fund investing is achieving consistent returns, the biggest test is actually dealing with manager hubris. Investors should seek managers who are driven by the intellectual challenge of investing and facing the challenges of the markets. Taking it a step further, the best managers are in fact mercenaries working for the common goal of the manager and the investors. The question that is raised is: how does an investor build a relationship with a mercenary and then deal with the manager when it is time to redeem?

REDEMPTION REQUESTS

The most frequent reason for redemption is performance results. Although performance-based redemption profiles vary according to investor class, many investors are merely return seekers. They chase the return; in the industry this is called "hot money."

The hot money is usually held by high net worth or family office investors. These groups usually do not go through the same painstaking stages or periods of due diligence to identify the manager; they simply look for managers with good returns and invest.

Institutional investors, including pension plans, invest for the longer periods and are more concerned about absolute return as well as meeting the liability portfolio requirement for their actuaries. Rather than chase returns, they are concerned with how hedge funds and fund of funds can act as a tool to reduce the volatility of the rest of their portfolios.

Institutional investors are generally concerned with alpha, but they are also concerned with volatility and Sharpe ratios. First we look at standard deviation, which measures the dispersion or spread of data around the mean value to measure portfolio volatility. It indicates the level of risk associated with the risk of the portfolio. As risk rises, portfolio value should increase as well. It boils down to this: The larger the variance, the greater the risk; the greater the risk, the greater the potential for gain or loss. In comparing the returns of managers within the same sector, investors should look at average annualized returns and then review the standard deviation.

How to Pick a Manager

Suppose you are looking at two long/short equity managers, both with a 15 percent return; however, one has a standard deviation of 9 percent and the other a standard deviation 12 percent. It is clear that one is more volatile then the other. Drilling down and looking at month-to-month comparisons, the overall return is the same, but the month-to-month volatility of the 12 percent deviation is much higher, which should cause investors to be concerned. Generally, the 9 percent volatility manager is statistically preferred, but further review will be required to determine how the returns are actually generated. It is not easy, it is not a science, but it is something that needs to be done.

The second factor that most investors look at is the Sharpe ratio. This is a risk-adjusted measurement used to calculate the return that is achieved, then it is compared with the level of risk that was taken to receive the return. Developed by William Sharpe, the formula uses standard deviation and excess return over the risk-free rate (generally Treasury bills) to calculate the ratio and to determine how the return compares for the risk taken. Expressed as a formula, the numerator is the average monthly return minus the risk-free rate divided by the denominator of the monthly standard deviation. Investors seek a high Sharpe ratio.

For example, a Sharpe of 1 indicates one unit of return per unit of risk, a Sharpe of 2 indicates two units of return per unit of risk, and a negative Sharpe indicates a loss or high level of risk taken to achieve returns. It tells us whether the manager is smart or took a high level of risk to achieve the returns. Strategies with lower volatility (standard deviations) have higher Sharpe ratios (e.g., fixed income or other types of arbitrage strategies), whereas long/short hedged equity will have a lower Sharpe. A Sharpe over 2.0 is very good and 3.0 is outstanding. At the end of the day, most institutional investors seek high Sharpe ratios and low standard deviation.

Institutional investors will closely monitor returns but are also concerned about quantitative evaluations of volatility and risk. They rely heavily on standard deviation and Sharpe calculation to make portfolio decisions.

Besides portfolio volatility and high levels of risk, additional reasons for redemption are varied, but the second most frequent cause for redemption is style drift in this unique asset class. Style drift can take many forms, but the most common is that the mandate of the hedge fund or fund of funds manager changed as the market grew. What started initially as a focused, low-volatility fund has morphed into a fund with multiple funds across a broad range of sectors. With the explosion of fund of funds assets, the manager may be more concerned with asset growth than with the performance results that were the primary focus in the early years. With the moderation of returns of assets as assets boomed, the manager may be less risk averse or less focused on returns. A fund that may have started several years ago as a small, focused fund may have now grown to a large behemoth with mediocre performance results. The problem may be too much money under management. The solution is to redeem.

Many firms that have also experienced robust growth have not adapted the infrastructure to handle the increased size of the assets. Consequently, they are unable to determine how to attract high-quality personnel and then manage the teams to operate infrastructure so as to both manage the money and deal with investors. Successful firms have integrated teams working together looking for investment opportunities. Some hire armies of young analysts who are actually filling seats completing forms. Many firms have handled the growth spurt well, while others have not. Thriving firms have been able to adapt to changing global markets, are tactically adept, and have performance results that reflect this. Others have failed. Early redeemers usually detect this deficiency.

FUND OF FUNDS DUE DILIGENCE ISSUES

Many fund of funds that participated in the credit market blowup of 2006–2008, took advantage of market opportunities, and were short credit and produced strong results. Other fund of funds did not understand credit, and also did not know how to participate or source ideas and trends; as a result, they got killed. With rapidly changing global capital markets, change is required, and the best investment managers regardless of structure seek new opportunities in new strategies with the aim of attracting new flows of funds to increase assets under management. Others languish. Personnel turnover or the strategies that are no longer viable all contribute to reasons for change. It is important to note that for fund of funds, due diligence, research, and allocation is an art, not a science, and certainly is not suitable in all situations. There is a lot of differentiation from one fund of funds to another, and sophisticated investors should be aware of the differences. Simply put, one size does not fit all; just as with snowflakes, no two fund of funds are alike.

After all, the decision-making process varies from traditional long-only to hedge funds to private equity managers. More often than not, the final decision about whether to use a specific hedge fund or fund of funds is a "gut" decision, and the investor must rely on his or her instincts and try to reduce the decision to a quantitative evaluation.

Remember this: strict and formal hedge fund due diligence investment procedures are important and should be adhered too. Due diligence must be consistent, and it must evolve and change as the markets evolve and change.

LESSONS LEARNED

There have been many lessons that investors have learned in the wake of the demise of Long-Term Capital Management (LTCM) and the 2008 market meltdown. The question is: are managers doing this differently today than they did in the late 1990s or in 2006 or 2007? The answer is not clear.

The good news is that institutional investors make investment decisions that take a long time to come to fruition, because they are making long-term capital commitments. Remember Sharpe ratio and standard deviation? The investor should not look at one calendar year unless something has changed dramatically with the hedge fund. Patience is a virtue that investors need to practice.

Fund of funds cannot easily change investment positions, do not make monthly decisions, and commit their assets for usually at least a year. This is how we believe most investors should act as well. Being late or early to the party is not an excuse. It is, however, sometimes quite rewarding.

There were several credit managers that were early to the subprime meltdown and started shorting in 2006. There were a few that were early to the commercial loan fallout who invested in 2007. The thesis was right; the timing was poor. Investors lost. Managers lost. Had they waited nine months, they would have made a killing. Unfortunately, in investing it's all about timing.

Taking it a step or two further, fund of funds are removed from the investment process of the underlying manager but determine global macro trends, evaluate opportunities for investment, and then put money to work at just the right time after the conclusion of the consistent investment and due diligence process.

HOT MONEY, COLD RETURNS

Hot money fund of funds—not the entire industry, just a small number—are often ready to redeem after one or two bad months in a row. As the derivative crisis of 2007–2008 demonstrated, investors will move money as soon as they sense that something is not going well. The holding period for underlying manager positions will vary from strategy to strategy, but certain strategies have limited or reduced liquidity inherent in them. Fixed-income arbitrage strategies, distressed, and derivative strategies have reduced liquidity, and in periods of market stress, it can get very dicey. Arbitrage strategies that depend on high levels of leverage also have reduced liquidity because of the overall increase in the size of the leveraged portfolio. If we look at the flow of capital into strategies that are deemed "hot" or the "next best place to invest" that no one else has discovered, what happens when the floodgates are opened for redemption because of investor dissatisfaction? Even assuming a moderate change in performance, the redemption by the largest or several large investors may cause a tidal wave of redemptions by other investors. Although hedge fund and fund of funds investing is part quantitative, part qualitative, there still is a herd mentality.

The arbitrage for the underlying manager is bad. The manager has positions (or assets) that may need a longer term to realize the economic benefit of the trade in the case of activist, event-driven, distressed, or various arbitrage strategies. The liability of the fund balance sheet is redeeming investors who want out at the same time. Will the manager sell positions to meet the redemptions? Or will the manager impose a gate to restrict redemptions?

The asset/liability mismatch of hedge fund balance sheets of security positions and frequent redemptions causes many hedge funds to extend redemption periods to protect partner capital and reduce the risk in the portfolio. The lengthening of the liquidity window has been occurring over the past few years as many managers have moved from monthly to quarterly to biannual, to annual; now, some put in place two-, three-, and four-year lockups. Before investing in a hedge fund, the fund of funds must decide whether the returns and benefits of the strategy are warranted by a longer lockup. With longer lockups, the investors must decide whether they are investing in a hedge fund or a private equity fund. They must ask, is hedge fund money the proper allocation for a private equity type of structure.

NEW CHALLENGES

Longer lockups for underlying managers present a new set of challenges for the fund of funds portfolio manager. One of the strengths of the fund of funds is its ability to dynamically reallocate capital and make changes in response to changes in the market, or to changes in the performance and structure of the underlying managers. With longer lockups and less liquidity, the fund of funds portfolio manager faces a new set of limitations. Despite the marketing material presented by the hedge fund managers, both investors and fund of funds learned in 2007–2008 that strategies that were not supposed to be correlated, in fact were. Longer lockups and imposition of gates made portfolio management more complicated and put pressure on performance results.

Size is very important in hedge fund land. Generally, according to a recent study compiled by Infovest21, new emerging hedge fund managers have better results than seasoned managers; in many cases, they put up really good numbers.

However, there is risk associated with investing in a manager who recently left a larger firm and has no track record. Other reasons include the fact that the manager truly has "fire in his belly" and eats, sleeps, and breathes his strategy. The manager knows every position in the portfolio intimately and can react to smaller positions and thereby maintain a higher level of liquidity. The manager may assume a higher and greater risk profile than a larger manager in order to demonstrate his trading and research acumen.

Another risk lies with organizational structure. Suddenly, the portfolio manager is managing a business—a portfolio—and trying to raise outside capital as well as manage investor relations. This creates a lot of tension; the markets have witnessed the self-destruction of many managers.

Darwin is alive and well in the hedge fund industry—perform well, and asset flows grow. Poor performance leads to an average life of hedge funds of approximately three years. It is, unfortunately, just that simple.

Redemptions are restricted by lockup periods with required notices before the actual redemption date. Hedge funds in general have an initial lockup that ranges from one to five years, with the norm being one year. During the past several years, many lockups have gravitated longer and have extended out to two to three years. The best performing funds, the ones that command greater pricing power, have the ability to demand longer lockup periods and set these restrictions in the private placement memorandum.

LIQUIDITY ISSUES

Fund of funds are wracked by additional liquidity issues. Often, the underlying funds may be forced to liquidate positions that are less liquid (or not liquid at all) or sell securities at a loss, due to redemptions requests. This reduces the performance of the underlying fund. The use of leverage may also exacerbate the magnitude of the loss, requiring the manager to sell larger chunks of the underlying positions, usually in periods of market stress.

As investors have learned repeatedly during various market gyrations, market selling begets selling and puts pressure on hedge fund redemptions. Fund of funds redemptions put pressure on hedge funds, contributing to the overall selling pressure. Investors must know what the notice period is for redemptions as well as the terms of any stated liquidity gates.

When the markets are in disarray, the selling pressure can create opportunity for funds that have liquidity and have restrictions on redemptions. These opportunities often lead to significant profits when those besieged with redemption requests seek liquidity.

Redemption Issues

Redemption issues represent another element of risk management for the fund of funds manager. The fund of funds may provide monthly, quarterly, semiannual, or even annual liquidity, but the underlying hedge funds that the manager may wish to redeem may have only annual liquidity. Within the varied liquidity requirements for the underlying hedge funds in the portfolio, this gives rise to the need of the fund for funds to have a credit facility to provide liquidity for redeeming investors. At the same time, the manager must be prepared to hold some of the unwanted positions longer than desired.

With a spike in market volatility—managers holding larger positions and an increase in the use of illiquid products—hedge fund managers are increasingly imposing gates as of 2008 to place restrictions on the proceeds that will be available for redemption on a particular date. A gate will place limits on the amount of capital that may be withdrawn at a particular period.

A 25 percent gate will allow investors to redeem 25 percent of the funds per period, usually quarterly, but that will vary depending on the portfolio's liquidity. This permits an investor with a one-year lockup to receive proceeds equal to 25 percent over a four-quarter period after the expiration of the lockup. The gate allows the manager to increase exposure to less liquid or longer holding periods for security positions. In addition, it discourages investors from making rapid movements of funds from manager to manager.

Gates encourage longer lockup investing, placing greater pressure on the due diligence process and ensuring that the manager selection decision was indeed correct. The longer lockup stability provides greater comfort to the hedge fund manager and limits flight of capital in times of market stress. In addition, it allows for longer planning, similar to the planning of private equity or real estate investing. In the end, gates limit investors from cashing out quickly.

Irwin Latner, a lawyer at the New York–based law firm Herrick Feinstein, has a specialization in hedge fund partnerships. He has said that "the gate is triggered when the aggregate redemption requests from investors as of a given date exceed the stated percentage threshold of the fund's net asset value."

"When the gate level is exceeded, the fund documents often permit the fund to defer excess redemptions above the gate level to the next permissible redemption date, and only satisfy redemptions on a pro rata basis up to the gate threshold," Latner added. "If aggregate redemptions on succeeding redemption dates exceed the gate, the fund may invoke the gate with respect to those succeeding redemptions as well until such time as the aggregate redemption requests fall below the gate level. Many but not all funds have gate provisions."

The due diligence process adopted by the fund of funds manager should focus on strategies that employ gates. Some of these strategies include asset-backed securities, private placements, and other hard-to-value securities. Generally, more liquid strategies such as long/short equity and traditional fixed-income arbitrage do not have gates.

"Gate provisions should be properly summarized in the PPM together with adequate risk disclosure with respect to their effect on an investor's ability to redeem its capital," Latner stated. "Investors must be made aware of which strategies employ gates and ask the fund of funds what happens in a 'what if' scenario."

The million dollar question is, "How can a fund of funds expect to get paid in the event of redemptions if the gate is imposed?" The answer is simple: It can't. Often, the imposition of a gate by underlying fund managers will negatively affect funds of funds that have invested in the gated fund because

- The fund of funds is often the investor that is seeking to pull out but is restricted by the gate.
- The fund of funds may be forced to impose a gate or other measure in its own fund if it is faced with redemption requests from its own investors and it cannot redeem a sufficient amount of its own capital from the underlying gated funds in which it is invested.

Along with high net worth investors, many hedge funds think of fund of funds as "hot money." When a fund of funds needs money to meet redemption requests, hedge funds with liquidity are the first to go from the portfolio. Fund of funds are usually the first to redeem, especially when they sense something not right in the hedge fund manager in terms of performance, style drift, and employee turnover. If fund of funds are not quick to pull the trigger, they themselves may be hit with redemptions. The key to successfully weathering a storm is communication. Both hedge funds and fund of funds must be proactive in communicating with the LPs in the fund and try to use moral suasion to keep their assets in the fund. The worst-case scenario for the hedge fund is to convey a sense of mismanagement or misrepresentation rather than just poor investment decisions.

High Water Marks

What sets traditional long-only managers apart from alternative investment managers is fee structures and the fact that the interests of managers of hedge funds, fund of funds, and private equity funds are aligned with their investors. Hedge fund and fund of funds managers manage for alpha and therefore are in the business of actually managing money.

Hedge fund and fund of funds managers continue to collect management and incentive fees as long as the fund is earning a positive return. If the investor makes money, the manager makes money. However, if the fund is losing money, the hedge fund manager receives only the management fee, which is calculated on the asset under management.

"The high water mark kicks in to prevent the manager from taking performance fees in subsequent periods until the fund recoups the prior period losses and becomes profitable again on a long-term cumulative basis," said Latner. "That's why it's called a high water mark."

Suspending Redemptions

Redemption halt or *suspending redemptions* are terms that cause hedge fund investors to shudder. Usually, it means that something bad is happening and the manager is literally sinking. When a fund suspends or halts all redemptions indefinitely, it means the fund is in liquidation, or better yet, the manager wants to liquidate and cannot price the portfolio because there is no liquidity. Halting redemptions is very bad. A gate prevents only redemptions that lie above the gate level; a halt or suspension of redemptions is enforced on all assets.

Most suspensions of redemptions are usually tied to a broader market disruption event or a difficulty in computing net asset value, whereas a gate may be invoked for more isolated reasons having to do with the operation of an individual fund. When a fund suspends redemptions, it is usually the death blow for its continued existence. After such a suspension, no new investors would come in, and the fund usually begins to wind down and liquidate its assets in an orderly manner. However, new high water marks allow for catch-up by investors to potentially recoup the loss.

Take a look at the Bear Stearns fixed-income hedge funds. Shortly after suspending redemptions, the funds declared bankruptcy due to the liquidity squeeze and inability to correctly price the securities. In short, many believe the suspension of redemptions was the first nail in the coffin.

While fund of funds managers have a challenge in dealing with the illiquidity issues of gates, it presents a greater problem for direct investors in hedge funds. In either case, it gives a severe case of "agita" to all when a fund announces or declares anything other than positive returns.

CHAPTER 9

Fees

One of the most contentious issues in the hedge fund and fund of funds industry is fees. According to PerTrac Financial Solutions LLP, a New York–based software company that aggregates hedge fund data and provides analytic tools for asset allocation, the average hedge fund charges a management fee of 1.50 percent and an incentive fee of 20 percent.

INCENTIVE FEE

Before the mid- to late-1970s, most managers that operated hedge funds charged just an incentive fee. This meant that if they made money for their clients, only then would the manager get paid. It also meant that if the manager lost money or the portfolio was flat, the manager had earned nothing. The interests of both parties were aligned. This alignment of interests is what A. W. Jones had in mind when he launched his fund in 1949, with just an incentive fee. The change came as fund complexes grew, overhead grew, and the management firms needed additional capital to operate their businesses.

The fee structure during most of the 1980s and the 1990s consisted of a 1 percent management fee and a 20 percent incentive fee. As the market grew and investor appetite for products grew, the fees increased; over time, they have settled into 1.5 and 20 percent. However, in light of the market dislocation of 2007, 2008, and 2009, don't be surprised if fees change again—this time, however, on the downside. In order to maintain assets and attract assets, some fund managers have lowered their fees and changed liquidity terms. This seems to be the trend going into the summer of 2009.

Remember this: The only people who complain about fees are those who cannot charge them. The market dictates the fees and, more importantly, puts a number or worth or value on the manager. Consequently, he or she can charge what the market allows—nothing more and nothing less.

In all the years that I (Dan) have been working with and writing about hedge funds, I have never met an investor who complained about fees. The only people I have ever come across who complain about fees are mutual fund and other long-only managers.

MORE OR LESS

The fees that fund of funds charge are less than the standard of single manager funds. Many fund of funds managers charge only an asset-based fee, which ranges from 1 to 2 percent, while others have both a management fee of 1 percent and an incentive fee. The incentive fee can range from 10 to 20 percent of net assets. The fees charged by the fund of funds are in addition to the fees charged by the underlying managers.

What does "1 and 10" mean in a fund of funds? If the underlying managers of a fund of funds earn 10 percent in aggregate, then the fees paid to the fund of funds managers would be a 1 percent management fee on the total assets and an additional 1 percent in incentive fees, because the underlying managers achieved a 10 percent positive rate return.

Are Fees Justified?

The fees are justified because the fund of funds manager has created a portfolio that achieved the target rate of return for the investors. However, because some investors believe that the fee structure is too high, many fund of funds managers have put in place benchmark hurdle rates that the manager must achieve before incentive fees are earned.

While absolute returns are important to many investors, many institutional investors view fund of funds as "LIBOR beaters" or "Treasury-bill beaters." The investors seek fund of funds investments that exceed short-term money market rates by a margin that is often based on these aforementioned benchmarks.

Therefore, an investor who receives a margin of 100 to 500 basis points in excess of the benchmarks will believe that the investment in the fund of funds is worth the additional fees. It all comes down to risk profiles and the ability of fund of funds managers to achieve their objectives for their investors.

Reasonable Costs

Additionally, one of the benefits of fund of funds investing is that investors have a single point of entry into a diversified portfolio of hedge funds at a very reasonable cost. Doing the research, completing the due diligence, making the allocations, and staying on top of the managers—it may not be cost-effective for an investor that allocates just a portion of overall portfolio to alternatives for less to take on this burden. Fund of funds provide an excellent way to gain exposure to hedge funds and other alternative managers for a very reasonable price. However, one thing is for sure—whichever way you go, it is important to perform due diligence. In light of the Madoff scandal, some well-known and well-respected fund of funds turned out to be simply investing with one or two managers, and this is just wrong. Funds of funds are supposed to be invested in a diversified portfolio, not a single manager. The idea is to reduce risk and exposure. In these funds, neither was achieved and the investors suffered greatly. You need to get answers and verify information about which managers to select and the amounts of money allocated by the fund of funds before and during your investment period.

MULTI-MANAGER FUNDS

In the post-Dot.com bubble and in the new era of corporate governance, many investors looking to make allocations have decided to allocate to another type of multi-manager funds. These products are called multi-strategy funds. The manager operates a team of investment professionals who trade various markets under a single fund structure. This differs from a fund of funds in that a fund of funds allocates to different strategies by investing in multiple funds, versus a multi-strategy fund which operates multiple trading desks under one roof. Multi-strategy funds will be discussed in greater detail in Chapter 13.

Recently, to say in the last three years, it seems that most investors have become frustrated with investment returns, and both hedge fund and fund of funds investors are concerned with two aspects of alternative investing: mediocre performance and fees. However, in years that hedge fund and fund of funds outperformed the benchmarks, major indexes, and frankly put up good numbers, nobody seems to care one bit about fees. It is important to note that fees are not indicative of performance. However, it is imperative for the investor to consider that what that fee includes is the cost "to run a research effort to service institutional investors."

Getting Returns

"The marginal cost to source, select, and service a portfolio of hedge funds can be close to 50 basis points," said Robert Schulman, the former chairman of Tremont Group Holdings, Inc.[1]

Naturally, most investors do not want to pay the fee to build out an infrastructure for a firm, they simply want the returns. However, this is just not possible. While the costs associated with operating a $2 to $3 billion fund of funds with a staff of 35 to 40 professionals can exceed $15 million, the margins may be thought to be excessive by institutional investors that are accustomed to paying fees of 15–25 bps for long-only investment services. However, remember, the fund of funds business is in the asset management business while the long-only manager is in the asset-gathering business. (If you don't understand this, e-mail us: dsrb@hedgeanswers.com.)

The challenge of many fund of funds managers is a struggle between cutting fees to acquire larger, stickier pools of assets while the cost of running the business like everything else in the world is going up. Most fund managers do not like to talk about fund discounts publicly; this is one of the final questions that many large investors ask as a final due diligence question. Many fund of funds managers are not as skillful in differentiation like hedge fund managers seem to be in their ability to command investors to pay "list price."

Differentiating

In order to differentiate themselves in the marketplace, fund of funds are introducing new products or are offering to provide advisory services or customized or private label funds for investors.

Fees are a critical issue for manager and investor alike. There are some investors who express dissatisfaction with fees especially when it comes down to concerns about the alignment of investors' interests with the manager. Many investors that we have talked to believe that fees should decline as the overall asset base of the fund of funds grows, but there has been no evidence that this is causing fees to shrink. And while the press seems to complain about fees in every article it writes about hedge funds and fund of funds, when investors are asked about the most important requirements in the manager selection process the answers are:

- Returns (source and repeatability)
- Professional staff
- Operational excellence
- Risk management systems
- Performance record and length

RESULTS VERSUS FEES

Investor dissatisfaction with fees is often caused by the fund of funds manager's inability to explain performance and the relationship to the benchmarks, the current market conditions, or the relationship of the managers' investment process and performance results. Fund of funds that are able to articulate the investment process in a timely and cohesive manner and with adjusting performance expectation as market conditions change, provide a high level of satisfaction for investors—and are more likely to see their business thrive and grow. Investors, regardless of market conditions, scandals, and political situations want to know what is going on. Communication is key—managers who don't communicate may make it for the short term, but in the long term they will go out of business no matter how good their performance.

Prior to the recent credit crisis and market meltdown, as the fund of funds turf grew quite competitive, consultants liked to boast to clients that they could save the investor 40 to 50 basis points in fees because they would be able to use their scale to demand discounts. However, in the summer of 2009, it seems in an effort to maintain asset levels and attract new capital that will stay locked up, managers are putting the sale sign up from the get-go.

The problem is like everything that gets discounted; just because something is cheap does not mean it is worth it and sometimes you do just get what you pay for. Fees are not what make a manager worth investing with or not; it is their ability to perform on a consistent basis. If the lowest priced fund can do this then go with it, but first make sure you do your homework. It comes down to "caveat emptor." Fees are linked to returns and capacity, and the markets will determine the point of equilibrium. Some people like to shop at Wal-Mart Stores, Inc. or other discount retailers and always pay the lowest price. Others go to Tiffany & Company and pay top dollar.

Making Smart Decisions

Making an investment comes down to a number of factors and the answer lies with the investor who should be making informed, prudent decisions. If not, use of a consultant or other investment professional will aid in the investment decision.

In the final analysis, fund of funds are justified if the manager executes the advertised strategy and achieves the targeted returns. Ultimately, the investor must determine if the fees have impacted the overall risk and return profile of the portfolio and if the investment is worth it.

CHAPTER 10

Leverage Facilities and Risk Management

Until the beginning of the 2007 liquidity crash, leverage was the friend of the hedge fund community. It also was a friend of the fund of funds industry, specifically those that were able to use leverage to "juice" returns. By adding leverage of 1x, 2x, or 3x to a "conservative" portfolio of hedge funds that had low volatility and low correlation to the public markets, hedge fund returns could be increased by hundreds of basis points. The cost was seen as nothing more than the spread between the price of the loan and the return achieved. Simply put, money was cheap, returns were high, and leverage was good.

LEVERAGE AND PRIME BROKERS

While several large investment banks—whose clients were prime brokerage clients—were big providers of leverage. Many commercial banks provided the same sort of leverage facilities to managers and welcomed the money with open arms. Many of the banks providing credit were banks that were not based in the United States, but several U.S. money center banks such as JP Morgan Chase, Bank of America, and Citibank, and international banks such as Banque Nationale de Paris and Société Générale SA, also created a niche to finance the leverage transactions. The reasons were the same for all the banks as it was for the managers: money was cheap, and the returns were high and consistent. Simply put, loaning money to hedge funds and fund of funds was a profitable business.

The transactions, while sophisticated on paper, were for the most part quite simple. The leverage provider (the bank) performed due diligence on the fund manager. If a fund of funds was involved, it was performed on the manager of the portfolio along with the manager's positions in the portfolio to determine the quality and liquidity of the assets and the levels at which they could loan. Once the process was complete, the bank would take a collateral position on the underlying hedge funds. The collateral pledge of the underlying funds reduced the principal risk to the lenders, a key ingredient for the lender. This was the same as when a bank would give a buyer a mortgage for a house. The better the credit of the borrower (the hedge fund), the better the rate and collateral requirements.

While many fund of funds used leverage to juice returns, many also used leverage as a cash management tool. Fund of funds use lines of credit to preinvest with a manager in anticipation of incoming funds from investors, or to meet redemption requests from investors in the event that the investor does not carry large cash positions. Liquidity and valuation go hand in hand, and as long as the liquidity of the underlying hedge funds is not stressed or under other pressures from liquidity or mark to market issues, use of the letters of credits to fund redemptions should be fine. However, when the markets are stressed and performance deteriorates, many banks will pull lines of credit, and this can cause significant headaches for both managers and investors. Some believe that using leverage is like playing with fire—you can get burned. However, others believe it is a necessary tool to make the markets function. Either way, the key for managers is to communicate to investors how leverage is being used and to make sure investors understand this aspect of the firm's operation.

If the credit crisis has taught us anything, it is that cash is truly king and that when money dries up, a desert can result. Therefore, investors and managers need to be prepared, because the unthinkable can quickly become the thinkable.

RISK MANAGEMENT

In light of poor performance, fraud, and other issues surrounding investments, institutional investors including fund of funds said to hedge fund managers, "show me the money." In other words, investors want to see what the manager has in its portfolio. Hedge funds, which are defined as secretive by the popular press, have come to the conclusion that they need to lift their veils of secrecy to maintain and attain investors in the post–credit crisis environment. Transparency is something that is now more then ever available to investors. Although hedge funds increasingly seem to be willing to cooperate and provide the information, many do not want to reveal their portfolio secrets. Many managers will give position detail to investment platforms and risk managers as long as the investments are kept confidential. At the same time, they will provide aggregate exposures and position-level transparency to investors, subject to high levels of confidentiality. All of this has been driven by the need for investors, particularly pension funds, to get a better handle on risk.

Investors and their consultants are simply stating, "If you want our money, we want to know what you're doing."

The origins of risk management may be traced by some to the origins of asset/liability management by the banking industry in the early 1980s. It was the failure of thrifts that funded short-term liabilities (deposits) with long-term assets—30-year fixed-rate mortgages. As interest rates peaked in 1980–1982, thrift earnings were negative because of the mismatch. Funding short-term liabilities with rising costs versus long, lower-yielding assets caused a mismatch of earnings. Looking for a solution to model or "stress test" earnings gave rise to asset/liability management.

The early asset/liability models were created to stress-test earnings in periods of rising or falling interest rates. The results may have satisfied the bank regulators at that time, but they were less than satisfactory given that the assumptions used implied an immediate shift in interest rates.

As risk management came to be used more and more, its implementation was acknowledged to be more an art than a science. The interest rate hikes of 1994 led to the fall of several mortgage-backed strategies, including fixed-income guru David Askin's Askin Capital Management's hedge funds. Askin was forced to liquidate his funds after a bet he made on interest rates using derivatives went against him, wiping out nearly $500 million.[1] Hedge funds were not the only losers in the derivative game; several other highly leveraged entities went under, including Orange County, California. The treasurer of the County, Robert Citron, purchased some derivative contracts that went against him, causing the County to lose $1.5 billion and forcing it to file for Chapter 9 bankruptcy.[2]

As the markets unraveled in the summer of 1998, combined with the meltdown of Long-Term Capital Management (LTCM), it became apparent that more sophisticated tools were needed to protect the assets of hedge fund investors. From this environment came the birth of quantitative analytics to measure risk.

Technology Tools

Over the years, it seems that risk management has developed into a science. But unlike true math, it has limitations. It is important for investors and their advisors to look for ways to protect their assets during good and bad times. Understanding the risk of any investment can make it that much more rewarding, which is something that cannot be overlooked. Most "sophisticated" investors use one of the two firms that have the lion's share of the risk management market—RiskMetrics Group, Inc. and Measurisk LLC—to measure portfolio risk and provide solutions for many institutional investors. Technology, however, is not enough by itself.

In the recent market volatility, many of the models did not work because it became clear that history was not repeatable. There is an old adage in the fixed-income markets: "All bull markets end at the repo desk." That fact has been repeatable, but all else has been a wild card. The failures of the highly levered Citron, LTCM, Petolon, Sowood Capital Management, or the many other fixed-income blowups all resulted from one thing—a margin call. The risk models did not calculate the resulting cost when whatever could go wrong did in fact go wrong. However, even the most sophisticated models could not detect the "when," or "how" the provider of credit or leverage would reprice the collateral or change "the haircut" (margin requirement) for the collateral.

Risk management technology remains a tool to be used, but investors must remember that this technical tool is still just a series of equations that crunch numbers. Investors need to combine the use of quantitative measurements with common sense and instincts to arrive at an independent and reasonable assessment of the level of risk in the portfolio.

Defining Risk Management

So, what really is risk management? The simplest definition is "knowing what you own." If you are a manager or an investor, you want to know what you own. Investors in a hedge fund or fund of funds may have access to holdings, but understanding the value, trading patterns, and liquidity of each individual security is another matter.

An analysis of hedge fund returns reveals that hedge fund managers make money in one of two ways: taking highly leveraged arbitrage bets or making unleveraged directional bets.

In the case of the highly leveraged bet, there have been winners and losers over time, depending on which side of the trade the manager is on when it is unwound. In the unleveraged directional bet, performance is bad when the bet is wrong. Yet, the loss may be the same in both cases. The role of the risk manager is to identify the risk, understand its structure, and determine how the outcomes of specific trades may affect the portfolio and investor returns. Or, in the words of the portfolio manager, "risk management is the level of volatility or drawdown that we can handle before investors redeem."

Information Needs

The key to risk management is taking the available data and turning it into information. This is hard for many to accomplish in an industry that is considered to be secretive. If a fixed-income manager provides complete transparency to investors and lists the entire portfolio of 500 positions (including bonds, futures, options, interest rate swaps, credit default swaps, and a few private placements with current market prices), the investor, along with the risk manager, now have a lot of data. It is a question not of how much data you have, but of what you do with the information.

You need information. The role of the risk manager is to take this data and turn it into valuable information that can be used to determine portfolio enterprise risk. The senior partner, managing partner, chief investment officer, and all investors want to know the answer to this question. It's not "where's the beef?" but "where's the risk?" While the frequency for calculation may be different depending on the status of the participant, access to this information should be readily available on a periodic basis.

Generally, in the hedge fund industry, there is a shortage of risk managers and people who actually perform risk management functions as both managers and investors. In many cases, the chief investment officer is the risk officer. In other cases, many hedge funds state that they have risk management systems, but in reality what they have is a report from the prime broker that indicates gross and net market exposures and shows liquidity trends of the portfolio. Many hedge fund managers will also explain risk management as "we limit our portfolio holdings to a maximum position size of 10 percent," or "we have a diversified portfolio of no fewer than 100 positions, limiting risk of concentration." Both of these statements are meaningless.

The biggest danger for risk managers is liquidity and funding. Risk managers and investors should ask how the fund survives in bad times. Hedge funds are generally long volatility. What happens when all goes awry? The biggest danger to most funds is liquidation along with the availability of unused capacity for funding.

Ask people who worked at Bear Stearns if what we have written is true. We know what the answer will be. If a bank has a liquidity problem and does not have enough capital to cover its trades, the side effect flows through to hedge fund clients and can pose a real problem.

Credit Crisis Affects Risk Management

In the wake of the collapse of Bear Stearns and the bankruptcy of Lehman Brothers, hedge funds are now looking at their prime brokerage relationships more closely and at the terms of the collateral that is held by the firm. Since hedge funds put up collateral that is held by the prime broker as margin for the hedge fund, many are now looking for other places to put the cash. What happens if the prime broker fails? What happens to my collateral and cash? This is the newest concern for risk managers, something that was unthinkable a year or two ago.

Risk management for the investor is a case of paying for the best diversification, not the best returns. Structuring a portfolio with several managers that have exceptional return patterns makes sense when blended into a portfolio with lower-volatility managers. Marketing meetings with managers usually provide significant insight into how they operate; each meeting is a window into the portfolio. Investors need to ask questions and receive answers to make informed decisions on what strategy is best for their portfolio. However, to completely understand how the portfolio is going to react, investors should look at macroeconomic themes as well.

Analysis of portfolio results for an interest rate move of 100 bps or 200 bps, or a decline of a 5 to 10 percent move in equity indexes does not reflect changing liquidity in the capital markets or sudden withdrawal by capital market financing. The combination of estimated portfolio results from the model along with practical evaluation should lead to a more realistic expectation of portfolio volatility.

Technological advances have provided a wealth of information for investors that use risk management systems. Third-party risk aggregators receive position-level data from prime brokers as well as administrators from nearly 1,000 hedge funds. This data is crunched in all sorts of ways and provides many fund of funds and large institutional investors with aggregated risk reports and specialized reports of customized analytics based on managers and positions.

Value at Risk

The credit crisis has taught many of us that in view of the challenges of pricing asset-backed securities (ABS) and collateralized debt obligations (CDOs), the risk model that Wall Street has used for the past several years has proven to be worthless. Wall Street firms such as Bear Stearns, Merrill Lynch, and Citicorp spent tens of millions of dollars each year on risk management; now two of them are dead and the other seems to be on permanent life support. In connection with risk tolerances and risk limits, the testing process failed when it came to the subprime market. The Wall Street failure resulted from both failure of brain power and failure to resist risk. In the end, the securities could not be valued, and if they could, the results were considered invalid. Wall Street disregarded risk in favor of business and size of market share. Value at risk (VAR), which is used to calculate the amount of risk that an investor, hedge fund, or Wall Street bank can lose at any given time from any given position, failed to detect the magnitude of the fallout resulting from the decline in residential mortgages and other credit instruments. Firms have now come to realize that algorithms are not a substitute for good old-fashioned due diligence. The meltdown of 2007–2008 demonstrated the flaws in the models, which could not calculate the idiosyncratic risk of ABS and CDOs. In addition, they failed to reject the risk that was inherent in the wake of greater profit potential.

Even a well-regarded firm such as Société Générale SA (SocGen) experienced a stumble, showing the other side of risk management. Banks have been proud to demonstrate the superiority of their controls and systems with checks and balances, but a junior trader was able to find a crack in the armor. Jerome Kerviel, a junior trader who supposedly was putting "vanilla futures hedging" trades lost more than $7.1 billion of the bank's capital.[3] His misdeeds were discovered only after a routine check found that a trade had exceeded his limit. Had the one trade not exceeded his limit, it is possible that the fraud might never have been discovered. As long as hedge funds or investment banks reward traders with bonuses for making big profits, managers may take risks that may be "dangerous to our financial health." Of course, with Kerviel, we see that simple checks and balances can uncover fraud but may not necessarily catch it before the losses materialize.

RISK

Investors must exercise a high level of on-site scrutiny to evaluate the actual risk profile and employ postinvestment monitoring to assess changes in risk limits that could lead to negative consequences.

As we have learned over time and were reminded again by the junior trader at SocGen, risk management and risk assessment are based on real-world procedures. Risk management is based on identifying risk and measuring risk. Risk is not bad; when properly used, it will increase returns. Without risk, returns would be minimal. However, when risk is mismanaged or not correctly priced, the investment outcome may not be satisfactory for the investors. All risk management models are quantitative and are supposed to be able to project market volatilities and variations, but the actual goal of the quantitative model should be to provide information to investors and related parties (trustees, advisors) about what will happen to the portfolio when the market zigs or zags. Quantitative measurement alone is not enough. Managers and investors need to employ a qualitative component that ensures that assumptions are correct and that before investment decisions are made both pieces of information are taken into consideration.

The risk manager should play an independent role in the process and should include and be constantly completing the following tasks:

- Recommending risk control parameters and changes in risk parameters to the executive board or finance committee
- Heading the risk committee
- Assisting senior management in educating the firm and traders about the risk management process to minimize unexpected events

Within the umbrella of hedge fund risk, risk takes many forms:

- Credit risk
- Interest-rate risk
- Market risk
- Yield-curve risk
- Leverage risk
- Derivative risk
- Liquidity risk
- Counterparty risk
- Operational risk

As discussed in Chapter 7 on systemic risk, any one or a combination of factors can throw the portfolio out of whack and push all assumptions to the wind. Investors must be aware of the interrelationship of each of the risks in the foregoing list and the impact each will have, both independently and collectively, on the value of the portfolio. The near default of LTCM represented a short-term setback to the proliferation and growth of hedge funds, but the hedge fund industry prospered thereafter. The systemic risk caused some pain, but once it passed, the world got back to normal.

LIQUIDITY ISSUES AT PRIME BROKERS

To make educated decisions, investors must understand the impact that hedge fund financing has on the global financial system. This is extremely critical in the fixed-income arena where many of the bond or credit derivative positions are highly customized and difficult to price, as SIV investors harshly learned in 2007–2008. In addition, because the prime brokerage business is highly concentrated among a handful of market participants, liquidity is complicated even further. The loss of Bear, Lehman, and Merrill certainly did not help.

VAR and available market data do not take into consideration the limited liquidity and the fact that a few credit market participants are providing liquidity to literally the whole bunch. Nor does it show the number of hedge funds with many highly specialized positions or hard-to-price securities. Thus, as more money flows into hedge funds and profit and leverage opportunities shift, investors must be sensitive to the flow of funds and the liquidity or illiquidity that may or may not exist as the markets expand and contract.

A walk down memory lane will serve investors and consultants well as they review the portfolio results in several different periods of significant market stress, including

- 1994—rising interest rates and yield curve inversion
- 1998—LTCM fixed-income spread widening and Asian contagion meltdown
- 2001—September 11 attacks
- 2000–2002—technology bubble burst
- 2006–2008—residential mortgage meltdown

This list will serve investors well in reviewing manager results during each of the stress periods as well as in other shorter, less well-publicized periods and will provide investors with the ability to evaluate manager results to see how each fund performed during these periods.

How to Evaluate Risk

As we look at our users' manual, investors must be cautioned that the performance numbers are only numbers and represent simply one factor of the investment decision process. Drivers who use GPS devices instead of relying on maps have often found themselves turning onto roads that don't exist; in the same way, the investment technology failed. It still pays to stop and ask questions, such as how do I get to this place or that place, or simply to look at a paper roadmap. The best question for hedge fund investors to ask and make sure they understand the answer to is: what is the risk of leverage?

Leverage can add significant amounts of return to a strategy. However, strategies that rely on high levels of leverage present a different risk profile when the rules change. As hedge funds and their investors learned to ask in 2007–2008, what happens when

- margin levels are raised by the stock exchanges or prime brokers?
- Wall Street dealers increase haircuts?
- liquidity disappears?

Regulation T of the Federal Reserve Board governs the amount of credit that brokerage firms may extend to customers and is limited to 50 percent. In other words, the investor may borrow $1.50 with $1.00 of equity. Because hedge funds are a profitable business to the Wall Street community, many prime brokers will extend credit at higher levels to hedge funds, based on various factors and positions. This is the profitable part of the puzzle. Before the credit crisis, the amounts varied depending on the strategy. Long/short equity managers were able to use leverage of two to four times; fixed-income leverage often ranged from five to ten times and in some cases often higher. For example, a fixed-income hedge fund used to be able to purchase $10 million of mortgage-backed securities with only $1 million equity capital. Today, things are different; but don't be fooled—leverage is available but expensive. If you are going to invest, ask the questions and get the answers.

Leverage and Its Risk

While leverage enhances returns in a flat market with low volatility, a shift in interest rates or a change in liquidity in the bond market presents an unforeseen challenge and can have devastating effects on a portfolio. In the markets of 1994, 1996, and 2007–2008, dealer haircuts were raised and liquidity disappeared in all cases when things got tough. The constant for most historical periods of market stress has been marked—or caused—by high levels of leverage that the Federal Reserve has intentionally or unintentionally sought to reduce, forcing the markets into a downward spiral. The chain of events goes like this: the Fed raises rates to cool the economy, bond prices fall, dealers raise haircuts, hedge funds are forced to sell bonds, spreads widen, stock prices fall, and leverage is reduced. But pain has been inflicted, and the evildoers have been punished; hedge funds along with numerous innocent investors lose billions.

While some fixed-income funds may flourish as bond spreads widen, most do not. Federal Reserve action to raise interest rates generally is a response intended to slow down or cool off the economy, or to wring leverage out of the system. Spread widening generally creates a challenging atmosphere for most bond investors, but particularly for highly levered hedge funds. Haircuts represent the margin requirements imposed by Wall Street dealers—either investment banks or commercial banks—that sell bonds to hedge funds. The haircut varies depending on the underlying collateral and may range from 1 percent to 10 percent for the most liquid securities, such as U.S. government bonds or agency securities such as Fannie Mae or Freddie Mac bonds, to 50 percent for less than liquid high-yield or distressed bonds. Before the subprime meltdown of 2006–2007, dealers gladly imposed haircuts on agency mortgage-backed securities from 1 to 3 percent, thereby encouraging hedge funds to use maximum leverage. A hedge fund could buy $100 million of Fannie Mae for $1 million to $3 million; now that's leverage! Although it may sound excessive to use 100 times leverage or 33 times leverage, U.S.-regulated, FDIC-insured banks historically used 15 times leverage, while Wall Street investment banks historically used 20 to 30 times leverage. However, the Federal Reserve action and that of the European Central Bank forced firms to lower leverage levels in an effort to bring sanity back to the credit markets. Sane we all may be, but the question is, was the cost worth it?

While spread widening hurts, a change in the haircut can amount to a body blow. The real death threat is the forced selling that occurs when bid/offer and interdealer market spreads widen, resulting in instantaneous losses. Analysis of the potential for a market spiral and systemic risk is part of the risk management process, but it brings us back to the realization that it involves the art, not the science to determine the effect of "what if" scenarios on a portfolio.

VALUATION RISK

In periods of market dislocation, one of the issues constantly raised is the basic question from each investor's questionnaire: "Please state how securities are valued." Sometimes it's a derivative of that question. However, the standard answer is "Monthly (or quarterly) we obtain three external market prices and take the average of the three to determine market pricing."

To understand valuation risk, the following questions relate specifically to fixed income strategies:

- Who provided the evaluations? Did the dealer who sold the securities to the hedge fund provide an evaluation, and what was the price—the highest?
- Are the final prices determined independently by the risk manager or CFO or by the portfolio manager?
- Does the prime broker or administrator obtain prices independent of the hedge fund?
- Is a pricing service used to obtain independent pricing?

For equity strategies, or less liquid positions, an additional question is to determine how prices are adjusted for positions that trade less frequently, have smaller trading volumes, or where the manager has a large position relative to the average daily trading volume. However, with the implementation of Financial Accounting Standard 157, it is very clear how managers, their administrators, and their auditors are going to price these sorts of positions.

Part of the due diligence required of the investor should include a review and understanding of the policies and procedures of the manager regarding pricing. Larger organizations will have systems of checks and balances to ensure that pricing is independent of the position trader. However, smaller firms need not be penalized by size as long as an independent verification of pricing occurs and prices can be justified. In the simplest terms, the hedge fund business is an industry of entrepreneurs who live by the age-old adage of Wall Street, "My word is my bond." Investors should feel comfortable with the explanations provided by the manager and his team. However, in light of the Madoff fraud, make sure you really understand it and that it works properly. One can never be too careful.

Portfolio Information

A key ingredient of risk management is understanding the individual fund positions held by a fund of funds. Some investors require that all prospective fund of funds managers release portfolio positions to its research team before investing and is happy to sign a nondisclosure agreement to reinforce the confidentiality of the holdings and its respect for the manager's work. This transparency is important and is used to monitor the manager, sector, and overlap of risk that may occur in the overall portfolio. Given that portfolio positions change over time, this transparency provides additional information about the manager's ability to understand risk and to evaluate the methods that are used to mitigate both systemic risk and market risk. By looking at individual hedge funds within the fund of funds, the investor will be able to determine the source of the fund's performance and evaluate whether the performance has been driven by strategy allocation or manager selection. If the fund of funds' results deviate from the expected targeted return, an interim call to or even a face-to-face meeting with the manager may be required. You need to get answers.

As with all portfolio management products, fund of funds investors do not get involved in the overall portfolio selection process but do want to understand the macroeconomic view the fund of funds manager has and how this influences the portfolio and the tactical allocation process. Although debate is always healthy, if investors feel that the manager's outlook is dramatically different from their own, redemption may be the only course of action.

A key strength of fund of funds managers is their ability to participate with strong results in good markets while preserving capital in periods of market stress. The drawdown history must be consistent within the risk guidelines and investment policy limits, and must offer a safer alternative than single-manager options.

Most fund of funds provide periodic performance update reporting at least monthly but sometimes more frequently, if available. As with hedge funds, fund of funds managers should also be available for periodic portfolio updates via conference calls. In addition, on-site visits are required at least annually, but preferably twice a year.

For many investors, accessing the flow of monthly information is always challenging. The lack of timeliness of delivery causes a constant headache for investors. Because of the lack of standardization or comprehensive or consolidated databases, prices, NAVs, and transparency reports are generally sent via e-mail or fax by the manager directly to investors or by the administrator to investors. Many hedge fund databases are not up to date in getting accurate performance results for funds, thereby compromising the timeliness and accuracy of reporting. Accessing complex derivative positions and side pockets adds to the confusion. As the hedge fund industry matures, administrators with new delivery technology will reduce the present reliance on manual reporting, which will improve the quality of data and market information.

THE DEMAND FOR BIG FIRMS

As the hedge fund industry grows, there are greater calls for the development of more robust organizations similar to those of their long-only brethren. Growth of assets in the period since 2000 has now given rise to the call for larger organizational structures and more transparency. The market meltdown has only helped this cause. As hedge funds and fund of funds seek higher levels of pension and other institutional assets, investors clamor for improved infrastructure and reporting systems. According to most allocators and consultants, despite the dislocation of 2008, the hedge fund industry is still poised for substantial growth over the next five to ten years. At the same time, moderation of returns will force investors to ask more questions and to demand greater transparency and risk management from the investment firms.

Investors expect to make a higher allocation to alternative assets, but are nevertheless frequently dissatisfied with performance.

There is a growing focus on governance, but the processes to make an assessment may be lacking.

The quality and scope of reporting needs attention, but investors must also learn to ask the right questions.

There is dissatisfaction among investors with some aspects of the current regulatory regime.[4]

PricewaterhouseCoopers published a financial services report in March 2008 titled *Transparency versus returns: The institutional investor view of alternative assets*. The report expressed several areas of concern, as shown on previous page.

With over 220 respondents to the survey, including institutional investors and alternative investment providers, risk management and transparency are as important as performance results but are still in the developmental stages at many firms. With the growth of the alternative investment industry, assets continue to flow to the firms that are building organizational structures.

In the early years of the fund of funds industry, many managers and investors alike believed that it was relatively easy operationally to manage a portfolio and manage the business. It is no longer a matter of getting the individual NAVs from each manager, aggregating the results, and reporting to LPs. By adding the value added of the fund of funds enterprise to the ongoing due diligence, the manager provides a wide range of indirect investment services and reporting, but investors want to know "How did you do last month?" If timing of the reports is often delayed, maybe it is time to put in a sell order. If the manager does not report the results in a timely, consistent manner, how can the NAV be trusted?

Never before has correct information, disseminated in a timely fashion, been more important.

CHAPTER 11

Recent Lessons Learned and Current Trends

The period 2006–2008 may go down in history as one that exemplified all that was wrong with Wall Street, Main Street, and global financial systems. In other words, just when you think you've seen it all, a tsunami strikes, and worlds and lives change in an instant. Fingers may be pointing for many years to come about who did what to whom and when; the subprime crisis and the subsequent credit freeze can be attributed to the excessive greed exhibited by all parties, including hedge funds, hedge fund investors, and the banking and mortgage industry.

Although some hedge fund investors may point to hedge funds that "took advantage" of their investors during this period, investors were more than satisfied with superior returns but did not ask "Why is my manager doing so much better than others." Alternatively, a better outcome may have been achieved by investors who believed that everything trades at a price for a reason and asked why the actual returns or projected returns were higher than historic industry averages.

A key principle of hedge fund investing is that hedge fund risk is different from traditional asset management risk because of

- The use of leverage
- The ability of the manager to short
- Reduced transparency
- The cultural background of managers to assume greater or different risk

However, as most investors understand, to make money you have to take some risk. Market-neutral managers who profess to make money consistently may not really be market neutral. There must be some risk inherent in the portfolio other than "zero" market exposure.

WHERE THE RISK IS FOUND

The key to understanding return is to understand the actual risk embedded in the hedge fund portfolio. Many equity and fixed-income managers claim to be "market neutral." Ask these professionals what happened in August 2007 or August 2008. Market neutral is supposed to offer no market exposure, but these funds suffered along with pretty much every other fund.

A risk management system does not eliminate risk; it should present the risk and reward in the portfolio in a fair and equal way. Even though the risk management system may present the "what if" in different scenarios, the quantitative portion represents only part of the analysis. The "gut check" lies in the practical understanding of what may happen in the market meltdown or doomsday scenario. The real purpose of the risk system turns out to be surprise avoidance, and only the manager can tell whether it really works.

Many investors believe that the market experiences a 10 standard deviation event (something that is extraordinary such as the collapse of an industry, a large company, or an economy) every four years, and that when this occurs fixed-income strategies become particularly vulnerable to this volatility. We believe that the markets have averaged a 10 standard deviation event nearly every year, starting in 1997 with the "Asian Flu" and continuing in 1998 with the LTCM blowup, in 1999 with the Brazilian crisis, in 2005 with the General Motors–Kirk Kerkorian chaos, and in 2008 with the bankruptcies of Bear Stearns and subsequently of Lehman Brothers.

Risk management cannot predict the next event, and the resulting output may be a flawed result of stress testing. One fact is clear: old-fashioned, well-thought-through intuition may be best, but it is far removed from the quantitative and qualitative analysis needed to make investment decisions.

Noncorrelated Investments

At the end of the day, hedge fund investors who have invested because hedge funds are "not correlated" to the capital markets must understand that their strategies may in reality be correlated to others and must attempt to understand strategies in different market scenarios. As we witnessed in 2007–2008, while nervous investors rushed to buy U.S. Treasuries (the standard flight to quality reaction in a downturn), bond spreads on agency and nonagency mortgage-backed securities (MBS) widened and fell in price because of the fear of the spread of delinquencies and defaults to these bonds. Even though the risk models may have indicated that Treasuries and agency MBS would go in the same direction, in fact, they did not. The widening of spread occurred in all sectors of the fixed-income markets—MBS, high-yield bonds, and distressed bonds—as well as in many sectors of equities, demonstrating the positive correlation of many sectors and disappointing both hedge fund managers and investors.

In periods of market stress, market risk and credit risk are interrelated, and stress testing may not detect this. In periods of stress, the markets often act irrationally. Many investors in hedge funds use consultants as a barrier for protection during meltdown periods. Investors are always looking to place the blame on someone else's shoulders. Managers are always quick to respond that the market is irrational and declare, "Our analysis is correct."

Successful hedge funds and fund of funds have strict written policies and procedures to deal with market or fund dislocation events; this often requires the manager to stick to stringent but flexible investment parameters. On the other hand, managers who lack written policies are generally the ones who encounter difficulties in tumultuous markets and deliver disastrous results to their investors.

Transparency

While obtaining hedge fund position transparency is always challenging, one of the best, if limited, public sources of information for equity position is quarterly 13-F filings that managers make based on Securities and Exchange Commission (SEC) requirements. The SEC requires that investment managers who manage more then $100 million file quarterly reports of the public securities it owns.[1] The data is limited, because it shows positions as of quarter end and is not a reflection of current activity. While the results will vary from period to period, generally the most commonly bought stocks outperform, while the most commonly sold stocks underperform. Market capitalization is important as well, with small-cap and mid-cap stocks having the greatest price volatility with concentration of hedge fund ownership.

The key issue for the hedge fund investor is to understand the concentration risk and its resulting impact on the liquidity of the individual positions "when the music stops." It adds another dimension to the risk—or rather the reality—of hedge fund liquidity. Sectors that hedge funds are buying or selling may have an impact on price performance and liquidity.

Periods of market stress also reveal weakness in hedge fund managers' back offices. Even though all hedge funds and fund of funds are quick to tell investors and potential investors that they have an annual audit performed by a major accounting firm, this action is completed just once a year. The increasing presence of institutional investors including large pension funds has altered the way hedge fund assets are managed and reported. High net worth investors and family offices are not subject to the same strict reporting requirements, but they want to receive the same level of reporting. Back-office problems often indicate weakness on the part of managers, who will unquestionably come under pressure in periods of market stress. A once-a-year audit, while fine for the government and the taxman, is not enough for any investor. Information needs to flow with regularity.

DELEVERAGE ISSUES

One of the centerpieces of hedge fund investing is buying when others are selling. As a result, hedge funds armed with leverage can buy securities that are being dumped by others, price the securities at a discount, and hold on to them for a long time in expectation of substantially higher future prices.

In 2007, commercial banks were saddled with hundreds of billions of dollars of unsold leveraged buyout (LBO) positions. The hedge fund community could not buy them, because prime brokers demanded higher haircuts on collateral and the accountants required greater transparency regarding pricing. The GPS is certainly a wonderful and practical invention, but still we ask, what happens when the battery dies? In the hedge fund industry, it's important to be able to read a road map as well as use the electronics device, but there is no substitute for good, independent judgment.

New Leverage Rules

As the hedge fund industry matures, reacts, and transforms itself in the aftermath of the 2007–2008 meltdown of the financial services industry and hedge fund industry, several trends are taking shape. The first is the changing face of hedge funds brought about by the actions of the Federal Reserve Board and the U.S. Treasury Department in a 10-day period during September 2008. Reacting to the deteriorating credit situation in the U.S. and global markets and the reduction in or freezing of the global capital and financial systems, Treasury Secretary Henry Paulson moved to seize Fannie Mae and Freddie Mac in an effort to reduce worldwide systemic risk. To prevent a run on the banks, he strongly recommended that Merrill Lynch, Morgan Stanley, Goldman Sachs, and Lehman Brothers seek merger partners within the commercial banking industry and that AIG raise $85 billion in new capital.

The story of what happened is no secret and probably does not need to be repeated. But for those who missed it, Lehman went bankrupt and Merrill Lynch was sold in a fire sale to Bank of America. Goldman raised money from Warren Buffett, and Morgan Stanley sold a chunk of its business to the Japanese company Mitsubishi UFJ Financial Group, Inc. Then under the cover of darkness, Paulson, under the direction of President George W. Bush, forced all of the large financial institutions to take billions of dollars in taxpayer money in return for preferred stock positions in the underlying companies in an effort to restore stability to the financial system. Needless to say, by June 2009 things were starting to right themselves. Both AIG and Citibank had gone to the trough again, and the others seemed to be holding onto whatever respect they had left in order to get out from under the federal government's thumb.

History will judge the "shock and awe" actions of President Bush and Secretary Paulson, but one fact is clear: the Feds wanted greater control of both the financial services industry and the hedge fund industry. It all happened during that 10-day period. The prime brokers, the purveyors of unbridled leverage, are now controlled by federal examiners. Leverage may not be gone, but it has been reduced. The Fed and the SEC also demonstrated that they would impose restrictions on shorting stocks to "maintain market liquidity."

While many shook their heads in disbelief that a far-right, free-market U.S. president could move to the left so quickly, several other things became quite clear. First, the hedge fund industry is no longer the bad guy on the block but rather one of many bullies taking advantage of the weak. Second, the days of unbridled leverage are over. Third, Darwin is alive and well on Wall Street, Main Street, and any other place that matters; only the strongest survive.

Despite the strong blow delivered by the Federal Reserve, inflows of new capital into hedge funds and fund of funds remain at high levels as many new entrants, including large pension plans, foundations, and endowments, are entering the alternative investment industry for the first time. Furthermore, the flawed calculations and the strategies that performed poorly have caused allocators and investors to review the entire due diligence and research process and are now looking to move money (whatever is left) to new funds.

FUND OF FUNDS FIRST

For many new first-time hedge fund market participants, investing in fund of funds will be the likely first choice. However, with the increased need for more customization of portfolios to meet specific asset allocations and lower fee structures, institutional investors with larger portfolios, probably in excess of $500 million, will likely evaluate options to bring their investment functions in-house. As this occurs, there will be a migration away from fund of funds to single-strategy investing. Benchmarks will be evaluated to compare peer group performance, with less reliance on industry-recognized reporting sources (e.g., the HFRI or Lipper indexes) in favor of comparisons to other pension plans or endowments, when such data is available.

Institutional investors will reexamine due diligence procedures to ensure that the existing policies and procedures have been reviewed and changed with the aim of reducing stress due to market forces. Institutional investors are likely to keep on preferring larger fund of funds and hedge funds over smaller managers. The multibillion-dollar fund of funds are expected to grow even more, and hedge fund sizes will grow to accommodate the large inflows of capital from institutional investors. However, given the poor returns of the 2007–2008 period and the redundancy of positions taken by many fund of funds and hedge funds, many investors are now moving toward smaller fund of funds in the range of $500 million to $2 billion to take advantage of niche strategies such as technology, emerging markets, or green or socially responsible funds. Smaller funds are more adept at identifying underlying niche managers and are more flexible, having smaller pools of capital to commit.

Both smaller fund of funds and smaller hedge funds will remain under pressure for performance returns but will gain a greater share of growing assets in an effort to compete with the large organizations. Contrary to popular thinking, performance may not necessarily be the primary barometer; size will continue to rule, and performance will follow. Despite being outperformaned by smaller funds, large management companies will continue to offer institutions greater comfort through their sheer bulk.

Portfolio Valuation

Valuation of securities will remain a key issue. As hedge funds have migrated toward more private equity, less liquid positions, in part funded with the LBO binge of 2005–2007, investors want greater transparency and more liquid positions. In the wake of the subprime debacle, investors in opaque strategies such as ABS and CDOs that seek to capitalize on the dislocation want to feel confident that the manager will provide a high level of clarity regarding the implementation of the strategy.

Because of the blurring of the lines between many strategies with lessened liquidity and increased private equity positions, hedge fund managers have lengthened redemption periods. While this may be an effective tool for the hedge fund manager and may reduce the outflows of capital, it presents a challenge for fund of funds that must find alternatives for funding redemptions of the underlying managers.

New Rules, New Products

Don't be surprised by future surprises. What once was marked "made in America" with subprime, Alt A, mezzanine financing, and an even longer laundry list, is now held by investors all over the globe. The crisis may have reached its peak, but investors must exercise a higher degree of due diligence in reviewing managers to anticipate what the next product or sector to cause global dislocation may be.

Strategies based on 130/30 will continue to grow in popularity as institutional investors resist higher hedge fees and look for cheaper alternatives that still provide greater transparency. It will take a period of a few years to measure the success of returns, not the growth of assets, in this arena.

Wall Street distribution of hedge funds will be limited and will come under pressure. The old business model of capital introduction by the prime broker has lost several key players, and hedge fund managers and specialized fund of funds will have to rely on internal marketing teams to raise assets.

Tighter regulation of hedge funds by global regulators including the SEC and the United Kingdom's Financial Services Authority, or FSA, will continue as the institutional client base grows. As more high net worth investors step up investments into more retail-oriented product, the test for high minimum levels of assets can be expected to become more stringent.

Thank You Bear and Lehman

In the wake of the failure of Bear Stearns and Lehman Brothers and the weakened balance sheets of investment banks, investor preference for bank balance sheets will be increased. Investors may feel less comfortable with the limited number of investment banks as derivative counterparties or providers of leverage and will seek hedge funds and fund of funds that use commercial banks for financing or as prime brokers for nonequity transactions. There has been a sea change in the environment for credit. Credit providers are aiming for a greater understanding of credit, particularly in the fixed-income markets. Leveraged strategies will be under increased scrutiny, with credit providers requiring greater liquidity and higher levels of margin. Repo-financed strategies may not be able to achieve the same level of historic returns as in past markets, given the lower levels of leverage and financing. Strategies that depend on short-term funding will be subjected to the increasing risk that the leverage provider will indiscriminately change the haircut and the term of financing.

At the same time, investors will again call for greater transparency, and prime brokers will continue to provide a greater flow of information to clients and hedge fund investors in the respective funds. Larger institutional investors and large fund of funds will demand separate accounts to achieve increased transparency and increased risk management. Heightened levels of due diligence will be performed by both investors and credit providers to avoid potential landmines and reduce the impact of systemic risk in other parts of the balance sheet.

Fund of funds will become larger. These firms must have an extensive infrastructure to build a scalable business and to be able to accommodate large inflows of new investment dollars.

Government regulators will exercise increased oversight. As their actions during September 2008 indicate, the regulators feel that the hedge fund industry had become too large, with its $2 trillion of equity and $10 trillion of market exposure. These figures do not include the potential trillions of dollars of off-sheet derivative exposure.

Will hedge fund fees of 2 and 20 percent at $200 million of assets work at $20 billion? Probably not. Does the manager have the same incentive to produce the same quality of results as the smaller shop? Are fund of funds that are now asset-gathering machines still concerned about producing results? The jury is out, but many believe that asset gathering is more important to management then true asset management.

THE END OF AN ERA

The golden age of investment banking is over. Fewer transactions reduce opportunities for many strategies but create new ones for flexible managers. The number of investment banks has contracted, and with greater Fed oversight and desire for lower leverage, the influence of the commercial banking industry will decrease, resulting in a lower risk profile and less compulsion to do deals for the sake of doing deals. To capitalize on the new opportunities, many hedge funds will need larger infrastructures.

Do investors understand the liquidity mismatch present in both hedge funds and fund of funds? Managers have longer-term positions and redemption liabilities that can change like the weather. Redemptions in 1998 and in 2007, even in good funds, amounted to investors rebalancing and seeking higher liquidity levels.

The question is why do many pensions go from allocating virtually nothing to 5 percent of their assets to hedge funds? Is it because of the lack of depth and expertise shown by the consultant while some large pensions have allocations similar to those of the successful college endowments?

One of the most talked-about investor classes that no one really knows anything about but everyone knows everything about is sovereign wealth funds (SWFs). Because of the large flows of capital resulting from the recycling of petrodollars and the growth in what used to be emerging markets, these investment entities have unprecedented levels of capital to put to work. Although many SWFs have become active in the capital markets by recapitalizing global financial institutions or purchases in the mergers and acquisitions (M&A) market, with total assets estimated to exceed $3 trillion and expected to increase substantially over the next five years, many estimate that their assets will flow directly into hedge fund coffers.

The Sovereign Wealth Funds

When hedge funds stop being front-page news, the next focus will be SWFs. Many of these funds have been around for many years, but with emerging economies such as Russia and China no longer emerging, and oil exporters Kuwait and Saudi Arabia seeing one-way flows of capital into their countries, the deployment of SWF capital will impact the capital markets globally as well as hedge fund strategies. We have already seen several high-visibility investments into U.S. and other global commercial banks with new capital to offset the decline of equity ratios concomitant with the write-offs due to poor commercial loan underwriting and exposure to subprime assets.

One of the largest and oldest SWFs is the Abu Dhabi Investment Authority (ADIA) established in 1976. ADIA has been investing globally in a wide range of countries and industries and owns large equity positions in Citigroup, Toll Brothers, and Apollo Management, to mention just a few. In spite of the large influence that it can wield, ADIA was rebuffed in its attempted purchase of U.S. ports.

Disclosure ranges from complete disclosure by Norway's governmental pension fund to required SEC filings of 13F equity holdings by many SWFs to low disclosure of holdings by many others. Because the investment objective varies among the various funds, many are oriented to absolute returns and positioned to achieve a higher risk profile. Although many invest in highly liquid securities, many SWFs invest in higher-return instruments. As a result, hedge funds, real estate, and private equity have experienced substantial inflows, with more expected.

SWFs Are BIG

According to a J.P. Morgan report dated May 22, 2008, SWFs currently own $270 to $340 billion in alternatives, or 6.8 to 7.5 percent of total alternatives, with half in private equity. Although much of investment mandate is managed internally by SWFs, each fund externally allocates substantial portions of the asset pools, particularly in the hedge fund sector. J.P. Morgan estimates that "roughly 60 percent of SWFs use external managers, with about half of SWF assets managed externally."[2]

In evaluating the impact of SWFs on hedge funds, the breakdown indicates that SWFs probably constitute about $150 billion of total hedge fund assets. While the amount is not large and will be growing, the conclusion is that the capital flows will be directed to the large managers that can accept large balances. Capital will also be directed to specific strategies that the SWFs want to have direct exposure to rather than to fund of funds with more of a multi-strategy investment approach.

As part of the due diligence process for hedge fund investors, it is important to know and understand what the total investor base profile of the hedge fund is, not just to know names but to understand and project what the investment objectives of the other investors may be. Given the volatility of the capital markets, highly fluctuating currencies, and ever-shifting geopolitical climates, investor funds may be sensitive to market as well as nonmarket factors, and well-informed investors should be prepared, along with managers, for sudden and unpredictable movements of capital. More investment funds will continue to be attracted to hedge funds by SWFs, especially in light of the decline of asset values in the developed world.

CHAPTER 12

New Products

As investors resist direct allocations to hedge funds, and fund of funds look for new ways to invest in hedge funds, several new investment products have been launched during the past several years to entice investors into a low-risk methodology of hedge fund investing. These products include the following:

- 130/30 funds
- Leveraged products
- Principal-protected notes
- Best-idea fund of funds
- Hedge fund replication
- Multi-strategy hedge funds

130/30 FUNDS

First are 130/30 funds, which are expected to have $1 trillion in assets over the next few years and are attracting large, sophisticated investors such as the California Public Employees' Retirement System, the Illinois State Teachers Retirement System, and many other pension funds. The first inducement is a lower level of fees that average around a 1 percent management fee and a small incentive-based fee, substantially lower than the 2 and 20 percent commonly found in single-manager hedge funds. The similarity to hedge funds lies in the use of leverage and shorting. The manager is long 130 percent and short 30 percent for a gross market exposure of 160 percent and a net market exposure of 100 percent. 130/30 is a structure, like 2&20, but not necessarily a strategy. The performance is based on the beta to the relevant index. One of the key ingredients of success in hedge funds is the ability of managers to short as well as to come up with good long ideas. Shorting in 130/30 is merely a by-product of the structure and not necessarily part of the strategy. While proponents claim that this strategy can generate alpha, the fund objective is still 100 percent net market exposure.

Why Mutual Funds Can't Short

In search of additional asset-based fee income, many traditional long-only managers are hearing investors clamor for new investment options with a hedge fund–like product. The quest for alpha has led many investors to seek new ways to allocate capital. The biggest risk is the untested ability of a traditional long-only manager to short stocks. As most hedge fund managers will readily state, shorting stocks is one of the most difficult strategies to execute successfully. After all, there are only a few short-only managers that have been able to survive during the past 20 years, while new long/short managers have prospered. If a manager is really good at picking shorts, why restrict the amount to 30 percent? This lack of experience by the long-only managers is a negative and can lead to underperforming risk-adjusted returns in many market environments.

Often referred to as "hedge fund lite," the small percentage of typical shorting that 130/30 managers use can be, in our opinion, quite risky. If a manager is good at managing long money and has the unique ability to pick shorts and prosper, why do it with a lower fee structure? More skill and resources are required in shorting stocks. Judging by the huge interest in this new product earned in a short period of time and the desire to seek hedge fund–like returns with un-hedge fund–like fees, investors and their consultants may be overlooking many steps in the due diligence process for the 130/30 manager versus investing with a hedge fund manager.

The rise in 130/30 has been a consequence of several academic papers that suggest that investors can achieve greater returns by altering the prohibition on shorting stocks. The assumption is that the manager will be able to demonstrate his skill set and transfer the long selection process to shorting stocks. 130/30 mandates have strict investment disciplines that may not always be present in hedge fund investing. The research papers indicate that 130/30 offers investors higher alpha, and while the product is still in its infancy, the jury is still out to determine if this approach will really deliver the returns, correlation, and volatility characteristics that have been suggested.

This product may fill a gap for pensions, but the road is littered with the carcasses of bright analysts and traders who could not transition to hedge funds. Will this product prove to be the next creation of Wall Street that does not work? At this point, 130/30 looks like a mutual fund with a limited ability to short stocks.

HEDGE FUND REPLICATION

Hedge fund replication represents another alternative to both direct hedge fund investing and fund of funds investing. As direct investors looked for the next methodology to reduce fees, investment banks' alternative investment creativity gave rise to the newest alternative investment product.

The objective of hedge fund replication is, as the name implies, to replicate the risk/adjusted returns of hedge funds. Replication can be limited to specific sectors or can encompass a broad range of hedge fund strategies. Using a model-based strategy, the investor can select the allocation based on standard regression analysis using variables to account for the difference in historic hedge fund returns. Factors that may be considered might include returns of long/short equity of small cap versus large cap, long value versus growth, returns of bond indexes, commodity market indexes, or foreign exchange returns. An investor who has a long lockup in a hedge fund strategy may want to have a short exposure to a hedge fund and thereby reduce overall exposure. Because this is an imperfect hedge, investors should evaluate the risk associated with this trade.

The goal of the structuring should include the determination of the historical period to review to estimated betas of the various indexes. The final phase of the analysis is to put the hedge fund returns through regression models against the selected factors over the selected time period.

Investors select hedge fund replication as a strategy for asset allocation that provides a dynamic tool for consultants and allocators to assist investors in achieving overall portfolio objectives. And, of course, to save fees! The goal of replication is to attempt to follow hedge funds in their ability to anticipate and participate in market trends.

The real positive to replication lies in transparency and liquidity. Since investors will have position-level transparency, active portfolio management results in a better understanding of sources of alpha and correlation to market indexes. Replication will allow investors to reduce portfolio redundancy and allocate to sectors that were previously underweighted. With the increase in transparency, investors will quickly be able to react to style drift, one of the dreaded concerns of all investors. The major positive for investors is transparency, and fraud risk is eliminated by the daily liquidity and high transparency.

Hedge fund replication has several limitations. Since the allocation is based on the self-selection process of specific strategies, it may be broadly defined as a market-timing strategy that needs to have additional research information besides the investment timing. Another shortcoming is exposed when short-term allocation changes are required. When hedge fund managers are quick to adapt to changing markets, the replicator may be few steps behind the hedge fund. The timeliness of performance also presents a challenge. As part of the modeling and regression analysis, the replication strategy should analyze returns over a longer time with more frequent results. Unfortunately, hedge funds report monthly results, resulting in fewer reporting periods and less reliable data.

The Cost of Replication

In determining the actual costs associated with replication, the due diligence costs of hedge funds are substantially higher. However, the limitations of replication are manifest in the larger amounts of capital required for investment. Because of the monitoring and constant review and adjustment of returns and strategies as well as the larger number of strategies in which to invest, replication is restricted to larger investors. In the end, there is one question that investors must ask: Is replication cheaper than investing in fund of funds, and is it worth it?

The answer most likely is that the strategies of fund of funds and replication products can go hand in hand. Even though the cost of fund of funds may be higher, these funds provide professional management and portfolio diversification, although they are a bit slower to make changes. Replication strategies provide higher transparency and a closer process for asset allocation. On the other hand, direct hedge fund investing will continue to provide the best source of alpha for investors who have the resources and staff to identify managers who meet the investor's investment objectives.

OPPORTUNITIES IN EMERGING MANAGERS

One of the newest buzzwords in the hedge fund industry is *emerging manager*. In the same breath in many cases, the terms *seeder* or *incubator* usually follows. The hedge fund industry is one in which it is often challenging to define terms or strategies. Difficult-to-define terms include *hedge fund*, just for starters. While most know what a hedge fund is with its ability to short, to use leverage, and to implement redemption requirements that are different from long-only investing, many skeptics define hedge funds as a compensation scheme, given its imposition of an incentive fee.

Definitions for an emerging manager are equally difficult to define. Technically, all new hedge fund managers without a track record are emerging managers. However, a manager with a pedigree from a well-respected Wall Street firm or a large investment management firm is not included in this category. If a Wall Street executive who has managed a trading desk for the preceding 10 years and has been actively involved in the day-to-day trading or research launches a fund with $1 billion, he should be considered an emerging manager. This team of professionals from the former firm may not have worked together as a team but did work at the same firm, and may have added several professionals from other firms to launch the new firm. Allocators do not consider this group "emerging," since they had a large asset pool at launch, but should really be considered emerging since they, too, have no verifiable track record.

On other hand, if a group of two lawyers, a distressed trader, and an analyst who worked together on the prop trading desk of a buy-side firm launch their new fund with $7 million of their own funds, they are also considered to be an emerging manager. This group can also point to the results that were achieved at the firm they used to work for, but they do not have an identifiable, audited track record. The difference in defining emerging appears to lie in the size of the asset pools at launch. For our discussion, we will refer to emerging managers as those that are newly launched funds that do not have a prior audited track and fall below a specific level of assets, such as $100 million. The hedge fund community usually refers to emerging managers as younger, smaller managers who are early in their life cycle rather than to the billion-dollar launch of a team that also has no track record.

An emerging manager has one additional distinction: the ability to raise capital is limited due to several challenges. First, the new manager may not be able to raise meaningfully significant capital levels at first because of a lack of a track record as well as not being able to identify the initial round of investors. Second, many hedge funds are unsuccessful in capital raising because of poorly prepared marketing material, inability to properly explain the strategy, or the manager's unwillingness to leave the trading desk to meet prospective investors. To raise capital, the new hedge fund must use other approaches.

Emerging Manager Due Diligence

As fund of funds look for new managers to add to their funds, emerging managers are always on the horizon. However, some fund of funds have minimum asset size requirements or length of track record required before a new fund is even considered for review. As a result, many emerging managers fail to make the cut. For those fund of funds looking at emerging managers, the major question remains, will it be a career-threatening decision to invest in the new manager?

For fund of funds that will review emerging managers for portfolio evaluation, hedge funds that have seed or incubating relationships have a new set of criteria that must be understood and explained during the due diligence phase. As a result, the due diligence process must be refined to understand who the seeder is; the objectives; the economics; revenue/equity ownership; and the additional services that may be provided. A meeting with the seeder is imperative to understand what the seeder's overall investment objectives may be.

At the same time, recent developments in the fund of funds industry have included several firms focusing on emerging managers and investing exclusively with emerging managers. Several of these fund of funds invest with managers who are new, niche, and emerging without any financial linkage. In other cases, the fund of funds invest with managers with whom it has a strategic alliance. While there may be advantages to both methodologies, the key issue for the investor is how quickly the manager can sever the relationship. As a fund of funds investor, I may not want to be involved in private equity–like transactions and want the fund of funds manager to have the ability to act decisively and independently in the event of a change in strategy or in market volatility. Linking the economics of the investment manager of the fund of funds and the investment objective of the fund of funds investor may not be compatible and may lead to an unwinding of the relationship.

All of this leads us to the question of why anyone should invest in an emerging manager? There is a belief in the hedge fund industry that younger, smaller funds have better performance results earlier in the developmental stages of their track record. The pro-small community argues that smaller funds are more nimble, more flexible, and more liquid because of their ability to move capital and make better decisions more quickly. Smaller funds take smaller-sized positions, which result in fewer liquidity issues. It is believed that smaller, emerging managers can concentrate capital in fewer, more focused positions. The anti–emerging managers' side of the investment community argues that small funds underperform because of the higher cost of their infrastructures, and many emerging managers may cut corners, having reduced levels of support and research staff to execute the strategy. This camp believes that there are fewer controls and investment policies in place, and the new manager may in fact have a higher risk profile to achieve higher returns.

Smaller managers may have a concentrated client base that could present liquidity issues in the event of a sudden change in market sentiment. The lack of an audit by a major hedge fund accounting firm can prove to be detrimental to the ability of the manager to attract capital and may also reveal internal reporting weaknesses within the organization.

The pro–big hedge fund manager camp believes that larger funds have better results. With a larger research budget, better access to company management teams, and access to the investment banking and brokerage community, big funds are more efficient. Larger funds may be less susceptible to unforeseen capital flows than smaller funds, and the larger capital base will enable them to deploy capital into different sectors to capitalize on changing markets or investment strategies.

RISKS ASSOCIATED WITH NEW HEDGE FUNDS

As all hedge fund legal documents and marketing material indicate, there are risks associated with investing in hedge funds. With newly launched strategies, the risk is the greatest. Although investors may claim that size reduces risk, in the case of the newly launched fund with $1 billion in assets under management, size may hide risk. Comfort may be afforded by the larger size of assets and infrastructure, but the facts remain; this new team has not worked together in the same organization as a team, and the new firm does not have a track record or any operating history. In most cases, the new team has not previously managed an independent, stand-alone business with its own profit and loss statement. Despite the size, the risk is great.

However, with startups, size does matter, and the risk is great for a small manager even though this group may have worked together for many years.

The perception by hedge fund allocators is that the small managers have the greatest business risk, resulting in increased challenges for capital raising and future growth. As a result, many new small managers will look for alternative methods to raise capital to get to critical mass and then reap the benefits of a successful strategy.

Many turn to seeders and incubators. Who are they, what are they, and what do they do? As the hedge fund industry went through its growth spurt during the late 1990s and into the early 2000s, new hedge fund managers were able to raise new capital from existing relationships, both large and small. Many took advantage of working with the capital introduction teams at the prime brokers. Others chose to use third-party marketing firms to find capital. With the institutionalization of the hedge fund industry and the demand for greater pools of assets and organizational infrastructure, managers needed to attract more capital to prove their worth to investors. Seeders and incubators were two groups that provided many funds with the ability to prove their worth.

Seed Capital Providers

Seeding operations take many forms. For many years, high net worth investors and family offices would provide "seed" capital to launch funds. The investor may have been the first outside investor to commit a substantial amount of capital relative to the size of the fund's assets under management, and the hedge fund manager could use the name of the investor to attract assets from other investors. For their capital, many seeders demand better terms than those offered in the private placement memorandum, resulting in lower management fees, incentive fees, or redemption terms than those offered to the masses.

As the need for larger pools of capital grew, one of the early entrants into the world of seeding was Capital Z Asset Management. Capital Z's staff say that they are presented with and review hundreds of strategies each year and have funded less than two dozen since its inception in 1998. While there are more than 30 firms in this space that represent themselves as seeders, competition is stiff, and each model differs. Some of the seeding firms provide capital only, while others may provide infrastructure and marketing capability. Some hedge funds want to build out all parts of their business and look for the seeder to help. Other managers look to be part of a platform and have only the administrative responsibility managed by the seeder.

The economics of each seeding deal differ as well. All seeders want the hedge fund to manage the business on a day-to-day basis and want the firm to be successful. The participation by today's seeder varies, with some providing a fixed amount of capital period (e.g., two to three years) in exchange for a share of the manager's revenue.

In other models, the seeder takes an equity ownership stake in the management company. The additional economic advantage to the seeder is the ability to reserve capacity for a fixed period of time and to profit in the success of the total business, not just their assets placed with the firm. Other seeders may share in the equity for a determined period of time. In this case, the seeder likes to play the role of partner and a minority investor in the fund while providing strategic support. The equity ownership stake may be for a fixed period or in perpetuity, with the manager having the ability to buy out the seeder after a set period of time based on various factors or assumptions.

Data Helps the Decision Process

Several academic studies have been conducted to analyze returns, standard deviation, Sharpe ratio, and alpha of small versus large. The results are mixed, with several stating that smaller funds do better, several stating that larger funds do better, and several stating that the results are inconclusive.

A recent study by Infovest21 reviewed past studies of data that compared big funds with small funds. According to George Martin, associate director of the Center for International Studies and Derivatives Markets at the University of Massachusetts, "Research on the performance characteristics of emerging managers suffers from several weaknesses: survivorship or other reporting bias, lack of consensus on the definition of what constitutes 'emerging.'" In other words,

- Are fund assets the definition?
- Is fund age the definition?
- Is manager experience the definition?
- Is it a combination of all three?

Martin said that assets under management, by themselves, do not make a meaningful statistical difference in performance when one controls for survivorship bias and strategy classification. He believes that there is no statistically significant return to investing in fund of funds that invest in emerging managers.

Young Funds Make Sense

A second study by Greg Gregoriou and Fabrice Rouah in the Winter 2002 *Journal of Alternative Investments* found that asset size has no impact on a fund's performance, whether adjusted (Sharpe and Treynor ratios) or unadjusted measures are used to evaluate one fund versus another.[1]

The Infovest21 report includes eight studies by industry professionals and academics. While the other results are varied, the Infovest21 study concludes:

> *The five studies examined conclude that younger funds have higher performance. One study said within the three years while another study found outperformance in the first year. Yet younger funds are also more vulnerable in the early stages and have higher mortality rates due to their limited infrastructure, and often they operate below breakeven levels. One study found the failure rate peaked at 28 months. Further studies on fund age and performance need to be updated to recent history and concluded over longer time horizons. Different methodologies need to be used to see if the conclusions are consistent. And, as previously stated, many factors contribute to the performance of hedge funds and it can't be determined solely by age.*[2]

Despite contributing to an overwhelming case for emerging managers, the data seems to indicate that newer, younger managers have an advantage in achieving better results over their older, seasoned brethren. However, the risks are greater in investing early on with a new manager. A decade ago, a trader could leave a larger firm, be joined by a teammate, launch a fund in the garage of one of their homes, and then grow and achieve good results before taking formal office space to begin the capital-raising process. Today, this is virtually impossible. With institutionalization of the market, some undefined level of critical mass and infrastructure is required.

The due diligence process of more established fund of funds managers is more complex, with great risk for the newest managers. Although some investors may "drop off some money," as one fund of funds manager stated, to reserve a place at the table, what happens if dinner is not served. Emerging manager investors must be prepared for poor performance and higher rate of disclosure in searching for the next best undiscovered manager. In addition, the emerging manager investor must adhere to a strict schedule of monitoring results and portfolio positions to anticipate any warning signs that may appear. While no manager regardless of size or track record is exempt from disclosure, greater scrutiny is required for emerging managers.

Given the tighter controls and surveillance imposed by the SEC and the UK's Financial Services Industry along with the accounting industry, hedge fund investors, and the U.S. Congress, hedge funds and fund of funds will be monitored more closely in the weeks, months, and years to come.

Most emerging managers will avoid the regulatory expense and scrutiny until critical mass is reached, providing little extra level of inquiry by outside examiners.

The overall size of the fund of funds may prove to be the key determinant to investing in emerging managers. Larger fund of funds may eliminate allocation into emerging managers unless a specific mandate calls for it, while many small- to midsized fund of funds—say with assets under $500 million—stress their unique ability to identify, research, and select emerging managers for inclusion into their funds. Smaller fund of funds, family offices, and high net worth investors are able to allocate smaller amounts of capital while enduring an extra level of due diligence and post-investment monitoring. In spite of everything, many large fund of funds, foundations, and endowments spend over 300 man-hours in the due diligence and review process before making the final decision to invest. In the end, the fund of funds or other investors must decide whether it has the skill or desire to add emerging managers to the overall portfolio along with its commitment to the tedious process required for investment approval.

CHAPTER 13

Multi-Strategy Funds versus Hedge Fund of Funds

If you ask seasoned hedge fund investors what keeps them awake at night, with very few exceptions you will get the same answer: the possibility of a massive drawdown. Such a drawdown can be classed into two broad categories: those related to poor portfolio management and trading decisions, and those caused by some exogenous factor outside the portfolio management process. To successfully navigate the universe of hedge fund investing, sophisticated investors have developed procedures to determine whether a drawdown could take place at a given hedge fund at any given time based on any given situation.

Despite the passage of time and the occurrence of other well-known blowups, hedge fund investors are still feeling the aftermath of the collapse of Amaranth in 2006 and the subsequent market meltdown in which some of the industry's greatest names went down 10, 20, or even 30 percent in 2008. As a result of these losses, many hedge fund investors are once again asking questions about the optimal investment vehicle to provide portfolio diversification. Many answers come down to two choices—fund of funds or multi-strategy funds.

DRAWDOWN ISSUES

Given the large pools of capital coming into the hedge fund industry, hedge fund investors proudly flaunt their unique due diligence processes and their ability to detect signs that a drawdown may occur. Sophisticated investors view the massive drawdown as an uncommon occurrence that their detection systems can sniff out with relative ease. Certainly, valuable lessons can be learned from what happened in 2008, but those events were essentially affirmations of their review processes. From time to time, a massive drawdown takes place within the hedge fund universe that goes beyond just questioning the investor's manager selection process and actually raises issues as to how investors view the industry generally. For such an event to take place, the drawdown would have to come from an established fund that may have avoided many investors' due diligence red flags.

As discussed previously, the demise of Long-Term Capital Management (LTCM) was the first such episode to raise fundamental questions about the hedge fund universe. Before the summer of 1998, hedge funds had come and gone, some more notable than others, but any major losses were seen as involving only a particular fund or manager. However, the events of the fall of 1998 forever changed the public's perceptions and investors' perceptions of the hedge fund industry; it was the sheer enormity of the situation as well as the number of players involved that had such an impact. Staffed with leading Wall Street executives and academics, LTCM was a vast institution that investors flocked to in droves; in fact, investors could not give the firm enough money. When the Russian government defaulted on its debt and fixed-income trades went awry (spreads diverging when they were supposed to converge), the dreaded massive drawdown that all hedge fund investors feared came about. A thorough postmortem ensued, and many important lessons that we take for granted today were first learned, albeit the hard way.

For the first time, questions began to be asked whether investing in individual hedge funds was the most efficient way to access the hedge fund management talent. While fund of funds had grown in number along with the growth of hedge fund assets during the 1990s, the aftermath of the LTCM debacle provided rationale for portfolio diversification through investments in fund of funds.

This review of history brings us to one of the past members of this infamous "Blowup" club—Amaranth. Like LTCM, Amaranth was a large and well-established multi-strategy fund organization. Unlike LTCM's, Amaranth's plunge was barely felt outside the circle of its own investors and employees, despite the loss of $6.5 billion. At the same time, many hedge funds and banks prospered at Amaranth's expense.

HOW BLOWUPS AFFECT THE INDUSTRY

Even though its overall effect on the hedge fund industry may have been muted, Amaranth's failure once again raised the age-old question: should I seek out a fund of hedge funds or a multi-strategy hedge fund manager? Institutional investment commitments are growing larger, and investors representing hundreds of billions of dollars are now deciding whether to invest with fund of funds or multi-strategy funds. After the LTCM blowup, much of the institutional capital that entered the hedge fund space did so through fund of funds, but over time, many of these same investors started investing directly with single managers. There are several reasons why this happened, but the Amaranth event has come to symbolize one prominent answer to this very question.

Arguably, the most common replacement for a fund of funds was the multi-strategy fund (multi-strat), which has attracted large inflows of institutional capital. As we review the multi-strat fund, we recognize once again that clearly defining this type of fund is difficult in spite of its simplicity. (Webster could probably publish a dictionary with hedge fund terms alone, but who would write the text?) A complicating factor is that until several years ago, multi-strats did not exist. Most managers did not start as multi-strategy funds but rather as single-strategy funds.

Robert Schulman, formerly of Tremont, states, "The best managers are always reinventing themselves, always looking for the new market opportunity or dislocation."[1] Historically, many of today's well-known multi-strat funds started out as either convertible bond arbitrage (as Amaranth did), risk arbitrage, or distressed managers; over time, they adapted to market conditions and morphed into multi-strategy complexes. Amaranth had become the poster child for multi-strat and had reignited the debate between fund of funds and direct hedge fund investing by the time it collapsed.

Funds of Hedge Funds

The first step in contrasting both structures is to compare the advantages, disadvantages, and distinctions of both classes of investment. Although both strategies seek to provide portfolio diversification, each strategy has many distinct defining characteristics. To begin with, the following two levels of fees apply:

- The underlying hedge funds management and performance fees (on average a 1.5 percent management fee and a 20 percent performance fee).
- Fund of funds managers' management fee, typically averaging 1 percent and sometimes including a performance fee of 10 percent.

Fund of funds invest in various hedge fund strategies through separate underlying hedge fund managers; the fund is responsible for the hiring and firing of each underlying manager. Because the underlying hedge fund managers restrict redemption frequency, fund of funds have reduced ability for frequent changes to the overall fund's portfolio allocation.

Security-level position transparency is limited because of the number of underlying hedge fund managers, which can exceed 40 to 50, each with hundreds (if not thousands) of positions. Many fund of funds, however, do provide individual hedge fund manager positions, which detail the strategy that the underlying hedge fund manager employs.

Due diligence and monitoring of each underlying hedge fund investment are performed by the fund of funds manager; the process includes understanding each underlying hedge fund manager's risk profile and relevant expertise. These funds are typically multiple strategies in orientation (although some are single-strategy focused), so their goal is to limit the fund's overall exposure to any one manager or strategy.

In some instances, fund of funds have access to closed funds by virtue of their length of investment. The breadth of possible investment is limited only by a fund of funds manager's ability to find appropriate underlying hedge fund managers. Since each investment is a separate legal entity, a massive drawdown in one underlying fund should have a small impact on other funds in the fund of hedge funds' portfolio. In the end, investors must ask: who is able to come up with the best trading ideas?

Will the fund of fund or the multi-strat argue that it is best equipped because it can go externally to source the best managers and ideas? Fund of funds will terminate strategies when the strategy goes awry, such as use of merger arbitrage when no deals are being done.

Multi-Strategy Hedge Funds

Multi-strategy hedge funds have only one level of management, and performance fees average at a 1.5 percent management fee and a 20 percent performance fee. It is also important to note that the performance fee is charged at the portfolio level. Other key attributes include the following:

- Multi-strats invest directly in strategies selected by the investment committee (or portfolio manager) responsible for the portfolio.
- Capital can be adjusted frequently, based on changing market opportunities, and is constrained only by the liquidity of the underlying position.
- Since many multi-strats manage large capital bases (in excess of $1 billion), they have the ability to attract highly talented trading and research teams dedicated to specific investment strategies.
- Multi-strat managers rotate capital allocations to strategies where opportunities exist and reduce capital allocations away from strategies with narrower profit potential.

- Multi-strat funds typically allocate more capital to arbitrage and process-driven strategies that use leverage to augment returns.
- To add additional strategies to the current multi-strat fund, new investment teams must be hired.
- Transparency varies from fund to fund, but multi-strats have the ability to offer clients better position-level information than fund of funds by virtue of managing every position.

Why Multi-Strats

Because the multi-strat is one fund with several underlying strategies, a drawdown in one strategy may affect other strategies. For example, investor redemptions may force the sale of illiquid securities to meet margin calls, resulting in a decline of overall portfolio value over a relatively short time. Furthermore, it may lead to the imposition of a gate to prevent the exodus of capital. In addition, one trader could cause a massive drawdown across the entire portfolio if not properly supervised.

One of the biggest challenges for multi-strat managers is to hire superior portfolio managers who are willing to work within the framework of an organization and sit on the bench waiting for market opportunities to arise that will enable the portfolio manager to come to bat. As Robert Schulman said, "If you're an expert in a field, do you want to hit every day? Or do you want to be a pinch hitter?"

Baseball may have batting specialists; some players hit lefties, others hit righties. The best managers want their players on the field every day. A good distressed manager or merger arbitrage manager has to be in the game each day, not waiting for market fundamentals to change to present opportunities for his strategy. After all, A-Rod plays every day, even when he is in a slump.

Without question, the choice to allocate to a multi-strat fund as opposed to allocating to a fund of funds seems to be driven by the quest for higher absolute returns. The data shown in Figure 13.1 confirms this statement. From January 2001 through December 2007, average multi-strat returns were 3.24 percent higher then those of fund of funds.[2] (We should point out that the data does have its limitations; please read note 2 in the Notes for this chapter.)

One difficulty is that all hedge fund managers can choose to classify themselves as they see fit. As a result, multi-strat managers are particularly difficult to distinguish from others in the hedge fund universe. For example, a hedge fund manager that runs a distressed merger arbitrage and capital structure arbitrage book could choose to classify the strategy as a multi-strategy manager or as a single-strategy event-driven manager. By the same

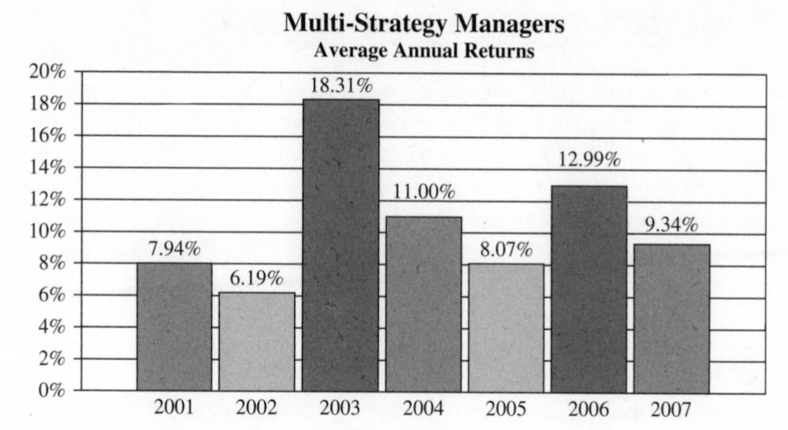

FIGURE 13.1 Multi-Strategy Managers Average Annual Returns
Source: HedgeFund.net.

token, a manager that primarily invests in convertible bond arbitrage and statistical arbitrage—very different strategies from those previously mentioned—could also choose to self-classify as a multi-strategy manager, but might choose relative value arbitrage instead. Needless to say, it is not an easy task to define the multi-strat vis-à-vis the long/short equity hedge fund manager space.

When evaluating the investment results, it appears that the return differential between fund of funds and multi-strats has several causes, some of which we have touched on.

- Fund of funds overall fees average from 1 to 1.50 percent higher, thereby reducing the net return to the end investor.
- Multi-strats typically use higher levels of leverage, both at the individual strategy level and at the overall portfolio level; this augments return but also increases volatility. By contrast, most funds of funds are not leveraged at the fund level; leverage is not applied to the portfolio unless the investor specifically requests it or the manager believes that it may enhance returns without dramatically raising volatility.
- Multi-strats have the ability to shift capital rapidly to react to changing market conditions; they can quickly take advantage of opportunities or reduce strategies when the strategies fall out of favor.

CONVERGENCE IN THE HEDGE FUND INDUSTRY

We have witnessed a convergence between hedge funds and private equity funds' investments into areas that previously had been the domain of private equity firms only. For many years, the largest component of hedge fund private equity investing had been private investments in public equity (PIPEs), but that component has grown recently to include real estate, traditional private equity, and levered loans. With the inflow of capital into hedge funds and private equity, this is one of the strategies whereby many hedge fund managers have expanded their traditional menu of investment options by adding hybrid securities and private finance capabilities to realize higher levels of return.

For many of these managers, these side pockets do not account for a large portion of their overall portfolios. However, the return targets necessary, given the illiquidity of these positions, can have a meaningful impact on the overall multi-strat. The manager can also enable certain investors, who so choose, access to their side pocket fund, which is a dedicated vehicle for illiquid investing. Fund of funds generally do not invest directly into the side pockets, given the nature of the redemption requirements of the overall fund.

Credit Crisis in Multi-Strat Funds

In the wake of the 2007–2008 mortgage meltdown, many multi-strats with specialized research and mortgage trading capabilities have added positions in highly illiquid asset-backed securities (ABS) and mortgage-backed securities (MBS). While the multi-strat looks for tremendous upside price movement for these bonds, their liquidity is reduced and longer holding periods for the funds are required.

In reviewing the volatility and correlation of both strategies, fund of funds have a beta of 0.1 to the S&P 500 and 0.03 to the Lehman Bond Aggregate Index, whereas multi-strats have 0.18 and –0.02, respectively. Standard deviation of the fund of funds index is 3.29 percent and for multi-strats is 3.94 percent. Thus, investors must evaluate the factors that drive the additional returns of multi-strats and determine whether the additional return is justified by the added leverage and exposure to sectors with reduced liquidity.

The search for alpha in the current market environment with moderate returns and the search for strategy diversification with larger hedge fund organizations may be the main forces driving investors toward multi-strats. On the other hand, the single manager blowup risk is the most compelling reason to invest in a fund of funds, where the risk is dramatically reduced for investors. In a fund of funds, each underlying hedge fund investment is viewed on its own terms; the liquidation of one underlying hedge fund investment does not affect the value of other investments held in the portfolio. Furthermore, the portfolio diversification employed by the fund of funds reduces the single entity risk by allocating to a broad range of strategies.

The Amaranth failure demonstrates precisely the additional risk level an investor in a multi-strat would have assumed. Let's suppose that a hypothetical fund of funds allocated to 20 underlying hedge fund managers, Amaranth included, each with equal weighting. Based on the reported Amaranth drawdown, the implied one-month drawdown at the portfolio level would have been approximately 3.25 percent if every other underlying hedge fund investment had been flat during that month. On the other hand, the Amaranth investor was shocked with an approximately 65 percent decline, offsetting several previously profitable years. The collapse of Amaranth has demonstrated that the diversification provided by a well-structured fund of funds can provide downside protection even with Amaranth exposure.

Allocations and Due Diligence

At the end of the day, the allocation decision is highly dependent on the due diligence process. Because of the varied risks inherent in fund of funds and multi-strats, the ensuing due diligence process for evaluating each investment vehicle is different. For example, additions to distressed or private placements, strategies that are relatively illiquid, or increases in arbitrage strategies, which typically use higher levels of leverage and may increase the risk of cross collateralization, will swiftly change the composition of the underlying multi-strat. As a result, the due diligence process requires a finely tuned understanding of each strategy and sufficient drilling down to the individual strategy level to evaluate each strategy independently and assess its impact on the overall portfolio. Sophisticated investors derive much comfort from their ability to spot the frauds, which are responsible for the majority of hedge fund failures.

Included in the assessment would be a review of the portfolio management, risk management, and investment teams. Strict attention must be paid to the infrastructure. Ultimately, success or failure depends on the management team, the risk/return objective, and the internal control systems. Thus, a strong back office that handles complex strategies and a legal staff that oversees investment activities are critical for the multi-strat, and to provide ample significant transparency to investors. While the largest and most sophisticated hedge fund operations are relatively lean organizations, even though they may boast hundreds or more of employees, the vast majority of funds are much smaller. Let's not forget that hedge funds are small businesses at their core and are generally run by the founding partners. There is no standard business model, and each fund has an enormous variation in structure, organization, and operational capability.

Review, Review, Review

In light of the latest chapters in the history of hedge funds, investors must review the due diligence process of the fund of funds and multi-strat that much closer to ensure that the following questions have been asked and satisfactorily answered:

- Is there sufficient diversification within the multi-strat?
- Is the risk management system central to the strategy or merely an afterthought to satisfy institutional investors' desires? Is the manager looking to improve the current system?
- Are all of the portfolio management, risk management, and trading personnel based in one location? If not, how is oversight conducted?
- Who has the responsibility for risk management within the organization, and is that authority independent? Can the risk manager take steps to correct deviations by portfolio managers from the stated policies?
- How are portfolio managers compensated? Is it based on the performance of each strategy or on the overall performance of the fund?
- Do investors pay additional fees for bonuses, rent, and other operating expenses?
- What type of risk reporting is provided to investors? How frequently is it reported, and from what date is it reported?

In our view, there are several lessons to be drawn from the Amaranth experience and other multi-strat meltdowns that should hopefully contribute to a more robust due diligence process. Large allocations to a big single-sector bet are always a reason of concern. Outsized returns from a single strategy should cause alarms to go off, given that most of the capital in the Amaranth strategy was dedicated to the natural gas bet at the time of the blowup. In this recent meltdown, as reported in the press, most of the assets that were advertised as "multi-strategy" were in fact primarily single-strategy dedicated to rising natural gas futures; the bet went out of kilter as gas prices dropped during September 2006. Many of the investors were large, blue-chip hedge fund investors, who presumably had done extensive due diligence and should have been able to understand the portfolio investments.

Realizing Risk

Misunderstanding or misrepresenting risk is an investor's nightmare. Rising volatility and returns at Amaranth should have been sufficient red flags to signal appropriate action. This case study provides a first-rate example of strategy drift. Investors must scrutinize the path that the manager took to arrive at the current strategy: was it organic growth or reaction to reduced opportunities within the original core strategy? In this failure, circumstances had changed a few years earlier, but many investors applauded as they were rewarded with higher absolute returns.

Outside the realm of due diligence, some other points are worth noting:

- The capital markets yawned at the Amaranth news, while investors sought to point fingers.
- Investors increased the call for greater transparency.
- Investors did not question outsized upside returns.
- While losses were incurred by some fund of funds, most fund of funds performed as expected with relatively minimal drawdowns.

Investors and consultants have always raised questions about the use and cost of fund of funds investing. With the trend toward investing in multi-strats, many investors are now raising new questions about the risk/reward profile and complexity of these programs. One path is apparent: investors must exercise superior judgment in the selection process for alternative managers, especially funds of funds and multi-strats. Even though risk is a fact of life in hedge fund investing, risk reduction should not be construed as the sole source of the generation of return. Risk must be identified and then controlled and monitored. On the other hand, if risk is eliminated, returns will disappear. While it would be anticipated that multi-strats will be subject to new and higher levels of due diligence and questioning, fund of funds will not be exempt from new inquiries either, especially those that have more opaque strategies.

If future trends follow those of the recent past, assets will continue to flow to both strategies. Investors must evaluate the higher returns, leverage, and volatility along with the reduced liquidity of most multi-strats compared with the lower return of fund of funds, but taking into account the independence of funds of funds to make changes to the portfolios, albeit at a slower pace. Despite the concerns about different fee structures, there is overwhelming justification for multi-strats in certain process-driven strategies such as fixed-income, derivatives, or event-driven. At the same time, fund of funds provide an approach for investors to gain exposure to a wide range of strategies managed by a team of professionals. As investors and gatekeepers look for investment opportunities in diversified hedge fund strategies, it is not a question of one or the other; both have a place in a diversified portfolio.

Ultimately, the real issue that comes out of this discussion is whether investors who moved or are contemplating a move from fund of funds to multi-strats or single hedge fund investments are capable of performing the necessary due diligence. By their very name, multi-strats evoke complexity—complexity of strategy, technology, and operations. Truly understanding the inner workings of a multi-strat is a much more difficult task than attaining a similar level of knowledge about a long/short equity hedge fund or a fund of funds. Investors need to think hard about multi-strat investing before embarking on it. Until investors can adequately evaluate the complexities of the multi-strat, they should stick with fund of funds. The marginal benefit in terms of increased return does not outweigh the cost of choosing the "wrong" multi-strat.

CHAPTER 14

How Fund of Funds Source Managers

Finding hedge fund managers for inclusion in a search for a potential investment by the fund of funds manager is a labor-intensive process, one that is underestimated by many. One of the first paths is for the research team to sift through the various databases and look for manager profiles that meet the investment parameters of the fund. Size, length of track record, performance results, and strategy are key ingredients for a "first cut" to determine whether a telephone call with the hedge fund is warranted and whether it is worthwhile to take the time to gain further understanding of the strategy.

WHERE MANAGERS COME FROM

Depending on the outcome, an on-site visit may occur next in the research process, if the manager believes that the hedge fund strategy is consistent with his or her fund's objectives.

Another starting point is the prime brokerage community. This is because hedge funds depend on the services of the prime broker. The prime broker offers a wide range of services for the hedge fund, including executing transactions, providing daily and monthly portfolio analytics, providing financing of securities positions through margin, and in some cases, actually providing office services and office space, including telecom, Internet, and Bloomberg access. One of the hallmarks of the prime brokers is to introduce hedge fund managers to a wide range of institutional, family office, and high net worth investors globally.

Montgomery Securities' prime brokerage division was a pioneer in creating the capital introduction capability in the mid-1990s by hosting a two-day event for hedge fund investors and Montgomery hedge fund clients.

Over 500 investors would sit in the ballroom of the Ritz Carlton in San Francisco for two days and listen to brief, rapid-fire manager presentations. The event was well coordinated by Montgomery, and each manager would discuss his strategy and team—but not performance results—in the allotted span of 12 to 15 minutes. Montgomery distributed a one-page summary of each manager's strategy and biography, and the brief talk and printed material provided prospective investors with an opportunity to decide whether a one-on-one meeting at the conference to gain additional insight was justified and, if so, to schedule a follow-up phone call or arrange for an on-site meeting.

Today, prime brokers provide various levels of capital introduction services created by the Montgomery model. The description of the prime brokers' services may range from capital introduction to capital solutions, but the objective is the same: to gain additional assets for the hedge fund managers. However, the prime brokers realize that all attendees (or all investors) who receive regular e-mails from them must indeed be accredited investors. Since fund of funds are the largest targeted investors for hedge fund managers, it is rare not to see one at these presentations.

Talk Is Good

One of the best methods of sourcing managers is good old-fashioned, unscientific word of mouth. Although the databases are useful tools, in most cases, the data is not complete. The databases do not include newly launched funds, which have no track records. They also do not report the many managers who choose not to provide performance results to a database. According to the PerTrac 2007 annual database study, "a significant number of hedge funds and fund of funds, about 12,000 in the eleven-database sample, appeared only in a single database."[1]

Given the limitations of databases, knowing the "right people" or having the "right" industry friends can be advantageous to finding not just new managers but good managers. One of the best sources of new managers is hedge fund managers themselves. Most managers will not admit to speaking to other managers, but they often meet at company presentations, known as road shows, with other investors. Hedge fund managers are always aware of who is trafficking in the stocks that they own or seek to own. They also know who the new managers are, especially if a new manager has a good pedigree. If the investor has a good relationship with some hedge fund managers, they can be a good source of information for new manager introductions.

The Inside Track

Fund of funds that have senior management teams with extensive relationships at both buy-side and sell-side firms have an edge. An alum of a Wall Street investment bank or a traditional long-only manager is able to gain an inside track in sourcing into both new and established managers that may be below the radar screen or unnamed road on the GPS. These organizations and professionals have an added advantage in being able to gain greater insight and references for due diligence to short-circuit the review and background process. The behemoth fund of funds may prefer not to openly discuss ideas and managers with other fund of funds—or with their own fund of funds investors—for fear of creating greater competition in the search for new managers. Smaller fund of funds, however, enjoy the cooperative spirit of collaboration and don't have the same "paranoia" about revealing a manager who may be up and coming.

Another source of identifying managers is simply to ask the managers in which the hedge fund investor is invested, "Do you know any new managers or have any buddies from your old shop that may look interesting for my firm to review." Many hedge fund managers are usually willing to provide insight. At the same time, the hedge fund manager who is not always receptive to giving free information may reply "Are there any new funds that you have seen that you like?" Or, "Have you met with the guys at such and such who just launched their fund?"

Third-party marketing firms have grown in popularity as a means for raising assets for hedge funds. If the marketing firm has an extensive database of hedge funds along with a referral network of financial industry professionals, the marketing firm should be able to provide a source of "below the radar screen" managers to market and introduce to fund of funds.

BLENDING METHODOLOGIES

At the end of the day, the most successful investors use a blend of all of these methods to identify new hedge fund managers for consideration and investment in their portfolios. The capital introduction sources are most effective for junior personnel within the fund of funds organization, whereas senior professionals with extensive and long-standing rolodexes are effective in reaching out to new managers from an established network of industry professionals and buddies. It takes time, it takes work, and it is something that needs to be taken seriously. Due diligence is not to be taken lightly. It is important to meet managers and do business with them, but it is also important to make sure they do what they say they are going to do, that their past records are not blemished, and that your money is safe. This, in the end, is the value proposition that fund of funds provide their investors and potential investors.

The question is, can these investment vehicles live up to investors' expectations and deliver? One of the scariest things to come out of the Madoff revelation is that many of the world's most respected fund of funds had invested so much if not all of their assets with one manager after telling investors that they were diversified. It remains to be determined what if anything these managers did wrong, and we are sure the courts will take some time to decide. Still, it is clear to us as outsiders looking in that these fund managers did not deliver on their value proposition.

CHAPTER 15

Conclusion

If you were not hiding under a rock, living in a cave, or staying on a island 300 miles west of Fiji during 2008 and early 2009, you probably believed that the hedge fund industry, the fund of funds industry, and Wall Street for that matter were all coming to end. That was the tone found in every article, news bulletin, and segment in the popular press. It seemed that without a doubt, the end was near or maybe even upon us. The collapse of Lehman and the fire sales of Bear Stearns and Merrill Lynch as well as the hundreds if not thousands of hedge funds that closed or went out of business have sent shockwaves through the system during this time. These actions have caused many to literally scratch their heads, wondering what, if any, future was left? Most were feeling this way even before the revelation about Madoff, which has only added more fuel to the fire and left many scared and frightened and asking why—and what comes next.

WHAT WE CAN AGREE ON

On more than one occasion in late 2007 and early 2008, the authors both agreed that there would always be a Bear Stearns. On more then one occasion in 2008, we both agreed that Lehman would be sold and would not go bankrupt, and on December 11, 2008, we both agreed that there was no excuse for being taken in by Madoff except for lack of due diligence and laziness. We were right about one of three.

Even with all of the aforesaid, the collapse of the banks along with Fannie Mae and Freddie Mac, the bailout of the auto industry, and the massive losses experienced by investors of all sizes, we both believe that hedge funds, fund of funds, and Wall Street will survive. More importantly, we believe that the United States and the rest of the world will survive the credit crisis and the economic crisis and that when we do come out of all this, we will be stronger and better equipped to weather such storms in the future.

To repeat, Wall Street is not dead, hedge funds are not dead, and fund of funds are not dead. In the coming weeks, months, and years, there will be continued consolidation, but mark our words: 5, 10, 15, and maybe even 20 years from now, there will be hedge funds, fund of funds, and some mythical place called Wall Street.

Continued Growth

In the near short term, such as by early 2010, we expect there to be renewed growth in new fund launches. We think that there will be consolidation and that many more traditional asset managers will begin to find ways, mostly through acquisition, to enter the alternative investment business. We believe that 2010 will be a year in which fund managers will develop new strategies. It will be a year in which managers retool, redevelop, rekindle their ability to perform in the marketplace, and grow bigger and bigger businesses.

Over the span of time this book was written, some funds have gone out of business because of their inability to perform and deal with liquidity issues. Some funds failed because they couldn't adapt to market changes. Some very large well-respected fund of funds, such as Fairfield Greenwich, Tremont, and Maxim were dealt death blows from their exposure to Madoff, while others have seen the need to drastically change their business models because investors were withdrawing whatever assets they had left.

This is okay. It is expected, it is needed, and it is what the market must do to fix itself and move on. These things work themselves out, which is, after all, what markets do. The year 2008 marked the first major retrenchment in the hedge fund industry.

Unfortunately, right now there seems to be an enormous amount of resentment between Wall Street and Main Street and everywhere in between. Hopefully, over the next year or so market conditions will improve and confidence will be restored. Time is a precious commodity, and it heals all wounds.

DON'T OVERLOOK DUE DILIGENCE

In reviewing the events of 2007–2008, one thing that we have all learned is that due diligence cannot be overlooked. It is a serious, meticulous, deliberate process. Madoff was exposed, not because he was caught in a due diligence review, but because the market forced his investors to withdraw and he could no longer feed his greed or need. While neither of us believes in the efficient market theory, it is clear that the efficiency of the market eventually caught up with Madoff. However, we believe that if Madoff's investors had performed comprehensive, in-depth due diligence, the fraud would have been exposed sooner. Clearly, the market allows for some funds to succeed and for some to fail. But for smart investors, this is not a way for anyone to make investment decisions, let alone use as an investment theory or plan.

This period of time has taught us that picking managers and understanding how money is managed and how wealth is created and opportunities are exploited is really important. There are no short cuts. We think that the single most important lesson that we all learned from the credit crisis, the Madoff and mini-Madoff frauds, and the rampant market volatility is that there is no substitute for good, solid, thoughtful due diligence, before and during the investment process.

Many investors learned, albeit too late, that many hedge fund managers had the same trade "on" and that when it went bad for one, it went bad for all. Many hedge fund managers were positioned in the same crowded trades. Portfolios were hit with significant losses because nobody could sell or get out in time or knew what many securities were worth. We do not know whether this could have been avoided, but we do know that many investors simply failed to do enough due diligence and frankly did not know what their investment managers were investing in. They simply believed in the manager and the returns and his or her experience and did not ask enough questions. Had they asked more or different questions, individual results would have been different, given that investors used so many funds that put on the same trade.

Due Diligence Helps Avoid Losses

Good due diligence would have caused some investors to reduce or avoid these losses. Had an investor taken the time to perform due diligence on Madoff, Agape, and others, they most likely would have weeded out the fraud, at least for themselves, maybe even for the masses. However, this is tough work; it is not glamorous, and it is quite a task. Madoff was, or shall we say is, a master manipulator. He preyed on emotions, greed, and envy and doing so allowed him to scam people for 30 years. Sure, Harry Markopolos and some others dropped dimes on Madoff over the years, but he was too good at his fraud to get caught. It is our responsibility as investors to perform the due diligence and always remember that if it seems too good to be true, it probably is. Think of how many billions of dollars would have been saved if the Madoff professional investors had practiced what they preached. The number is mind-boggling. In this instance, greed and envy proved not to be good for anyone.

There are many who are saying that they performed solid due diligence on Madoff and that they were simply scammed; that has been the defense of many feeders in response to investor lawsuits. The courts will decide whether these claims are true. We believe, however, that one of the ways to avoid making the same mistake twice, or even for the first time, is to focus on how a manager actually manages money. It is important during the due diligence process to ask how the investments are made—not simply what counterparties are used to execute the orders but the process behind the decision making. It is clear that everyone on "the Street" talks to each other. It is clear that many use some if not all of the same trading strategies, but you need to know this and you need to demand answers.

HINDSIGHT IS 20/20

The losses of 2007 and 2008 in the fund of funds industry showed us that some fund of funds turned out not to be as diversified or noncorrelated as they claimed, and that some fund of funds were not performing the level of due diligence required to avoid the problems experienced by others. The events of 2007 and 2008 demonstrated that strategies that were supposed to be noncorrelated were, in fact, correlated, and managers were exposed when the financial markets ceased to function. Trades were taking place, but not at rational levels. We believe that many fund of funds were not doing enough research into portfolio management and, as a result, their performance did not deliver the steady results they once provided. However, remember that one bad apple does not spoil a bunch, nor does it mean that the whole industry is spoiled. Quite the contrary; the fund of funds industry is alive and well and thriving in the post-meltdown world. That's the beauty of what the hedge fund industry is all about.

To use another produce analogy, if you peel back an onion, you find various layers, one after the other, until you finally reach the core. The same can be said for the fund of funds industry. Due diligence is the knife that lets you get to the core and allows you to find the right fund to fit your specific needs. The hedge fund industry is multi-layered as well. It truly offers something for every investor, regardless of the level of assets. Whether it's a multi-strategy fund, a separate account product, a sector-based or diversified fund of funds, or even many different single-manager products, the industry has something for everyone. The problem is figuring out the right fit. Never settle for unsophisticated due diligence or poor manager selection processes. They will do you in.

Playing Both Sides

Investors understand the value proposition of being able to go long and short the market. There is a simple truth that everybody who invests understands: markets don't always rise. One needs to be prepared to make money when markets rise as well as when they fall. Hedge funds are supposed to be the tool that delivers on that need and fulfills that promise. Fund of funds are supposed to create diversified portfolios of hedge funds that meet and exceed this expectation. What we learned in 2007 and 2008 is that many funds were unable to fulfill that promise or deliver on that need and, as a result, many fund of funds did not diversify their investment portfolios. In other cases, fund of funds managers invested in strategies that they did not fully understand; they just wanted to follow the crowd. This tells us one thing of great importance: we need greater levels of due diligence. We need to understand how money is managed on all levels. As investors, it's our responsibility to ask questions and get answers.

It's the responsibility of the money manager to provide good answers, and it's the responsibility of the investor to follow up and confirm whether or not those answers are true. This is not something that stops once the investment has been made. It is something that is ongoing and should be done continuously. Fund of funds get paid for postinvestment monitoring and review.

The lesson we've learned is not that not all hedge funds are bad, not all fund of funds are evil, and not all separately managed accounts are negative. What we've learned is that we must do due diligence. That is certainly not something that we learned yesterday or three years ago or one year ago; it's something that everybody has known. But because of the pace of growth in the industry and the pace of growth of those providing services to the industry, we think that due diligence has been lacking because people just did not feel they had to do the work. Now they know the consequences.

STILL, WE BELIEVE

On a going-forward basis, we think there's an opportunity to continue to achieve noncorrelated returns in hedge funds and fund of funds, and that each provides a unique and different service within the marketplace. The key is for investors to make sure that the funds to which they allocate deliver on the promise that they offer. Due diligence involves understanding how money is being managed, by whom, and who is checking on it to make sure the data is correct. It's about asking questions, getting answers, making sure the answers are understood, and making sure that what you see is really what you get. What we've learned since 2007 is that a lot of what we saw was not what we got and the only way to ensure that it is, going forward, is to have constant contact. It's a matter of following up, demanding meetings, and making withdrawals if you don't get the answers you want.

There are plenty of good money managers out there; the hard part is finding them. Once you find the ones you like, make sure you establish a good relationship with them. It is a lot of work, but it's your money so, to quote the Nike Corporation, "Just do it!"

It's important to realize that if you, as an individual or institutional investor, have a relatively modest amount of money to invest, somewhere less than $5 million, fund of funds are probably the best way to access the hedge fund industry. However, you still need to perform a substantially high level of due diligence. If you are an institutional investor, fund of funds can be even more important, because you are able to offload a significant amount of the work to trained professionals as opposed to doing the work yourselves. Again, you still need to be constantly performing due diligence.

We don't believe that fund of funds or single-manager strategies are the end-all or be-all for everybody; nothing is. Everybody is unique. Everybody has different issues. Everybody has different wants. Everybody has different needs. And frankly, everybody needs different money managers and different strategies.

The only thing that determines whether the right investment choice is for a particular portfolio instead of someone else's is that the investor believes the manager will deliver on the promise made in the marketing pitch, in the meetings, and in the performance once the money has been invested. It's not saying, "Well you're a square hole, so we'll put the square peg in you." No, it's quite the opposite. It's finding out what actually fits instead of just trying to fit something to what you need. When you make an investment, you must make sure that it is the right investment for your specific needs.

THE ANSWER ON FEES

People have asked us over the past 12 months as we've been researching and writing this book, "Where do you see fees going? What do you see happening?" While we both agree that fees are fees and some funds are able to charge some fees while other funds aren't, we also believe that fees for the most part will remain under pressure as managers react to the changing sentiment and poor results of 2008. As funds continue to try to gather assets, they will offer sale prices or discounts—a mistake, in our opinion. Once the price is lowered, it most likely will never go up. Discounting to gather assets sets a level of worth and puts a lot of pressure on the manager. After all, in the wake of the fallout of 2008, managers are now required to build out more robust infrastructures including managed accounts, and that is costly. Do the math—lower fees, higher expenses. It sounds as though either higher returns are needed or more assets. By discounting, the manager may take risks that he would not normally take in order to achieve higher returns. Possibly, the manager has decided that he really wants to be in the asset-gathering business and manage for mediocrity.

On the fund of funds fee front, we believe that fees will also remain under pressure. There may be some funds that eliminate or reduce the incentive fee in lieu of a higher management fee. Investors need to pay attention to the manager and how he is managing the fund assets. Separate account management platforms will increase as investors demand asset pricing verification, security collateral protection, and greater transparency.

We also believe that regulatory oversight is good and should be enhanced. Hedge funds increasingly are being bound by rules that make them more like mutual funds in terms of standardized reporting (i.e., forcing managers to be Registered Investment Advisors), and this is also a good thing. The problem we have is that for the regulations to be meaningful and protect the investors, they must be enforced. The regulators seemed to completely drop the ball when it came to monitoring, investigating, and dealing with one of the largest frauds of all time. Like many others, we have a real problem with what happened with Madoff and other frauds. We want the regulators to regulate, and we want Congress to make sure that the government agencies are doing their jobs. Regulations aren't worth much more than the paper they are printed on if nobody enforces them. We believe that regulation that is done simply for window-dressing purposes is pointless.

Our goal is not to call for more or less regulation; we want investors to make their own decisions with good information. Our goal is for you to understand that you need to make an educated decision, a decision that is right for you. If you make a good decision that you continually monitor, you most likely will achieve your portfolio aim. There may be losses; that is okay, it is to be expected. However, you have no one to blame but yourself if you don't do the work. So do the work. Check with the auditor. Pay for a background report. Understand how the hedge fund or fund of funds fits in your portfolio. Ask questions. It's your money, and you need to pay attention to how it is being managed.

Epilogue

Turning Points

As we started our book, we began with the December 2008 date that has forever altered the landscape of investing and certainly of the hedge fund industry. On the other hand, several significant dates in history have created unparalleled economic opportunities because of the changing geopolitical climate at those historic times:

- **May 4, 1904.** With the support of President Theodore Roosevelt, construction began on the Panama Canal.
- **May 6, 1954.** President Dwight D. Eisenhower signed the Federal-Aid Highway Act of 1954 creating the Interstate Highway System.
- **May 25, 1962.** President John F. Kennedy announced an ambitious effort to send an American astronaut to the moon by the end of the decade.

A review of the historical background of these major ground-breaking projects shows that national security was the driving force behind each achievement. The construction of the Panama Canal was driven by the need to quickly move the U.S. Navy fleet from the Atlantic to the Pacific Ocean and to avoid the two months needed to travel around Cape Horn at the tip of South America—a 12,000-mile journey. The Interstate Highway System was created during the post-Korean, Russian Cold War era to allow troops to move quickly to different parts of the country in the event of a military attack. President Kennedy, in an announcement before a joint session of Congress, announced the space program to "catch up and overtake" the Soviet Union in the "space race." The common theme connecting each of these major historic events was national security.

Although much less publicized, July 11, 2008 also marks a noteworthy date in the history of the nation and serves as an inflection point for nations around the world: crude oil peaked at $147. With the United States fully engaged in a presidential campaign, a new term surfaced in the national debate—energy security. Homeowners, drivers, truckers, and industrial users everywhere were suffering from record-high oil prices. In the United States, both major presidential candidates increased the rhetoric and created a heightened sense of awareness of the economic stress created by rising energy prices. Both of the candidates also expressed their commitments to invest in alternative and renewable energy as well as to develop a cap and trade market system to reduce greenhouse gases. The idea was simple: the planet was suffering, the economy was suffering, and something needed to be done. Discussions surrounding the use of alternative, cheaper, safer fuel solutions were now becoming part of both the national and international debate. Alternative energy became part of the global lexicon and is starting to create new financial opportunities for investors worldwide.

WHAT IS CLIMATE CHANGE?

Scientists have been evaluating the impact of climate change and global warming for several decades. However, the spike in crude oil prices in July of 2008 caused many to take this issue more seriously than ever before. Interest in alternative energy sources seemed to surpass the levels noted during the gasoline shortages of the 1970s.

Scientists' estimates of the increase in the Earth's temperature range from 1.8 to 4.0 degrees Celsius (or 3.2 to 7.2 degrees Fahrenheit) by the year 2100. Anyone who reads a newspaper, watches National Geographic, or simply pays attention to global warming issues, should be aware that the Arctic Cap is shrinking, glaciers are melting, and Australia and parts of Africa have been suffering from a year-long drought.

According to Rick Smolan and Jennifer Erwitt in *Blue Planet Run*, "Two-thirds of the world's population will suffer from water shortages by 2025."[1] That's 5.3 billion people.

Climate change is largely caused by human emissions, driven by economic growth, of greenhouse gases (GHG) into the earth's atmosphere. This is a process that has been accelerating since 1750, with the onset of the Industrial Revolution. Many believe that the resulting impact on our climate is significant. Climate-sensitive sectors of the global economy, including agriculture, fishing, forestry, and tourism are all experiencing some form of impact. Damage to coastal areas due to sea-level rise has been documented, as have increased energy expenditures for heating and cooling. With rising temperatures, we are also likely to see nonmarket impacts, such as the spread of infectious diseases, massive loss of biodiversity, and the relocation of hundreds of millions of people due to rising sea levels, loss of water resources, and increasing desertification.

Countries around the world banded together in 1997 to adopt the Kyoto Protocol (Kyoto). Kyoto, which went into effect in 2005, was intended to reduce greenhouse gas emissions to 1990 levels by 2012. This has been recognized as a first attempt to decrease greenhouse gases and a first step toward acceptance by industrialized countries of the need to make the world a better place. In an attempt to curtail these emission practices, world leaders met in Kyoto, Japan in 1997 and negotiated a treaty that would lead industrialized countries to make a collective cut in emissions. The Kyoto treaty aimed to cut emissions by 5.2 percent globally over the period 2008–2012, compared with the base year 1990. The goal was to stabilize the concentrations of six greenhouse gases in the atmosphere by putting an individual cap on countries' emissions, which would effectively put a price on carbon by limiting the supply. The agreement would be implemented once it had at least 55 signatories, covering at least 55 percent of global emissions.[2]

The United States, which was the world's largest emitter at the time,[3] was initially very much involved in the negotiations, but the Senate passed a 95–0 vote against committing to any agreement if it "would result in serious harm to the economy of the United States." The United States was opposed to the differentiation of responsibilities under the Protocol, saying it would put developed nations at a disadvantage.[4]

Congressional leadership under both President Clinton and President Bush declined to support Kyoto, but a sea change occurred in the middle of the presidential campaign season in 2008. Following Barack Obama's election and with a high level of support in both the House and the Senate, as of mid-2009 it seemed as though legislation aimed at reducing the emissions of greenhouse gases in the United States was on track. Several facts are clear:

- World populations are growing, and affluence is increasing in many parts of the globe, putting greater stress on natural resources.
- The rise in the concentration of CO_2 in the atmosphere is raising the heat of the Earth with catastrophic impact.
- There is a shortage of water globally and an increase in contaminated water.
- There is a growing awareness of global warming and a resulting increase in carbon reduction strategies.

On the other hand, the causes of several phenomena are not as clear, including the increase in the number and severity of hurricanes to strike the

Gulf of Mexico in 2005. Storms on both sides of the equator in the Pacific also indicate that something is happening in the Earth's environment, but nobody really knows the cause of these changes. While the science is not clear—we are financial professionals and not climatologists—the evidence points to climate change.

Europe and parts of Asia have been pioneers in supporting climate change rules and have been approaching this problem over the past decade. Although California has been on the forefront of dealing with this issue since the 1980s, the rest of the United States has delayed implementation of aggressive programs to address climate change. However, all of the delays or inaction changed in 2008 during the presidential campaign, which brought a newly heightened sense of awareness. Following President Obama's inauguration and his immediate addresses to Congress, agreement on the need to stabilize (and ultimately reduce) CO_2 emissions has started to swing in a positive direction.

RECENT PROGRESS

Ever since the United States retreated as a major force in the international environmental community, many people perceived the world's efforts to curb greenhouse gas emissions to be at a standstill. However, after facing growing opposition both at home and abroad, the United States finally agreed to let the discussions move forward during the meeting in Bali in 2007 that was described by some observers as a U-turn in U.S. negotiations.[5] At the meeting, the assembly acknowledged the research findings and observations and concluded that evidence for the warming of the planet was "unequivocal" and that delays in reducing emissions increased the risks of "severe climate change impacts." This led to the "Bali Action Plan," which is a two-year process for finalizing a binding agreement during the negotiations set to take place in Copenhagen in December 2009. The goal of the Copenhagen meeting is to reach an agreement that can replace the Kyoto Protocol when it expires in 2012.

One of the first positive signs of a new outlook is the proposed legislation that is working its way through Congress for adoption in 2009. As new programs are signed into law, segments of the capital markets are poised for long-term growth and development that may far exceed the technological boom of the 1990s.

Renewable energy, including wind, solar, and hydropower, and new technologies, including smart grids, electric metering, and improved usage of electric products, are just a few of the revolutionary changes that are starting to take place. *Smart grids* are modernizing the way in which energy is generated and used. It improves both energy efficiency and the integration of renewable energy with the grid, but it also requires synergy between the utilities, the consumers, and ultimately the regulators. Smart grids shift energy generated by solar panels and wind to the utilities and incorporate demand management that can be shifted during peak and non-peak usage periods. Sensors and meters can detect fluctuations and disturbances that signal trouble spots in areas that need to be isolated.

Clean technology includes some of the following sectors for investment:

Alternative energy: solar, wind, hydro, tidal, geothermal, and low-carbon power

Energy distribution: fuel cells, flywheels, transformers, cabling, grid infrastructure, and turbines

Energy efficiency: lighting improvement such as LEDs, green-building efficiency, thermal protection using glass, energy management systems, increased use of rails, and remote metering

Waste recycling: water and wastewater filtering, infrastructure, pipes and filters, and desalinization of water

Other segments: weather, agriculture, biofuels, and fertilizer and seeds.

Billions of dollars are being spent on research for electric vehicles and for technologies to make automobiles more efficient and less expensive to operate. President Obama has announced new fuel standards for auto emissions that will significantly raise fuel economy by 2016.[6]

WHERE IS THE OPPORTUNITY?

On the education front, a "green wave" is appearing all over America. In Daniel Esty and Andrew Winston's book, *Green to Gold*, the authors point to companies that have recognized how to incorporate environmental strategies into the daily operation of business. GE's Jeffrey Immelt announced "ecomagination," and Wal-Mart has committed to reducing energy usage by using renewable energy sources and improving the efficiency of its massive fleet of vehicles. Early adopters of the green wave who recognize and understand climate change and understand that financial institutions can work hand in hand with climate change efforts to reduce the stress on the Earth should benefit financially as well as environmentally.[7]

Renewable energy is in an early growth stage. Globally, cumulative installed capacity is increasing; Europe, Japan, and China have been leading the way for several years, and North America is now starting to catch up. Global policies are becoming synchronized with the promotion of renewable and alternative energy sources. Many new power projects are being started that rely on renewable energy, including wind and solar, while reducing reliance on fossil fuels.

As investors look for new opportunities for investments, the green sector appears to be poised for a bright future with many new industries and companies being created. During the technology bubble of the 1990s, which focused on the birth of the Internet and hundreds of successful companies, the market was littered with failures that focused on "eyeballs and clicks," new search engines, or home Internet grocery delivery companies. The world of 2009 and beyond, however, is different. It's about energy security and the stewardship of our planet.

Role of Hedge Funds

Hedge fund managers seem to be on the cutting edge when it comes to developing strategies; they appear best equipped to capitalize on the global change and inefficient markets. Many new manufacturing companies will be born out of these initiatives, including manufacturers of solar panels or thin films that offer higher levels of efficiency and companies that make products to monitor or replace 40-year-old electric transformers. In addition, many companies will not have access to the capital markets for new financing for product development and will fail, or using a term coined during the tech bubble, companies will "run out of runway." Opportunities exist on the long side of the market with new and innovative companies, but also with shorts of companies that have poor products and weak balance sheets.

The green wave, in reality, has created the newest emerging market for environmental and financial investing. Historically, new capital flows for clean technology and renewable energy have come from the venture capital community, and once again, we are seeing a convergence in the hedge fund industry. In the past, venture capital projects have had a long life, often approaching 10 years. With the credit implosion of 2008–2009 and banks moving to the sidelines, many projects that require shorter time frames, such as project finance for biofuel or solar installations, have attracted specialized hedge funds to deploy capital with higher risk/reward profiles than traditional investments.

For hedge funds, once again it is the perfect storm in 2009: high energy prices, increased environmental momentum, misunderstanding of strategies and products, and absence of traditional financing for many projects and new technologies. Still, despite a global slowdown, energy demand is expected to rise as global economies recover and commodity prices are expected to rise once again.

Cutting-Edge Strategies

One of the first strategies for hedge fund opportunities is carbon emission trading. The Kyoto Protocol was implemented with the intention of creating a system that would allow the European Union (EU) to have a pricing system in place at the beginning of the Kyoto compliance period. The EU Emissions Trading Scheme (ETS) started trading emissions in 2005 under a three-year trial period. placing over 12,000 emitting facilities in the EU under an absolute cap of CO_2 emissions. Under this scheme, target emission levels are established for individual countries, and their industries are then issued tradable emission allowances called European Union Allowances (EUAs). If any market participant exceeds its targets, fines of 100 per ton can be avoided only by buying EUAs under the flexible mechanisms. This fine also serves as an implicit ceiling for the price, since at this point it would be cheaper to pay the penalty than to buy credits at a higher price.[8]

The total carbon market is generally divided into two sectors: the compliance market, which is regulated under the Kyoto Protocol, and the voluntary market. The voluntary market trades in offsets that are not mandated by regulation but often mimic the flexible mechanisms under the Kyoto. The participants in the voluntary markets are often motivated by either corporate sustainability and green marketing initiatives or precompliance efforts in preparation for upcoming legislation. While most participants in both markets are compliance buyers (e.g., utilities, manufacturers, and other industrial users), financial participants are also actively involved in the trading of emission offsets.

The main part of the voluntary markets is made up of two segments: an over-the-counter (OTC) market and the Chicago Climate Exchange (CCX). The CCX currently accounts for a significant amount of the total volume in the voluntary market. The CCX is a membership-based trading system for emissions, the members of which voluntarily agree to legally binding emission reductions that vary depending on the type of membership. According to the CCX, members with considerable GHG emissions commit to a target that reduces their emissions by 6 percent by 2010, compared to a baseline calculated either from the members' average annual emissions 1998 through 2001 or over the single year 2000, depending on when they joined the exchange.[9]

The OTC market is made up of bilateral trades that take place outside an exchange; this market is not as standardized as the CCX, and there is not much publicly available information. According to a survey taken by

Ecosystem Marketplace and *New Carbon Finance*, 79 percent of the buyers in the voluntary OTC market were private businesses, and non-governmental organizations accounted for 13 percent. The same report stated that about one-third of the offsets purchased in 2007 were for speculative or investment purposes, whereas the majority were for marketing and corporate sustainability purposes.[10]

A CLIMATE OF GREEN STIMULUS

As global economies slipped into recession during 2008, governments decided that they needed to seek solutions to pull their economies out of the financial malaise. With China and the United States leading the way, spending on a massive scale was determined to be an efficient method to get the economic engines jump-started.

The initial amounts of spending on renewable and clean technologies are staggering: $223 billion in China,[11] $100 billion in the United States,[12] $16 billion in Japan,[13] and $325 billion in the EU. Governments are approaching the credit meltdown and economic contraction with a large dose of medicine to "stimulate" their economies, deal with climate change, and reduce energy insecurity. China is spending its capital on rails, grids, and water infrastructure, and U.S. spending will be directed to renewable energy resources, including wind and solar, building efficiencies, mass transit, and grids.

As global governments shifted gears, policymakers reacted to the sharp rise in energy prices, recognizing that a low-carbon economy could create jobs at a time when unemployment was rising. From November 2008 to January 2009, over 20 countries in Asia, Europe, and North America passed stimulus packages totaling $2.8 trillion, with significant amounts earmarked for green projects. All of this is being accomplished in time to prepare for the year-end 2009 Copenhagen meeting to extend the Kyoto Protocol and to allow for the stimulus to stimulate.[14]

Climate Change Is a Game Changer

Shortly after the Obama administration came into power, the Energy and Commerce Committee of the U.S. House of Representatives under the leadership of Rep. Henry Waxman began work on comprehensive energy legislation that includes reducing greenhouse gas emissions. For the first time, the United States appears ready to adopt a cap and trade system of allocating and selling pollution permits from large industrial sources. In anticipation of the year-end 2009 Copenhagen meeting to advance the next phase of Kyoto, the House of Representatives moved forward with a new plan to soften the blow for consumers and commercial users with a big, first step: passage of the American Clean Energy Security Act of 2009. Shortly after the July 2009 passage, the Senate began its debate.

According to Bloomberg pricing, on July 6, 2009, carbon traded at $1.00 on the CCX, where trading is voluntary, but it currently trades at €13.05 (or $18.27) in London, where compliance requirements are mandatory. The difference in pricing is due to several factors, including voluntary and/or mandatory requirements in different geographical regions. One of the other major reasons for pricing differences is the low level of liquidity in the U.S. markets. Not many firms are actively trading carbon, and that contributes to the inefficiency of the markets. Most of the trading participants are compliance buyers that practice buy and hold, with few financial players that are generally more active traders of securities. As a result, bid/offer spreads may be wide, and large amounts of either buying or selling will move market prices widely.

The other key driver of short-term carbon prices is politics, and politics can be challenging to predict or to model. Two things to keep in mind:

- Carbon is still relatively illiquid, indicating that it might be challenging to liquidate large positions without causing significant price disruptions.
- There is still uncertainty regarding whether the multiple exchanges will consolidate and which standard of carbon permits will prevail and what the final form of legislation will be in the United States.

For hedge fund investors, this uncertainty clearly presents a new opportunity as investors seek to capitalize on the arbitrage that exists or for investors who seek to make a directional bet about the future of carbon prices. As previously discussed, uncertainty and inefficient markets have been the cornerstones of hedge fund investing, creating opportunity for astute hedge fund managers. While there is not yet a centralized database to indicate the number of hedge funds active in emission trading, we believe, based on our research, that the number of active trading firms is probably less than two dozen, creating a unique prospect for investors.

In addition to the position trading or portfolio arbitrage of the actual carbon permits and other emissions, the global equity markets present opportunities for investors with hedge fund managers who are able to establish long or short positions in the global companies that have manufactured products that address the energy policy changes required by the United States and the world. Managers who employ this strategy seek to take equity positions in companies that constitute the entire value chain of a particular renewable energy source. For example, generating wind energy requires manufacturing turbine parts, assembling turbines, and operating the actual wind farm. After doing fundamental analysis of companies operating within each sector of a specific value chain, managers will establish long positions in companies that provide the most attractive risk/reward profile or short positions in companies with weak or flawed products.

Technological progress dictates that many of today's technologies may well become obsolete tomorrow, or prices may drop dramatically. Ongoing scientific debate is focused on which technologies are more efficient and likely to prevail. Therefore, companies that might have significant growth prospects today may find that their technology has become outdated and costly later on. Managers that exercise extreme caution when performing financial valuations and modeling must also have a high level of expertise to analyze the individual companies, and they should benefit from these unexplored and unexploited opportunities. On the other hand, stock prices that reflect extraordinary, unrealistic growth expectations may be subject to wide and downward price swings. In short, opportunities are present for investors looking to participate and capitalize on the new green wave niche.

As in the technology bubble of the late 1990s, when new technologies were developed, there will be both winners and losers. Thus, many hedge fund managers seek to add short positions to their in portfolio in order to add alpha. Depending on their portfolio objectives, many hedge fund managers will seek to profit from companies that may fail due to inefficient or costly technology or weak management teams and weak balance sheets. As discussed previously in connection with the convergence of the public and private markets, many promising renewable energy companies are in the developmental stage and are privately held. In select situations, hedge fund managers might choose to invest in private placements in expectation of upside potential with liquidity events, including future initial public offerings. In most instances, these illiquid investments are held in a specialized class or a side pocket.

With the recent growth of the green and renewable industry during the past few years, new equity indexes have been developed to measure the performance of the underlying companies. One of the most well-known indexes is the Wilderhill Clean Energy Index (ECO), started December 30, 2002, which as of the end of the third quarter of 2009 tracked 52 global companies, including First Solar, a manufacturer of solar modules; Yingli Green Energy, a China-based manufacturer of solar modules; and American Superconductor, an energy technology company that manufactures electronic convertors. For investors seeking to trade ETFs rather than individual stocks, the Powershares Wilderhill Clean Energy Portfolio was created as an ETF to mirror the ECO index.

DON'T FORGET!

In reviewing new strategies, don't forget what we've already discussed. We are enthusiastic proponents of environmental strategies based on sustainability along with the unique opportunities available for early adopters and investors, but recognize that this sector may exhibit higher volatility. While there is a great benefit to investing in many of these new companies through a diversified portfolio of renewable and clean energy hedge fund strategies, the overall due diligence and research must be subject to the same standards that we have previously detailed. No one gets special dispensation just because of the benefit of sustainability. With new managers popping up and professing expertise in technology—or as one manager stated, "I was a biotech analyst for many years"—there are no shortcuts to investing in this space. The underlying managers may have specialized expertise in research, investment banking, or related industries that include energy, science, or trading or financing commodities.

Remember this: we do not want to invest in science projects. We are looking to invest with proven managers with proven skill sets who understand how the markets function. We are still looking to invest with good old-fashioned hedge fund mercenaries whose interests are aligned with those of the investors.

As we have researched the new green hedge fund space, including carbon trading funds, we have been able to identify over 100 hedge funds globally. Clearly, this represents a relatively small portion of hedge fund assets. The good news is that this developing and emerging market has not attracted much attention from the hedge fund community; this is a positive for hedge fund investors who may have tired of seeing the same ideas recycled by many managers. Although many of these funds provide project finance, carbon arbitrage, or trade 1,000 companies globally with both long and short positions, the new locomotive now pulling the train is climate change. In the United States, the train is starting to move—with greater efficiency and fewer emissions.

Given the smaller number of managers active in this space, the selection process has become even more critical. The deployment of the 2009 U.S. Stimulus Act will provide hundreds of billions of dollars to many companies as well as other global governments providing billions of green stimulus, but vigilance in the due diligence process is critical. In spite of the urge to get ahead of the crowd with green investing—or any new strategy, for that matter—caution is still required.

Appendix

DISCLAIMER: THIS MATERIAL IS TO BE USED ONLY AS AN ILLUSTRATION AND NOT FOR PREPARATION OF DOCUMENTS; NOR DOES IT IN ANY WAY CONSTITUTE LEGAL OR ANY OTHER FORM OF ADVICE.

STANDARD DUE DILIGENCE: (NAME) FUND

General Information

(1) **Please describe all the strategies you deploy in the (NAME) Fund (e.g., fixed income arb, convertible arb, event arb, long/short equities, etc.).** The core tenet of (NAME)'s investing strategy is relative value investing. In general, relative value investing in the (NAME) Fund involves the purchase of undervalued securities and hedging with fair value or overvalued securities. Regardless of the specific asset class, this is the core of the strategy. Current asset classes involved in the multi-strategy portfolio include Mortgage Arbitrage, Global Fixed Income Arbitrage, Convertible Bond Arbitrage, Event Driven Arbitrage, and Capital Structure Arbitrage. The asset allocation is dynamic, dependent upon current market conditions and opportunities in specific asset classes. The expectation is that the multi-strategy fund will have an improved risk/return profile, since the fund has a wide investment universe and a large set of markets to explore for hedging purposes.

(2) **Do you operate in all markets globally or do you limit yourself to specific markets?** Globally.

(3) **What do you consider the revenue prospects to be for the strategies you exploit?** We anticipate a Libor + xxx basis points to LIBOR + xxx basis points annual return profile with a minimum of volatility and drawdown. The strategy is designed to be market neutral, so market conditions should have limited impact. There is no guarantee of performance.

(4) **Please describe for each of your major funds, their name, whether they are on- or offshore, the strategies followed, and fees.** x% Management fee accrued and paid monthly with a xx% Incentive fee accrued monthly and paid annually.

- (NAME) Fund, LP and Convertible (NAME) Fund, Ltd.: with onshore and offshore spokes. Convertible Securities Arbitrage.
- (NAME) Global Fund LLC and (NAME) Global Fixed Fund Ltd.: Global Sovereign debt, GSE, MBS, ABS, and corporate debt relative value trading.
- (NAME) Fund LLC and (NAME) Fund Ltd.: with onshore and offshore spokes.
- (NAME) Global Fund LLC and (NAME) Global Fund Ltd.: with onshore and offshore spokes. Directional value/correlation positioning fund.

A. Investment Process

(1) **How do you identify profit opportunities in each of your strategies? What quantitative tools do you use?** In each of the strategies, we perform intense analysis of individual securities, identify undervalued securities, and develop hedging plans. The combination of the security and its hedge are stress-tested to assure the efficacy of the hedge. Risk Management reviews portfolios to assure compliance with fund guidelines. Additionally, stress-testing is an ongoing process in which we monitor possible changes in market conditions. (NAME) possesses a rare combination of technology, experience, and discipline, all of which are utilized in the investment process. All quantitative tools have been developed internally, and are subject to constant review and improvement.

(2) **What is your investment time horizon?** Typically, strategy horizons from entry to exit range between x and x months.

(3) **Risk management: a) Please describe the key risks to each strategy (e.g., interest rates, prepayment, credit, etc.).** Risks are detailed more fully in the Private Placement Memorandum of the fund and investors should consult this for a more complete description.

(i) Mortgage-backed securities: Risk in any strategy is determined by five factors:

- **Interest rate risk.** Portfolios are managed on a duration-neutral basis. Consequently, portfolios will have minimal exposure to movement in interest rates.
- **Yield curve risk.** Mortgage securities may have specific and varying exposures to certain parts of the yield curve. Key rate duration is

performed on all securities (and is part of the hedging process), which enables (NAME) to negate this exposure.

- **Spread risk.** As (NAME) Mortgage Arbitrage portfolios will be long mortgage securities and generally short something other than mortgage securities, mortgage basis risk is present. However, diligent security selection is one of the many techniques designed to minimize this risk.
- **Convexity and volatility risk.** Convexity and volatility exposures are hedged by offsetting instruments and options strategies.
- **Liquidity risk.** In general, under certain circumstances, repurchase markets may slow down and cause liquidity constraints. Consequently, term financing arrangements are pursued, which better match the investment cycle and are largely protected against short-term liquidity issues. Additionally, multiple borrowing relationships are utilized to diversify away dependence on any specific lender.

(ii) Global fixed income arbitrage strategy:

- **Interest rate risk.** Portfolios are managed on a duration-neutral basis. Consequently, portfolios are structured to minimize exposure to movement in interest rates.
- **Yield curve risk.** All fixed-income securities may have specific and varying exposures to certain parts of the yield curve. Key rate duration is performed on all securities (and is part of the hedging process), which enables (NAME) to negate this exposure.
- **Liquidity risk.** In general, under certain circumstances, repurchase markets may slow down and constrain liquidity. Consequently, term financing arrangements are pursued, which better match the investment cycle and are largely protected against short-term liquidity issues. Additionally, multiple borrowing relationships are utilized to diversify away dependence on any specific lender.
- **Spread risk.** The global fixed-income arbitrage strategy is based on spread relationships of correlated instruments. The security selection process isolates advantageous situations, so the risk from adverse spread movements is minimal.
- **Strategy correlation risk.** The portfolio is stress-tested under varying market environments to assure the expected minimal correlations across the portfolio. Positions will be added to minimize ongoing risk.

(iii) Convertible debt arbitrage strategy:

- **Spread risk.** Convertible arbitrage comprises unique security positions, which may narrow or widen relative to Libor or government bonds depending on market conditions. "Beta" hedges on the portfolio including the arrangement of credit-oriented swaps mitigate the potential spread risk.

- **Convexity risk.** Convexity is hedged by offsetting instruments and listed options.
- **Volatility risk.** In general, convertibles are long the conversion option, therefore in most circumstances, there is long volatility. This is managed through diversification and trading of listed options.
- **Issuer risk.** This is subsumed in the spread and volatility risks, but it is critical that solid fundamental and credit analysis guide investment decisions are used to minimize single-name or sector-specific risks.

(iv) Event-driven strategy: Risk in any event-driven transaction is determined by several factors, some of which include:

- government and regulatory agency intervention risk,
- fundamentals of the companies, their balance sheets, and other relevant information,
- general market conditions that affect deal prices, the collar bands being exceeded, etc.,
- appearance and effect of other interested parties on the deal table such as competing acquirers, consumer groups, and active shareholders.
- **b) Please detail the investment process from trade assessment, execution, and risk management.**

Core Exposure Management:
(NAME) attempts to:

(1) Minimize fund exposures to the outright level and direction of interest rates (if it is a relative-value/arbitrage investment vehicle).
(2) Minimize fund exposures to the outright level and direction of equity prices (if it is a relative-value/arbitrage investment vehicle).
(3) Control drawdowns and help preserve capital by running and analyzing risk exposure reports, stress tests, and managing correlations. Traders must monitor and judiciously manage, and if necessary, liquidate positions whose realized performance profile does not match prior analysis, payoff criteria, expectations, or else changes in market fundamentals change the position's or portfolio's original risk-return characteristics.

The Process of Front–Line Investment Analysis and Risk Management:
The process of risk assessment and management ranges from trade identification, to execution, to trade risk management, and through to operations. This process is continuous and proceeds generally as follows:

(1) Dimensions of anomaly/dislocation/arbitrage/investment opportunity relative to market information and events, and economic or mathematically determinable relationships are identified and analyzed.

(2) Dimensions of arbitrage opportunities relative to historical and experiential data; core economic/technical/market reason for the existence of arbitrage opportunity are identified and analyzed; estimates of temporal duration and persistence of arbitrage opportunity are obtained; and probabilistic and economic assessment of further movements in the securities is evaluated.
(3) The correlation of a proposed investment position with current portfolio of investments is determined. Investment opportunities, which reduce the correlation risk in the portfolio, have a significantly higher likelihood of being executed.
(4) Availability of hedge instruments, which allow for the isolation and extraction of the relative value opportunity and minimize exposure to other market risks is identified and calculated.
(5) Financing (e.g., repurchase agreements) markets, liquidity, and opportunity are reviewed. For example, liquidity of relevant securities and execution channels ensuring optimality vis-à-vis transaction costs is analyzed.
(6) An exit strategy in terms of profit-taking and loss minimization is developed.
(7) Ensuring security type, trade sizing, and risk exposures do not exceed any regulatory limits or limits specified in investment strategy guidelines.
(8) Trader/Portfolio Manager performs trade checking at the system input stage.
(9) Subject to the guidelines established by the Risk Management team, the portfolio management team's judgment and analysis also plays a role in the assessment of overall risk and its management; that is, the sum total of portfolio manager assessments of all available information, statistical estimates and general/specific market conditions are vital tools in accurately assessing trade and portfolio risk.
(10) Portfolio management teams are held primarily responsible for trade input into the operations system. Therefore, portfolio management teams must check out trade ticket entries.
(11) All portfolio management teams must adhere to any limits set by Risk Management at all times.

Summarizing, at the portfolio level, factors such as interstrategy correlation, size of the exposure, and fit for the portfolio are to be considered in order to ensure that the portfolio does not have any one-way positions across the portfolio, and the diversification across strategies is maintained. Existing positions may be modified depending on the opportunities in the marketplace and assessments of different, portfolio-specific diversification requirements.

From experience and investment philosophy, portfolio managers are instructed when warranted to be relatively quick in exiting losing positions.

Finally, tail event and systemic risks must be monitored and managed through (a) purchase of options in the tails, (i.e., options which cover extreme market moves); (b) purchase of default protection for credit exposures; (c) overall portfolio structure.

Operations:

The firm has an Operations division whose functions range from:

(1) Trade verification and checkout.
(2) Day-to-day operation cash-flow management and securities handling duties.
(3) Delivery of risk and position reports and p&l's to desk and principals.
(4) Coordination with technology and systems division for ensuring appropriate operational management of all relevant operational functions.

Oversight Function of Risk Management Policies/Protocols: All portfolio management teams have a joint morning meeting daily, chaired by the firm's Chief Investment Officer, where they report and discuss major positions, major exposures, market developments, and impact on every portfolio. The firmwide risk-management team evaluates all positions and monitors their progress to:

(a) Ensure adherence to prescribed regulatory and investment guidelines.
(b) Help define risk exposure levels, in consultation with senior portfolio managers, and ensure that these levels are maintained (this will depend on the type of trade, investment strategy).
(c) Assist in structuring trades which attempt to minimize risk and withstand systemic/tail events.
(d) Oversee the generation of daily risk and position reports in the Risk Management System. This requires the Risk Management team to coordinate efforts with research and technology, and operations.
(e) Lead and coordinate development of risk management technology and tools with portfolio management and systems development teams.
(f) Ensure portfolio stress and scenario analysis are run, updated, and made available to portfolio management to enhance decision-making.
(g) Examine risk reports and stress test analysis to detect any unintended or unanticipated or incidental risk exposures, and ensure such are rectified immediately by trading team.
(h) Coordinate and oversee efforts with documentation team to ensure counterparty credit agreements are drafted and executed with terms that are in the best interests of clients, and are fair and equitable to all

parties concerned, and in keeping with industry standards and practices.

(i) Work with (NAME) Legal team to assist in ensuring relevant documents provide clients with the suitable and equitable terms.

(j) The risk management team reports directly to the Chief Investment Officer of (NAME), who oversees portfolio risk for all clients. The CIO reports directly to the President and they advise portfolio managers as and when they see fit.

Finally, for a complete description of potential risk factors for the (NAME) Fund, please see the "Risk Factors" section, pages xxx, of (NAME) Fund's Private Placement Memorandum.

- **c) How do you calculate your hedges and what instruments do you use?** With all strategies, all identifiable risks are analyzed and relevant ones are hedged as desired in a cost-effective manner. Certain basis risks may exist as a structural necessity. Hedge instruments include other securities, treasuries, swaps, and options.

(1) *How much leverage do you typically use?* Leverage is achieved through repurchase agreements and levels of leverage depend very much on the risk-reward opportunity and relative liquidity of the instruments being traded by the fund. 1) Mortgage arbitrage: The recent average has been around xx. 2) Global fixed income arbitrage strategy: Recently, the leverage has ranged between xx and xxx. 3) Convertible arbitrage strategy: Leverage has recently averaged xxx. Leverage is achieved through margin borrowing in the convertible strategy.

(2) *Describe your cash management policy?* Cash positions including those in margin accounts are reconciled daily by our operations department. The Fund's custodian, the (NAME), holds cash, collateral, and securities. Our financing trading team is charged with ensuring that we optimize in terms of return on cash, and this is implemented by our active participation in the repo market. Finally, we strive to maintain sufficient levels of unencumbered cash in the fund which are more than enough for operating under regular market conditions and allow the fund to deal with unforeseen contingencies in times of market dislocations

(3) *What systems (programs, etc.) are used for fund management on a regular basis?* Of the many in-house systems, a sample includes (a) models to generate yield curves (splines, etc.) for bond and swap valuation, (b) PCA and related analyses to evaluate yield curve strategies, (c) models evaluating the basis and different delivery options

between futures and cash markets, (d) term structure models ranging from Hull-White to more complex factor models, (e) Multicurrency models, (f) models for evaluating volatilities cash, futures, swap markets, etc.

The primary system for risk analysis/monitoring is a proprietary interactive system called (NAME). In brief, this system allows one to analyze every fund managed by (NAME). (NAME) has drill-down abilities for a plethora of analyses from basic risk measures to batteries of stress tests beginning at the fund level all the way down to the single position level.

The (NAME) is the proprietary system used by the (NAME) to process all trades related to portfolio management. It is more than just a ticket entry system since every trade executed follows a number of stages with full documentation and accountability of any changes or updates made at each point. Additionally, the in-house applications provide tools to independently verify P&L, hedging, and position maintenance parameters (i.e., cash flow, margins, cancel/corrects, claims, collateral mgmt.).

(1) *How many positions do you typically hold?* The number of positions depends primarily on market opportunities, and desired level of diversification.

B. Turnover

(1) *Approximate annual turnover:* Mortgage-backed securities: xxx%; Global arbitrage: xxx%; Convertible arbitrage: xxx%

C. Investment Information

(1) *Macro outlook for your strategies and revenue potential:* Our investment strategy is generally not dependent upon macro market conditions. Current conditions suggest a favorable environment for arbitrage strategies.
(2) *Fund performance and net asset value:* Since several asset classes are involved in many different strategies, we find such attribution of P&L varies considerably depending on markets and hence not entirely meaningful. In positions and strategies, contributions to P&I may differ considerably year over year.

D. Company and Management Information

(1) *People: any changes, particularly to key professional staff:* (NAME) currently employs a staff of xxx employees (see organizational chart).

(2) *Infrastructure: any substantial changes:* Improvement is an ongoing trend in all areas: systems, client service, and our trading process. We continue to evaluate our process in respect to changes in the marketplace and make the appropriate improvements

E. Company Information

(1) *Who are the major shareholders (more than, say, 10% holding) in the company?* The company is owned by a holding company, which is owned by (NAME). In addition, there are x principals, but they do not have an ownership stake.
(2) *Please provide details on the people in your firm.* See attached organizational chart and biographies.
(3) *Employee compensation.* Employees receive a salary and an annual bonus, which is determined by the principals. It is based on overall firm performance and employee contribution in achieving the same.
(4) *Is the company financially sound?* Yes.
(5) *Who are the offshore fund's administrators? (NAME)*

F. Infrastructure

(1) **Please describe the trade execution, confirmation, and posttrade accounting and valuation process, identifying which stages are automated.** (NAME) has developed a number of modules and utilities used for daily trading: The system used by (NAME) to process all trades related to portfolio management is more than just a ticket entry system. Every trade executed follows a number of stages with full documentation and accountability of any changes or updates made at each point: 1) Initial Entry—done by the trader, 2) Checkout—trade details confirmed with the counterparty, 3) Confirmation—on settlement date. Major emphasis in the design of the system has been placed on minimizing the input required by the user with specific focus on minimizing and preventing entry errors. For a security trade, the only input needed by the trader is the name of the security, the face amount, and its price. All the relevant trade details (CUSIP, factor, accrued interest, and total cash) are provided or calculated by the system to prevent possible entry errors. All the operations handled by the system are designed to increase reliability and efficiency and as a result, decrease the number of employees required to handle a very large trading volume. The integrity of the trading system is protected by its ability to restrict different users of the system to perform only specific operations. Settlement processing, security pair-offs and cash pair-offs are much easier to manage and monitor by combining the trading and financing functions within a single

system. A large number of reports are available to the user, including cash availability, profit and loss statement, future activity, principal and interest payments, and claims. The system currently handles the trading, financing, and hedging activity for all the funds managed by (NAME).

(2) **Who is responsible for trade execution, confirmation, and posttrade accounting and valuation? What controls are in place to maintain these separate from portfolio management?** The trading desk works as a team on the portfolio. All executed trades are input into our proprietary ticket system. Trading and settlement areas are segregated. The back office works directly with our counterparties and our custodian to settle trades. The step-by-step process is as follows:
   - Trades are entered into the system by the trading desk.
   - Our back office immediately accesses the information, and is responsible for verifying the details of the trade and implementation of the settlement process with the relevant counterparties.
   - Accounting reports are generated by our system and are compared with the administrator and custodian on a daily basis. This process alleviates any problems or questions that may arise on settlement date.
   - We receive confirmations on each trade, which are then matched against our records.
   - Monthly statements from brokers are received and filed accordingly.

(3) **How are positions valued and priced?** Please refer to Memorandum for a detailed description.

(4) **What contingency arrangements do you have in place?** We have set up several levels of defense against contingencies to prevent any disruptions. (NAME)'s portfolios are backed up daily on multiple network servers and distinct hard copies are also generated every day. The systems are maintained and backed up so that in the event of an emergency, they can be managed from two remote locations, one in (NAME) and the other in (NAME).

G. Liquidity & Fees

(1) **Liquidity terms & conditions.** Subscriptions are monthly. Redemptions are quarterly with xx-day prior notice. The minimum investment is $xxx.

(2) **How liquid are the instruments in the portfolio?** This would be dependent on market conditions.

(3) **Please detail all fees and expenses:**

- Management fees: x%
- Performance fees: xx%
- Up-front fees: N/A
- Redemption fees: Redemptions are quarterly with xx days notice. x% redemption fee if initial investment is withdrawn within the first twelve months.

H. Compliance

(1) **Who is responsible for compliance in the firm?** The CFO works in conjunction with the Legal Department.

(2) **With regard to contractual agreements with the companies with which you trade, what types of controls are in place with regard to updating the agreements? Are they updated on a regular (e.g., every 5 years) basis?** Counterparties are selected and authorized by the CFO. Upon approval, (NAME) is notified and documentation is put in place. Contractual agreements with counterparties are updated in keeping with market practice. Our in-house counsel reviews all counterparty agreements to ensure compliance with all rules and regulations of regulatory authorities. (NAME) carefully monitors the market value of securities pledged and received to and from its counterparties. A daily reconciliation of all collateral positions maximizes the use of cash and collateral. All mark-to-market requests issued by counterparties are carefully reviewed by the manager of operations who has many years of front and mid-office experience. When warranted, market valuations will be reviewed with the applicable portfolio manager. All legal issues at the firm are dealt with by our in-house legal team and whenever necessary we search advice from external legal experts.

(3) **Please list your accountant and attorney of the company.** See Private Placement Memorandum

(4) **Are there any material, criminal, civil, or administrative proceedings pending or threatened against the firm or any of its principals, or have there been any such matters?** There have been no complaints, proceedings, etc. involving the Fund (NAME) or its principal's investment/securities activities. (NAME) was previously involved in arbitration with a third-party consultant wherein most of the consultant's claims were dismissed. (NAME) is presently involved in arbitration with a third-party consultant regarding the consultant's fees. We do not believe their claims to have merit, and in any event, they are not material to the firm's business. (NAME) has interposed a counterclaim against the third party consultant for breach of contract, which exceeds the claimants' claims for damages. To the best of the firm's knowledge and belief,

there have been no complaints, proceedings, etc. involving (NAME) employees' investment management activities.

(5) **What are the account dealing procedures for the firm's employees?** Employees are responsible for reporting and receiving approval for any transaction that may be similar to transactions entered in to by the firm. Duplicate monthly brokerage statements are maintained on file for each employee. A more detailed description of this procedure is outlined in the firm's employee manuals.

(NAME): IMPORTANT DISCLAIMERS

The information contained in these materials (collectively, the "Materials"), is exclusively for investors in Funds sponsored by the (NAME) and select prospective investors. **These Materials shall not constitute an offer to sell, or a solicitation of an offer to buy, any securities, including an interest in any Fund described herein.** No such offer or solicitation may be made prior to the delivery of such Fund's confidential private placement memorandum. The memorandum is important and should be read in its entirety, along with all its exhibits, before any offeree decides whether to invest.

These Materials are intended for educational, illustration, and discussion purposes only and are qualified in their entirety by reference to the more detailed information and disclosures contained in each Fund's memorandum and constituent documents. These Materials do not attempt to set forth all of the terms and conditions regarding an investment in any Fund. These Materials contain certain information about certain Funds and their respective investment strategies, objectives, portfolios, performance, investment terms, and other information, and do not attempt to describe all of the Funds or investment strategies utilized by (NAME). No representation is made that the Materials contain complete information about any Fund, including its summary of investment strategy, or complete information about all of the products and services offered by (NAME). The investment strategies described may not be suitable for all investors. These Materials are not intended to be and do not constitute investment advice by (NAME), nor an opinion or recommendation by (NAME) regarding the appropriateness of any investment.

All performance information is net of fees and as of the dates shown. **There is no assurance or guarantee that a Fund's investment strategy or objectives will be successful or that a Fund will be profitable or will not incur losses.** Investment results may vary substantially over time. No representation is made that any investor will or is likely to achieve results comparable to those shown. Investors should not place undue reliance on such performance in making a decision to invest. Past performance is no guarantee of future results.

Any example, graph, or similar information regarding (NAME)'s or a Fund's investment strategy, risk, investment results, portfolio profit and loss, allocations, or investment process is presented for educational and illustration purposes only and is intended to be used in a discussion of investment strategy, risk, and/or process, not to suggest investment performance. This includes certain trading information which otherwise would only be available to traders and or analysts of (NAME). No representation is made that the information is complete or timely. The information is not necessarily indicative of the performance or profitability of a Fund, (NAME), or any investor in the past or future. Any statements or investment examples are nonfactual in nature and constitute only views, beliefs, opinions, or intentions as of the date shown, which are subject to change due to a variety of factors, including fluctuating market conditions. No representation is made that such nonfactual statements or examples are now, or will continue to be, complete or accurate. No statement, example, graph, or similar information should be construed as an investment recommendation.

Certain information provided herein is based on third-party sources, including data obtained from recognized statistical services, issuer reports or communications, and other sources. Although such information is believed to be accurate, we have not verified such information and do not make any representations as to its accuracy or completeness.

Indexes and other financial benchmarks are provided for illustrative purposes only, are unmanaged, reflect reinvestment of income and dividends, and do not reflect the impact of advisory fees. Investors cannot invest directly in an index. Comparisons to indexes have limitations because indexes have volatility and other material characteristics that may differ from each Fund. For example, a Fund may typically hold substantially fewer securities than are contained in an index. Indexes also may contain securities or types of securities that are not comparable to those traded by a Fund. Therefore, the Fund's performance may differ substantially from the performance of an index. Because of these differences, indexes should not be relied upon as an accurate measure of comparison.

These Materials are being provided to you on a confidential basis. Accordingly, these Materials may not be reproduced in any manner, in whole or in part, and may not be delivered to any person without the prior written permission of (NAME).

Glossary

absolute-return fund An absolute-return fund attempts to perform positively for investors regardless of general direction or market conditions by investing in a range of long and short positions with low correlation to the markets. An absolute-return fund measures the gain or loss of the portfolio as a percentage of capital invested.

ABX ABX, also known as the asset-backed securities index, is a credit derivative that has asset-backed securities underlying it.

accredited investor Rule 501 or Regulation D of the Securities Act of 1933 defines an accredited investor as any of the following:

- A bank, insurance company, registered investment company, business development company, or small business investment company.
- An employee benefit plan, within the meaning of the Employee Retirement Income Security Act, if a bank, insurance company, or registered investment advisor makes the investment decisions, or if the plan has total assets in excess of $5 million.
- A charitable organization, corporation, or partnership with assets exceeding $5 million.
- A director, executive officer, or general partner of the company selling the securities.
- A business in which all the equity owners are accredited investors.
- A natural person who has individual net worth, or joint net worth with the person's spouse, that exceeds $1 million at the time of purchase.
- A natural person with income exceeding $200,000 in each of the two most recent years or joint income with a spouse exceeding $300,000 for those years and a reasonable expectation of the same income level in the current year.
- A trust with assets in excess of $5 million, not formed to acquire the securities offered, whose purchases a sophisticated person makes.

administrator A service provider hired by an investment manager to calculate performance and net asset value for the fund, perform record-keeping functions, perform fund accounting, act as transfer agent, and maintain all books and records for the fund manager.

alpha The premium investment return of an investment over a benchmark index such as the S&P 500. Positive alpha indicates that the investment manager has earned a premium over the index and returns are driven by the manager, not the index. The stronger the investment results relative to the index, the stronger the management team and research process of the investor.

alternative assets Alternative assets include any nontraditional investments that would not be found in the standard investment portfolio. Alternative assets include hedge funds, private equity funds, real estate partnerships, forestry investments, and oil and gas partnerships.

arbitrage An investment strategy that attempts to exploit the price difference between the same or similar financial instruments, commodities, or currencies. An arbitrageur may buy a contract for crude oil in the New York market at a lower price and simultaneously sell it in the Chicago market at a higher price.

assets under management (AUM) Assets under management includes all investments that are managed by a fund manager to gauge the amount of fund balances.

average annual return (annualized rate of return) Cumulative compounded gains and losses divided by the number of years of a fund's existence.

average rate of return Sometimes referred to as ROR, the average return of investment over a fixed period of time. ROR is used to compare returns on investments over a period of time, and is usually expressed on an annualized basis.

back testing Back testing uses historical data to evaluate past performance results. Often referred to as a hypothetical portfolio, it simulates investment returns over a past period of time to determine the performance outcome if the strategy had been followed in the past.

basis points One basis point is 1/100th of a percentage point or 0.01 percent. Conversely, 100 basis points (bps) is 1 percent.

bear market A market that is characterized by a period of falling prices that may last from several months to several years.

beta The measure of volatility or risk of a security or portfolio in comparison with an index. Beta represents the percentage change in the price given a 1 percent change of the index. The higher the beta, the higher the risk. A beta of 1.0 indicates that the asset follows the index, whereas a beta less than 1.0 indicates that the asset has lower volatility.

black box A computer program in which a series of inputs are processed using preprogrammed logical procedures to return an output. This output is then used by traders to determine whether to buy, sell, or hold a security. A black box is an integral part of any quantitative strategy fund.

Bloomberg terminal A proprietary software and hardware system that enables its users to view and analyze market data movements and securities trades in real time.

bull market A market that is characterized by a period of rising prices that may last from several months to several years.

Calmar ratio Used to determine return on a downside risk-adjusted basis. It can be computed by dividing the compounded annual return by the maximum drawdown (*see* **Drawdown**).

cap and trade A system to provide economic incentives for firms to reduce emissions by allowing their reductions to be converted to and traded as credits in given emissions markets.

capital structure arbitrage Consists of investors profiting from a pricing inefficiency within the capital structure of a single firm. For example, an investor can go long convertible bonds and short the underlying common stock.

carbon emissions trading A cap and trade system particular to carbon dioxide emissions.

CDX CDX, also known as the credit default swap index, is a credit derivative that represents a basket of credit securities pertaining to various credit entities. The CDX index contains only companies from emerging markets and North America.

clearing The process of reconciling transactions between a fund manager and broker dealers and the prime broker after trades have been entered, executed, and settled involves the process of clearing.

collateralized bond obligation (CBO) A structured credit product backed by high yield bonds placed into separate tranches, with corresponding credit ratings—senior tranches, mezzanine tranches, and equity tranches. Losses flow upstream from the junior tranches into the senior tranches; therefore, the riskier lower tranches offer higher coupon rates (*see* **coupon rate**).

collateralized debt obligation (CDO) A structured credit product backed by fixed-income assets, including pools of bonds, loans, and other assets, placed into separate tranches, with corresponding credit ratings—senior tranches, mezzanine tranches, and equity tranches. Losses flow upstream from the junior tranches into the senior tranches; therefore, the riskier lower tranches offer higher coupon rates (*see* **coupon rate**).

collateralized loan obligation (CLO) Similar to a collateralized debt obligation with the difference being that in the case of the CLO, only loans are packaged into the security.

commodity trading advisor (CTA) A person or entity that provides expert advice to investors on investments in commodity futures, options, and foreign-exchange contracts is referred to as a CTA.

compounded average growth rate (CAGR) The year-after-year growth of an investment for a specified period of time.

coupon rate The term used to describe the interest rate on a bond when it is issued. The name originates from the fact that some bonds have actual coupons attached to them that can be removed and used for redemption of interest payments.

credit crunch An abrupt reduction of the availability of loans or a sharp increase in the cost of loans.

credit default swaps A credit derivative that involves two counterparties. Party A makes periodic payments to party B, and in exchange, party A has the promise that if a third party, party C, defaults, party A will receive the full payoff from party B. Therefore, party A is said to be the "buyer" of credit protection and party B is the "seller" of credit protection. Party C is referred to as the "reference entity." Credit default swaps are used to hedge credit risks when making loans.

custodian A bank, trust company, or other financial institution that holds the fund assets and provides other services, including receiving funds from investors, distributing redemption proceeds, providing safekeeping services, and reporting fund transfers.

delta The ratio that illustrates how the change in the price of an asset affects the price of an option. For example, if a call option has a delta of 0.5, an increase of $1 in the price of the asset will result in an increase of $0.50 in the price of an option. Conversely, for a put option, a delta of 0.5 followed by an increase in price of the asset of $1 would result in a decrease in the price of the option of $0.50.

derivative A financial instrument that is valued based on the underlying value of another security or benchmark index. Derivatives include options, credit default swaps, futures, interest rate swaps, and interest rate caps and floors.

diversification A portfolio strategy that is structured to add investment positions to lower portfolio volatility and reduce exposure to reduce the upside and downside volatility.

drawdown The amount of decline from the prior peak return level of the fund.

due diligence A process that describes the research of a manager and the strategy used by an investor that involves the performance results and operational procedures of an investment partnership and investment team. While the term originated by broker/dealers for business transactions, it refers to the overall detailed review of a hedge fund strategy and activity to ensure that the fund manager complies with the marketing documents and legal documents governing the fund and strategy.

emerging markets Emerging economies in countries that are developing and becoming mature. The term refers to developing economies including Russia, Mexico, Brazil (and Latin America in general), India, China, much of Southeast Asia, and Eastern Europe.

enterprise risk The risk associated with the creation and management of young businesses and their transition from start-ups to more mature companies.

equity market neutral An expression used to describe a strategy that is free from any market risk in the equity markets to which it could have exposure.

event-driven A type of strategy in which the manager invests in stocks of companies that are termed "special situations," such as in distressed, in the process of being acquired.

exposure The extent to which an investment has the potential to change based on changes in market conditions. In hedge funds, exposure is measured on a net basis. Net exposure takes into account the difference between the long positions versus the short positions. For example, if a fund is 150 percent long and 65 percent short, the net exposure would be 85 percent. Gross exposure takes into consideration the total exposure, such as 235 percent gross in the preceding example.

fair value The price at which a security would trade between parties.

financing risk The likelihood of a loss based on the duration of the repayment period.

forward contract An agreement in an over-the-counter derivative instrument that requires one party to sell and another party to buy a specific security or commodity at a preset price on an agreed-upon date in the future. The forward price of the contract is contrasted with the spot price, which is the price of the asset at the spot date.

fund of funds An investment fund that implements an investment strategy that invests in other hedge funds or other investment vehicles to provide portfolio diversification for a wide range of investors. Generally, a fund of funds does not own securities directly.

futures contract An agreement to buy or sell a specific amount of a commodity or security at a specific date in the future.

gamma Measures the rate of change of delta with respect to the price of the underlying asset.

general partner The general partner is one or more individuals or a firm that operates, develops, and runs a limited partnership and is responsible for the debts of the partnership.

haircut A percentage that is subtracted from the value of an asset used as collateral in order to reflect the perceived risk associated with holding the asset.

hedge fund A global term used to describe investment vehicles that are exempt from registering under the Securities Act of 1940.

high water mark A reference in the offering documents that provides for the manager to earn an incentive fee only after the fund's performance surpasses its highest net asset value from the prior period.

hurdle rate A minimum rate of return that the fund must achieve before the fund manager receives an incentive (performance) fee. The hurdle rate may be a fixed rate such as LIBOR or the one-year Treasury bill rate plus a fixed spread of basis points.

incentive fee (performance fee) A fee that a fund manager receives that depends on profits generated in the portfolio. The compensation fee is generally 20 percent of all profits over a fixed level.

inception date The specific period on which a fund begins trading.

internal rate of return (IRR) The annualized compounded rate of return that an investment could potentially earn, based on past performance.

leverage The amplification of results, either negative or positive, through the use of borrowed funds or debt creation.

limited liability company (LLC) A legal structure often used by investment partnerships in which the owners of the LLC receive limited personal liability for operating the business.

limited partnership A business organizational structure in which the general partner manages the business, assumes the legal obligations for limited partners, and receives the economic benefit of the business for the benefit of the limited partners, who receive the cash flow but have no corporate or legal obligations.

liquidity The ability of an investment to be sold or converted to cash without dramatically affecting its price in the market. Liquidity varies according to market conditions, size of the position, and the historic trading volume of the security.

lockup The term for which an investor must maintain an investment in the fund until the first period before redemption is permitted. Initial lockups generally are for one year but may range as long as five years for some specific-purpose hedge funds.

long position A position of an investor who buys a security (or derivative) and expects the value of the security to rise in price.

management fee The fee that investment partnership investors pay to the investment manager to offset the operating expenses of the underlying fund. The annual fee generally ranges from 1 percent to 2 percent of the investor's capital account balance in the fund and is usually collected on a quarterly basis.

margin call The order from a broker/dealer for an investor that is using margin in a securities account to provide additional monies or securities to bring the account up to the minimum maintenance level required by the lending firm. It also may be called a house call or maintenance call.

market neutral A strategy that seeks to reduce risk exposure to the market index. Also referred to as zero beta, the strategy seeks to achieve a return that is a spread to an index, such as Libor, by hedging long positions and will have no correlation to the underlying index. This term is often misused as the strategy should be long and short equal levels of market capitalization, sectors, and industry positions to be judged market neutral for an equity strategy.

mean reversion A method for investing in stocks whereby the mean price at which a stock is traded is calculated. The investors then either purchase additional stocks when they are priced below the mean price or sell stocks when they are priced above the mean price.

minimum investment The smallest amount that an investor is permitted to invest in a hedge fund as an initial investment. Minimum investment requirements generally range from $500,000 to $5 million.

net asset value (NAV) The market value of a fund's total assets.

net exposure The percentage of a portfolio's assets invested in long positions minus the percentage of a portfolios assets invested in short positions. For example, if a portfolio is 80 percent long and 40 percent short, net exposure will equal 40 percent (80 – 40).

offshore fund A private investment company open to a limited range of accredited investors that is set up outside of the United States, generally in an offshore financial center such as the Cayman Islands. It is available for investment to non-U.S. citizens or non-U.S. taxpayer entities such as foundations and endowments. These offshore domiciles offer significant tax benefits for eligible investors.

onshore fund A private investment partnership that is open to a limited range of accredited investors set up in the United States. Available for investment to U.S. citizens only.

operational risk The risk associated with a company's operations; it is not inherent in either financing risk (*see* **financing risk**) or systemic risk (*see* "Systemic risk"). It can be thought of as the risk associated with a business that is failing due to human incompetence.

option A contract that gives parties the right to buy or sell a specific asset or security at a specific strike price at a specific future date.

performance fee A fee paid to the investment manager that is based on the increase in net asset value of the underlying fund. Performance fees are generally 20 percent of the increase of NAV and are assessed annually.

PerTrac (PerTrac Financial Solutions, LLP) A commercially available service that provides an investment platform for portfolio analytics for hedge fund and traditional long-only investment.

poison pill A strategy used to increase the likelihood of negative results for an investor that attempts a takeover of a company.

portfolio risk The overall risk presented by the securities in which a portfolio's assets are invested.

prime broker A reference to the full range of investment services provided by an investment bank or commercial bank to hedge funds. It includes operational services, trading, reporting, securities lending, technology support, and financing.

private-equity fund A pooled fixed-life investment vehicle that makes equity or debt investments in companies, with a management fee and carried interest paid to the management company.

private placement memorandum (PPM) A document that sets forth the offering term for the fund and includes all business terms such as fees, restrictions, and a detailed description of the investment strategy.

pro forma (from the Latin, meaning *for the sake of form*) A method of describing projected figures for a current or future investment. It is important to remember that pro forma figures are estimates and do not satisfy generally accepted accounting practices (GAAP) rules.

quantitative analysis Security analysis that uses objective statistical information to determine when to buy and sell securities.

quantitative fund A hedge fund that employs solely quantitative analysis and models to decide how to allocate and trade its assets and securities respectively.

quantitative model A model that utilizes numerical information to determine whether a security is attractive (*see* **black box**).

redemption The sale of all of an investor's interests in a fund.

redemption fee A fee often imposed by a hedge fund manager if the redemption occurs before the end of the first redemption period.

redemption notice period The official notice period that an investor must provide to the hedge fund manager before withdrawing the investment from the fund.

Regulation D (Reg D) A Securities and Exchange Commission (SEC) regulation concerning private placement exemptions; it allows companies to raise capital through the sales of equity or the creation of debt, without the need to register any of these securities with the SEC.

repurchase agreements Also known as repos or RPs, repurchase agreements occur when a seller sells a security for cash by agreeing to repurchase it at a premium at a later date.

rho A measurement of the rate of change in the price of a derivative relative to a change in the risk-free interest rate.

risk arbitrage A practice whereby investors bet on potential mergers or acquisitions of companies by shorting the stock of the acquirer and going long the stock of the potential target, hoping that if the transaction takes place, the acquirer's stock will fall and the target company's stock will rise.

Section 3(c)(1) A provision in the Investment Company Act of 1940 that permits hedge funds to have less than 100 investors, provided all investors are qualified purchasers, and allows the exclusion of the funds from registration with the SEC.

Section 3(c)(7) A provision in the Investment Company Act of 1940 that permits hedge funds to have more than 100 investors, provided all investors are qualified purchasers and allows the exclusion of the funds from registration with the SEC.

Sharpe ratio Developed by Nobel Laureate William Sharpe, the ratio measures the reward of a portfolio's excess return relative to the volatility of the portfolio. It represents the absolute return less the risk-free interest rate divided by the standard deviation of returns.

short selling The practice of borrowing a stock, selling it at a high market price, hoping that the market price will decrease and, thus, the stock can be repurchased at a lower price and returned to its original owner. The difference is then pocketed by the short seller. Nowadays, it is possible to short sell by using options that enable the exerciser to sell options at a strike price which, if higher than the market price, will enable the short seller to profit.

short-sell rule A regulation created by the Securities and Exchange Commission (SEC) that prohibited short sales from being placed on a downtick in the market price of the shares. In July 2007, this rule was changed, enabling short sales of securities on any price tick in the market.

standard deviation A measure of the dispersion of a group of numerical values from the mean and indicates the level of portfolio volatility. The higher the number, the higher the level of volatility. It is a basis of comparison of volatility of different investment strategies.

statistical arbitrage An opportunity for investors to profit from price mismatch between securities identified through the use of sophisticated mathematical modeling techniques. StatArb, as it is often abbreviated, involves very short holding periods and a large number of securities traded, as well as a powerful IT infrastructure.

style drift A term used to describe manager behavior that consists of a divergence from the manager's initial investment style.

survivorship bias The tendency of mutual fund companies to drop their worst performing mutual funds, resulting in a better track record and a distortion of the data used to describe past performance.

systemic risk The risk presented by the market itself; it impacts all securities encompassed in that particular market.

theta Measures the rate of decrease in the value of an option as time passes.

traditional investments Products whose performances are correlated with broad stock market or fixed-income markets.

treynor ratio Measures returns earned in excess of those that could have been earned on a riskless investment per unit of market risk. It is calculated by subtracting the average return of the portfolio and subtracting the risk-free rate and then dividing the answer by the beta of the portfolio.

vega A measure of how sensitive the price of an option is compared to a 1 percent change in implied volatility. It is the derivative of the option price with respect to the underlying asset.

VIX The ticker symbol for the Chicago Board Options Exchange Volatility Index, often used as a measure of the S&P 500 Index options.

Wilderhill Clean Energy Index An index used as a benchmark for investments in the alternative energy space.

GLOSSARY SOURCES

Global Value Investing: www.numeraire.com/margin.htm

Hedge Fund Alert Glossary: www.hfalert.com/NewPagesIndex.cfm?Article_ID=61250

The Free Dictionary by Farlex: www.thefreedictionary.com/Hedge+funds

Venture Japan—Hedge Fund Glossary of Terms: www.venturejapan.com/index.htm

Notes

CHAPTER 2

1. The 2003 Securities and Exchange Commission Report, "The Implications of the Growth of Hedge Funds."

CHAPTER 3

1. FINRA is the largest independent regulator for all securities firms doing business in the United States. According to its web site, it oversees nearly 5,000 brokerage firms, 173,000 branch offices, and 656,000 registered securities representatives. Its chief role is to protect investors by maintaining the fairness of the U.S. capital markets; as such, it regulates all mutual funds. Visit www.finra.org/index.htm for more information.
2. According to PerTrac.
3. Personal interview done by Richard S. Bookbinder, April 25, 2008.

CHAPTER 4

1. Google search, April 13, 2009: www.google.com/search?hl=en&q=hedge+funds&btnG=Google+Search&aq=f&oq=.
2. Regulation T, www.finra.org/Industry/Compliance/RegulatoryFilings/RegulationT/index.htm.
3. Regulation FD, www.law.uc.edu/CCL/regFD/index.html.
4. 2007 PerTrac Hedge Fund Database Study, March 4, 2008.
5. Ibid.
6. Ibid.
7. *New York Times*, "Company News: Bank of New York Acquires Ivy Asset Management," August 10, 2000, sec. C, pg. 3. Management at Ivy and The Bank of New York refused to confirm or deny the rumors of the decrease in assets.
8. The Financial Services Executive Forum First Quarter 2008, American Banker and Greenwich Associates.
9. This number is taken directly from the Madoff investor list, which has been published on numerous news and information web sites.

CHAPTER 5

1. Federal Reserve Bank of New York web site, www.newyorkfed.org/aboutthefed/fedpoint/fed02.html.

CHAPTER 6

1. Christine Williamson, "Top 1000 funds drop close to $1 trillion," January 26, 2009, *Pensions and Investments*. www.pionline.com/apps/pbcs.dll/article?AID=/20090126/PRINTSUB/301269981/-1/PENSIONFUNDDIRECTORY.
2. ABP Statistics—ABP at a Glance, www.abp.nl/abp/abp/english/about_abp/about_us/abp_at_a_glance/default.asp.
3. PricewaterhouseCoopers, "Transparency versus returns: The institutional investor view of alternative assets," March 2008, www.pwchk.com/webmedia/doc/633422068336988144_fs_trans_vs_return_mar2008.pdf.

CHAPTER 9

1. This quote is from a meeting Daniel Strachman and Richard Bookbinder had with Schulman at Tremont's offices at 555 Theodore Fremd Avenue in Rye, NY, on November 5, 2007.

CHAPTER 10

1. John Greenwald, Massimo Calabresi, Thomas McCarroll, Sribala Subramanian, Jane Van Tassel/New York, and William McWhirter/Chicago, "The Secret Money Machine," *Time*, April 11, 1994, www.time.com/time/magazine/ article/0,9171,980522-4,00.html.
2. Orange County Information, http://en.wikipedia.org/wiki/Orange_County,_California.
3. Alan Katz and Gregorary Viscusi, "Trader Turns Société Générale Report into a Nightmare," January 25, 2008, Bloomberg, www.bloomberg.com/apps/news?pid=20601087&sid=awdX2SvGEIgE&refer=home.
4. PricewaterhouseCoopers, "Transparency versus returns: The Institutional investor view of alternative assets," March 2008.

CHAPTER 11

1. Securities Exchange Act of 1934, Section 13F, www.law.uc.edu/CCL/34Act/sec13.html#f.1.
2. J.P. Morgan Research, "Sovereign Wealth Funds: A Bottom-up Primer," May 22, 2008, www.econ.puc-rio.br/mgarcia/Seminario/textos_preliminares/SWF22May08.pdf.

CHAPTER 12

1. Greg N. Gregoriou and Fabrice Rouah, "Large versus Small Hedge Funds: Does Size Affect Performance?" *Journal of Alternative Investments*, Winter 2002, Volume 5, Number 3.
2. Infovest21 White Paper, "Performance: Small/Emerging Managers vs. Large/Established Managers - Analysis and Compilation of Studies," January 2008.

CHAPTER 13

1. This quote is from a meeting Daniel Strachman and Richard Bookbinder had with Schulman at Tremont's offices at 555 Theodore Fremd Avenue in Rye, NY on November 5, 2007.
2. Our source of information is the Hedgefund.net database as of January 22, 2007 with YTD results through December 31, 2006. There are two indexes used: HFN Fund of Funds multi-strategy (HFN FOF) average with 1,781 reporting funds, and HFN Multi-Strategy (HFN MS) average with 358 reporting funds.

CHAPTER 14

1. 2007 PerTrac Hedge Fund Database Study, March 4, 2008.

EPILOGUE

1. Rick Smolan and Jennifer Erwitt, *Blue Planet Run: The Race to Provide Safe Drinking Water to the World*, Earth Aware Editions, November 28, 2007.
2. BBC News Channel, "Demand for 'Kyoto tax' on the US," December 6, 2003, http://news.bbc.co.uk/1/hi/sci/tech/3296819.stm.
3. BBC News Channel, "Climate Change: The Big Emitters," July 4, 2005, http://news.bbc.co.uk/2/hi/science/nature/3143798.stm.
4. Ibid.
5. CNN World News, "In U-Turn, US Agrees to Global Warming Deal," December 15, 2007. www.cnn.com/2007/WORLD/asiapcf/12/15/bali.agreement/index.html.
6. Domenick Yoney and Autobloggreen.com, "President Obama Announces $2.4 Billion for Electric Vehicles," March 20, 2009, www.autobloggreen.com/2009/03/20/president-obama-announces-2-4-billion-for-electric-vehicles/.
7. Dave Douglas, *BusinessWeek*, "Carbon Advantage, Competitive Advantage," January 2, 2008, www.businessweek.com/technology/content/jan2008/tc2008011_569637.htm.
8. Low-Impact.net, "What is an Emissions Trading Scheme (ETS)?" July 7, 2008, www.low-impact.net/index.php/20080707/what-is-an-emissions-trading-scheme-ets/.

9. Chicago Climate Exchange, "Emission Reduction Commitment," www.chicagoclimatex.com/content.jsf?id=72.
10. Katherine Hamilton, Milo Sjardin, Thomas Marcello, and Gordon Xu, "Ecosystem Marketplace & New Carbon Finance; Forging a Frontier: State of the Voluntary Carbon Markets 2008," May 8, 2008, http://ecosystemmarketplace.com/documents/cms_documents/2008_StateofVoluntaryCarbonMarket.4.pdf.
11. Fiona Harvey, "Stimulus Plans Threaten Green Gains," *Financial Times*, March 3, 2009, www.ft.com/cms/s/0/69dfdef0-081d-11de-8a33-0000779fd2ac.html?nclick_check=1.
12. Katie Fehrenbacher, Earth2tech.com, "Obama Should Spend $100B on Green Stimulus," December 11, 2008, http://earth2tech.com/2008/12/11/report-obama-should-spend-100b-on-green-stimulus/.
13. PointCarbon News, "Japan Earmarks $16 Billion of Stimulus for 'Green' Measures," April 9, 2009, www.pointcarbon.com/news/1.1094390.
14. Climate Conference, Copenhagen 2009, December 6-18, 2009, www.erantis.com/events/denmark/copenhagen/climate-conference-2009/index.htm.

GLOSSARY

1. Some of the entries were previously printed in Strachman, D., *The Fundamentals of Hedge Fund Management,* Hoboken, NJ: John Wiley & Sons, 2007.

Index

ABP, 70
Absolute return, xi–xii
Abu Dhabi Investment Authority (ADIA), 132
Accounting rules, 31–33
Accredited investors, 16–17
Ackman, William, 22
Activist investing, 21–22
Advertising, prohibited, 17
AIG, 22, 128
Alaska Permanent Fund, 60
Allocation strategies, 39–41
Alpha:
  defined, 3, 15
  delivering of, 47–48
Alternative investments:
  hedge funds as, 24–25, 66–67
  origins of, 11–13
Amaranth, 14, 33, 38, 40, 145–146, 151–153
American Clean Energy Security Act of 2009, 175
American Superconductor, 176
Asian Flu, 11
Askin Capital Management, 112
Asset-backed securities (ABS), 22, 115–116
Asset class, hedge funds as, 17–18
Asset managers. *See* Managers
Auditors, due diligence and, 89–90
A. W. Jones & Co., 4, 5–6

Background checks, due diligence and, 90
Bali Action Plan, 170
Bank of New York, 42–43
Barclay Group, 26, 27
Bayou Hedge Fund Group, 38
Bear Sterns Asset Management, 14, 25, 76–77, 104, 115, 159
Bloomberg, 20–21
Blue Planet Run (Smolan and Erwitt), 168
Boldt, Bob, 62, 65
Boutique investing, 41–42
Buffett, Warren, 44, 127
Bulge bracket, 40
Bush, George W., 128, 169

Capital Z Asset Management, 141
Carbon emissions trading, 22, 173–176
Catastrophe bonds, 22
Cerberus, 22
Chicago Board Options Exchange Volatility Index (VIX), 46
Chicago Climate Exchange (CCX), 173–174
Chrysler, 22
CISDM (Center for International Securities and Derivatives Markets), 27
Citicorp, 115, 128
Citron, Robert, 112
Clients, interests aligned with managers, 3, 25
Climate change, investments and, 22, 168–176
Clinton, Bill, 169
CogentHedge, 27
Collateralized debt obligations (CDOs), 115–116
Concept Capital, 89
Conflicts of interest, outlined in private placement memoranda, 17
Consultants, challenges for, 64–68
Crecelius, Kathryn, 70–71
Credit arbitrage, 21

Credit crisis, 2007–2009, 78–79
hedge funds and, 16–17, 114–116
leverage and, 127
multi-strategy funds, 150–151
Credit spread, as driver of returns, 45
Credit Suisse/Tremont, 26

Data mining, 49
Day traders, press myths about, 35–36
D. B. Zwirn, 14, 38
De-leverage issues, 127–128
Derivatives:
leverage and, 28
myths about, 34
Direct investing:
education needed for, 69
by family offices, 59
by institutions, 65–66
lack of diversification and, 14
Disclaimers, 17
Diversification, 13–14
Drawdown issues, 144–145
Due diligence, 79–94
auditors and, 89–90
continued importance of, 129, 130, 160–164
emerging managers and, 138–140, 143
fees and, 91, 106–107
fund of funds and, 80–82
issues to consider, 19
key components of, 84–86, 89–94, 179–191
by leverage provider, 110–111
managers and, 47–48, 157–158
marketers and, 52–54
monitoring and, 55–56, 67–68
multi-strategy funds, 151–152
redemption and, 97–98
replication, 137
Request for Proposals and, 54–55
risk-reward profile and, 80
tips for productive meetings, 83–84
transparency issues, 83, 85–86
weakness of reporting requirements, 27–28

Economic crisis. *See* Credit crisis, 2007–2009
Education, importance of client's, 67, 68–70
Emerging managers, opportunity and, 137–143
Emission Trading Scheme (ETS), of European Union, 173
Endowments, 62, 63–64*f*, 70–71
Environmental investing, 22, 168–176
Erwitt, Jennifer, 168
Esty, Daniel, 171
Eureka, 27
European Union Allowances (EUAs), 173
Executive compensation practices, of AIG, 22
Executive Forum First Quarter 2008 survey, 43

Failure of funds, myth of effect on markets, 33–34
Fair value, defining of, 32
Family offices, 57–59
Fannie Mae:
government seizure of, 127
leverage and, 77
systemic risk and, 75
Federal Reserve:
2007-2008 crisis and, 128
Regulation T, 34–35, 119
Federal Reserve Bank of New York, 74
Fees, 105–109
as barrier to investing, 30
costs of operation and, 107–108
due diligence and, 91, 106–107
fund of funds and, 37, 38–39
future of, 164–165
multi-strategy funds and, 147
outlined in private placement memoranda, 17
press myths about, 36
results versus, 108–109
third-party marketers and, 49

Financial Accounting Standards Board, FAS 157, 31–33
Financial Services Authority (FSA), 23, 130
First Advantage Investigative Services, 90
First Solar, 176
Fixed-income arbitrage, leverage and, 28
Foundations, 62
  direct investing by, 65–66
  education and, 67, 68–70
Freddie Mac:
  government seizure of, 127
  leverage and, 77
  systemic risk and, 75
Freeman & Co LLC, 30
Fund of funds:
  allocation strategies, 39–41
  asset gathering, 48–51
  benefits of, 13–14
  boutique investing, 41–42
  common requirements of investors, 57
  defined, xi
  fees and, 37, 38–39
  future of, 128–131, 159–165
  growth of industry, 30, 60–61*f*, 61–62
  investors in, 38, 57–61
  multi-strategy funds, 144–154
  value of managers, 38

Gabelli, Mario, 22
Gate provision, redemption and, 32–33, 101–102
Germany, 23–24
Global funds, 23–24
GMAC, 22
Goldman Sachs, 127
Graham, Bruce, 67
Green hedge funds. *See* Environmental investing
Greenhouse gas emission. *See* Environmental investing
Green to Gold (Esty and Winston), 171
Gregoire, Jim, 92
Gregoire Capital LLC, 91–92, 121
Gregoriou, Greg, 142

Harvard University, 62
Hedgefund.net, 26, 27
Hedge fund replication, 136–137
Hedge Fund Research, 27
Hedge funds, 31–43
  activist investing and, 21–22
  as alternative investment, 24–25, 66–67
  appeal of, 2–3
  as asset class, 17–18
  credit crisis and, 16–17
  defined, 16
  as efficient investments, 12–13
  global, 23–24
  history of, 3–8
  industry growth, 1900 to 2007, 9–10f, 11–13
  institutional investors and, 12, 14–15
  institutionalization of, 29–30
  liquidity and, 18–20
  manager and client interests aligned, 3, 25
  press myths about, 33–37
  pricing and, 31–33
  private equity and, 22–23
  size of market, 26–29
  sophisticated investors and growth of, 8, 11
  technology and, 20–21
Hedge fund wraps, 24

Icahn, Carl, 22
Illiquid securities, pricing of, 32–33
Immelt, Jeffrey, 171
Incentive fee, 105–106
Infovest21, 27, 142
Institutional investors, 12, 14–15, 16–17
  future of, 128–130

Institutionalization, of hedge funds, 29–30, 36
Insurance premium finance, 22
Interest rates, as drivers of returns, 45–46
International Organization of Securities Commission (IOSCO), 23
Internet, as due diligence tool, 20
Investment banking, future of, 131
Investment strategies, press myths and, 36
Ivy Asset Management, 42–43

Johns Hopkins University, 70–71
Jones & Co., 4, 5–6
Jones, Alfred Winslow, 3–4, 105
Jones, Meredith, 27
Jones, Tony, 5–6
Journal of Alternative Investments, 142
JPMorgan, 132–133

K-1 forms, 93
Kerviel, Jerome, 116
K-Mart, 22
Kyoto Protocol, 169, 170, 173, 174–175

Lampert, Edward, 22
Landmark Management, Inc., 58–59
Latner, Irwin, 102–103
Lehman Brothers, 127, 159
Leverage, 110–123
  de-leverage issues, 127–128
  increased scrutiny of, 130
  liquidity and, 77–79
  LTCM and, 73–74
  myths about, 34–35
  providers of, 110–111, 117–118
  redemption and, 99
  reporting and, 28
  risk and, 118–120
  uses of, 18, 19, 111
Life settlement contracts, 22
Lighthouse Partners, 88–89
Lipper HedgeWorld, 27
Lipper/Tass, 27
Liquidity:
  low levels of, 18–20
  redemption and, 100–103
  replication and, 136
Long/short equity leverage, 28
Long-Term Capital Management (LTCM), 7, 11, 73–74, 112, 145
Lowenstein, Roger, 7

Madoff, Bernard L., fraud of, 1–2, 25, 34, 43, 160–161
Managed account platforms, 86–89
Managers. *See also* Due diligence
  allocation strategies, 39–41
  emerging managers, 137–143
  interests aligned with clients', 3, 25
  sources of, 155–158
Marketing, to gather assets, 48–51
  due diligence and, 52–54
"Market neutral," 125
Markets:
  hedge funds place in, 35
  myth of effect of failures on, 33–34
Market size, of hedge funds, 26–29
Marking to market, 31
Martin, George, 141–142
Massachusetts Pensions Reserves Investment, 60
Measurisk LLC, 113
Merger arbitrage, decline in, 21
Meriwether, John, 7, 73
Merrill Lynch, 115, 127
Minimum investments, 16
Mitubishi UFJ Financial Group, Inc., 128
Monitoring, importance of, 55–56, 67–68. *See also* Due diligence
Montgomery Securities, 155–156
Morgan Stanley, 127
Morningstar, 26
Morningstar/Altvest, 27
Mortgage-backed securities, leverage and, 28
MSCI Hedge Fund Indices, 27
Multi-strategy funds, 107, 144–154

Mutual funds:
paid for assets managed, not performance, 61
regulation of, compared, 60–61

NACUBO endowment study, 63–64*f*
Napolitani, Frank, 89
Non-correlated investments, 125–126
Non-public information, press myths about, 35–36
Norway, 132

Obama, Barack, 22, 169, 170, 171, 174
130/30 funds, 130, 134–135
Orange County, California, 112
Over-the-counter market, carbon trading and, 173–174

Paulson, Henry, 127–128
Peltz, Norman, 22
Pennsylvania State Employees Retirement System, 60
Pension plans, 60, 62, 65–68
direct investing by, 65
education and, 67, 68–70
130/30 funds and, 134
Pensions and Investments Magazine, 54, 62
Perkins, Kelly, 88
PerTrac Financial Solutions LLP, 27, 28, 42, 105
PIPES (private investments in public equities), 47–48, 150
Portfolio insurance, 8
Powershares Winderhill Clean Energy Portfolio, 176
Press, myths perpetuated by, 33–37
PricewaterhouseCoopers, 122–123
Pricing problems, 31–33
Private equity, 22–23
Private placement memoranda, 17
Program traders, 8

Rahl, Leslie, 66, 69, 71
Redemption, 95–104
gate provision and, 32–33, 101–102
liquidity issues, 100–103
longer lockups and, 99–100
patience and, 88
standard deviation and Sharpe ratio, 96–97
suspensions of, 103–104
Registered Investment Advisors, 165
Regulatory issues. *See also* Securities and Exchange Commission (SEC)
in future, 165
mutual funds compared, 60–61
Regulation T, 34–35, 119
Replication, 136–137
Reporting. *See also* Transparency
due diligence and, 92–93
weakness of requirements of hedge funds, 26, 27–28
Request for Proposals (RPFs), 54–55
Returns, drivers of, 44–48
RiskMetrics Group. Inc., 113
Risk/risk management, 29, 111–112
credit crisis and, 114–116
as "knowing what you own," 113–114
leverage and, 118–120
locations of risk, 125–127
multi-strategy funds and, 153–154
new strategies and, 140
technology and, 112–113
10 standard deviation and, 125
traditional asset management differences, 124
types of risk, 117
valuation risk, 120–122
Robertson, Julian, 6, 57
Rouen, Fabrice, 142

Samson, Trip, 58–59
Schulman, Robert, 40, 107, 146
Sears, 22

Securities and Exchange Commission (SEC):
  future of regulations, 130
  non-public information and, 36
  study of hedge funds' value, 22–23
  13-F filings and, 126–127
Seed capital providers, 140–141
Shain, Randy, 90
Sharpe ratio, 96–97
Short selling, 4–5, 135
Smolan, Rick, 168
Société Générale SA, 116
Sophisticated investors, hedge fund growth and, 8, 11
Soros, George, 6, 57
Sovereign wealth funds (SWFs), 131–133
Standard deviation, 96–97
State employee pension funds, 60, 62, 65–68
Steinhardt, Michael, 6, 57
Stock market crash, 1987, 8
Stock prices, as driver of returns, 45
Structured investment vehicles (SIVs), 76–77
Style drift, 19, 97
Subprime debt, 74–77
Suspending redemptions, 103–104
Swan, Rob, 89
Systemic risk:
  leverage and liquidity, 77–79
  LTCM and, 73–74
  sub-prime lending and, 74–77

Technology:
  due diligence and, 27
  as industry aid, 20–21
Testaverde, Peter, 11
Third-party consultants, due diligence and, 81
Third-party marketers, 49, 157
13-F filings, 126–127
Transparency:
  due diligence and, 19, 83, 85–86, 92–93
  fees and, 30
  managed account platforms, 87
  need for greater, 42, 51
  portfolio information and risk, 121
  press myths and, 36
  replication, 136
  risk management and, 111–112
  13-F filings and, 126–127
Transparency versus returns: The institutional investor view of alternative asset (PricewaterhouseCoopers), 122–123

Underperformance, 19
University endowments, 70–71

Valuation risk, 120–122
Value at risk (VAR), 115–116
VIX (Chicago Board Options Exchange Volatility Index), 46
Volatility, as driver of returns, 46–47

WalMart, 171
Waxman, Henry, 174
Weather derivatives, 22
Weber, Eric, 41–42, 71
When Genius Failed: The Rise and Fall of Long-Term Capital Management (Lowenstein), 7
Wilderhill Clean Energy Index (ECO), 176
Winston, Andrew, 171
Wolfel, Scott, 91

Yale University, 62
Yield curve, as driver of returns, 45
Yingli Green Energy, 176

Zwirn, 14, 38